...N'S (IDE

ENGI 3H

C IRC ES

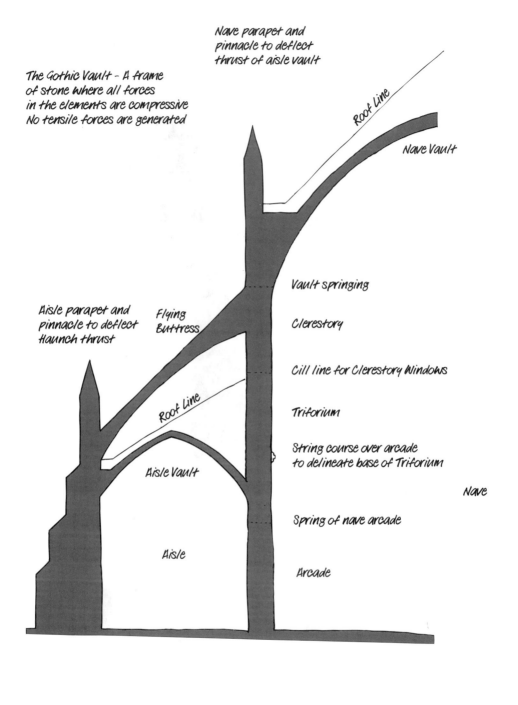

The Gothic Vault - A frame
of stone where all forces
in the elements are compressive
No tensile forces are generated

Nave parapet and
pinnacle to deflect
thrust of aisle vault

Roof Line

Nave Vault

Vault springing

Clerestory

Aisle parapet and
pinnacle to deflect
Haunch thrust

Flying
Buttress

Cill line for Clerestory Windows

Roof Line

Triforium

Aisle Vault

String course over arcade
to delineate base of Triforium

Nave

Spring of nave arcade

Aisle

Arcade

JORDAN'S GUIDE TO ENGLISH CHURCHES

by

Owen Jordan

The King's England Press

2000

Jordan's Guide to English Churches is typeset in New
Century Schoolbook by Moose Manuscripts
and published by The King's England Press,
Cambertown House, Commercial Road,
Goldthorpe, Rotherham,
South Yorkshire, S63 9BL.

ISBN 1 872438 37 7

First printed 2000

Printed and bound in Great Britain by
Woolnough Bookbinding, Irthlingborough,
Northamptonshire.

Contents

Preface

'Cast out from Paradise'

It is part of the very nature of human existence that what one man builds is no sooner completed, than another declares its supercedence, a third its redundancy and a fourth seeks to tear it down. We have even geared our taxation system to favour this process, and passed laws to prevent the repair of old buildings (you will find them under 'Planning', and 'Listed Buildings'). The survival of not just a few samples, but a whole family of structures with a history commencing in the Dark Ages, is something not just extra special, but truly to be wondered at.

The genesis of this work is in the tradition of the authors of commentary on church architecture over the past century, yet written against a backcloth of change that, while foreseeable in the decades prior to the Second World War, and seemingly both desirable and inevitable in the twenty years after that war's conclusion, has, as far as architecture is concerned, completely rewritten the textbooks on building. Where fifty years ago stone and native hardwood would have been fairly common in better quality construction, now they are so rare as to provoke comment. Decoration applied epicurean style to building exteriors is almost *verboten*. New work in either the Gothic or the Classical style almost unheard of. In our taste for new we have distanced ourselves from the old so firmly that a gulf has emerged between the generations, a gulf of time, place and understanding that puts us as far distant from Mee or Pevsner as they were from Pugin, and he from Inigo Jones.

In that gulf we can observe the tattered remnants of the fetters that bound thinking to the two styles; perhaps now free of the religious overtones that caused battle to be joined thereon, we can now look all the more objectively at the past's great buildings. We are not, and cannot however be independent of the underlying philosophy that is organized religion, for this powerful mover of men is the very reason that the subject works have survived, almost to spite reason itself.

This book is intended to be a handbook of English church architecture, a guide to what you can see, what it is you are actually seeing, how and why it was built, and to a degree, where it can be seen. The limitation of the book to the notional boundaries of England is to recognize that it is in England that society, since the dawn of feudalism, has created conditions that are unique; conditions that enabled the Church of England to thrive in a manner without parallel elsewhere. The decision to exclude Scotland, Wales and other foreign parts who have their own distinct histories, is deliberate, for they are not to be construed as England's more remote bits where the people speak in strange tongues and with odd accents. There is also a good architectural reason which should unfold with the tale. I will say now that I intend to bend this rule, partly for egotistical reasons, but mainly for the sheer delight of rule bending. The reasoning should be revealed in due course.

Owen Jordan
Pengwaunsarah
Ochrywaun   November 1999

Chapter One:
The Christian Church
in England

In two millennia, the Christian faith has spread from being a lesser sect among many within the Roman Empire, to be a major world religion. For rather more than half that span of years the Church has been firmly established in this country. From that period of about twelve centuries down to the present day, with relatively few exceptions, the churches that survive to grace the English land or townscape, stem from two major periods of building activity. Firstly, commencing at the end of the eleventh century, we have a series of buildings that run chronologically through to the mid fifteen hundreds. This period has given us buildings that have, both individually and as a group, a unique place in architectural history.

The second phase of church construction commenced with the rise of the Nonconformist movement, and the emancipation of the Catholics, at the end of the eighteenth century, and is even today only just reaching a conclusion. History has not yet had time to pass judgment on the staying power of these more recent structures, though many have already passed away or been converted to other use. This combination of a major phase of church building coinciding with significant demolition and conversion to alternative use may be a modern phenomenon, but it is not necessarily so.

Before and between these ages of major activity, and perhaps also in recent years, we have substantial periods in which both religion and church building were in serious recession, when churches were frequently regarded as quarries of pre-packed stone, and when repair was a rare event. Nonetheless, though few churches survive as examples, what little was built is characterized by a few rare gems, as at Tetbury, where we can appreciate the skill of the architect, and in London, where just eleven of the Wren collection have made it undamaged to the start of the third millennium.

To the casual observer then, how many churches have graced the landscape of England? To this question there is no 'correct' answer, but a rough calculation is quite instructive, and the result not a little surprising.

A Herculean Achievement

There are over sixteen thousand parishes in England; ten thousand were in existence at the Norman Conquest. Ignoring for the present the domain of the Dissenters and the Catholics, and the imports of the last ten decades, we are still talking about a lot of buildings. The majority of these parishes are both rural in origin, and remain to some degree rural in character today. Excepting those parishes generated by the Victorian age to supply the urban masses, most parishes had already built their first church, and not infrequently a second one too, by the end of the eleventh century. Of those early buildings there are relatively few intact survivors, and a new church plus various extensions is the norm after 1100.

Unsurprisingly, much of this effort required major repair or rebuilding before the end of the sixteenth century, to the extent that complete and unaltered examples of late Norman/ Early English churches are also rare. To survive the ecclesiastical dark age from the middle of the sixteenth century to the end of the eighteenth, all the structures that continue to grace our landscape from this period required periodic overhaul, repair, and not infrequently, rebuilding.

To add to this tally, there were over six hundred monastic foundations, with abbey churches, minsters, collegiate churches and chantries adding around a further two thousand churches and similar buildings to the score. Many of these have disappeared without trace, though some are picturesque ruins, and some, like Howden, are in use but partially ruined.

The frenzy of economic activity that was the Industrial Revolution in turn produced its spate of new churches, including many replacements for mediaeval structures that had passed the point of no return (and some that hadn't, but fell victim to the zeal for new that still plagues us today). Substantial numbers of new churches on urban sites were however built to minister to the heathens in the new conurbations, many actually funded by the state.

At a conservative estimate then, over forty thousand churches have been built by the 'official' Christian faith in England, over the last twelve hundred years. To this must be added the contributions of the Dissenters, and the Catholics, mostly since the end of the eighteenth century. That contribution continues apace; something approaching half of all Catholic churches are post-1945; and overkill in terms of numbers has been a feature of the dissenting churches, with even quite. small villages sporting three or four varieties, betwixt whom the outsider is hard pressed to insert the proverbial credit card, when looking for differences.

Man's capacity to build in honour of God is difficult to overestimate.

Within this impressive tally, the distribution of architectural gems is widespread, but uneven, both geographically and chronologically. In chronological terms the Saxon church is rare, a rarity only exceeded by Georgian Gothic. The Victorian Gothic in basically unaltered form is numerous, if only because the Victorians were faced with a need to both provide large numbers of new churches, and to rebuild or replace many semi-derelict mediaeval ones. The true Gothic church of the Middle Ages, while also numerous, is almost never to be found in unaltered form, with extensions lengthways, sideways, vertically (in both directions) making the larger structures complex histories in their own right.

Of the rest, there are some Gothic churches that date from, at least in part, post-1550. Outside the towns the Classical church has no great presence, and Wren's frolic with the coal tax in London has been relentlessly whittled down from fifty one, to thirty in 1939, and eleven unscathed examples six years later. Towns and cities are notoriously dangerous places for ancient buildings. A century ago and earlier, hungry eyes would be cast on the rich store of materials an empty church presented, and recycling would not be long delayed. Now demolition means the salvaging of a few of the more

11

precious pieces at best, and the reduction of the rest to low grade fills, fit only for road sub bases or disposal.

What this book looks at therefore is buildings that have achieved maturity, either as an agglomeration of the work of successive builders over several centuries (the majority) or as more or less unsullied monuments to their creator's genius (very much a small minority). *This* book shows how the churches were built, why those you can see didn't fall down, and why some of the ones you can't see did. At the same time the book hopes to broaden the understanding of a unique part of England's heritage, and to provide viewers with a vocabulary that is not the preserve of the few.

At this juncture we can draw in those worthy souls after whom architecture is christened (it could not be the other way round, could it?). While architects were a feature of classical times as an intellectual hierarchy, rather than the profession we see today, they do not have any role to play in this tale, until it is half complete. The tale would not, however, be complete without them.

Architects

The term 'architect' did not enter the English language until the mid-sixteenth century, and as the story unfolds the discerning will distinguish the difference between buildings that have been designed by an architect and those that haven't. The architect as a profession emerges with the commencement of the Battle of the Styles, about a hundred years after the end of the main phase of Gothic construction, and at the point in history when many of the Gothic splendours, those that had survived ten decades of large scale iconoclasm that is, were beginning to lurch, lean and crumble in a most disconcerting manner.

The arrival of the architect signified a shift in the balance of wealth in the country, indeed it could be argued that the architect could not have survived and prospered within an economy that was almost entirely rural. While the majority of churches this book examines are thus exemplification of the surplus generated by a rural economy, it is in the towns and cities that you will find the architect's efforts.

12

Towns and Cities

Churches in towns and cities have an important niche in history, for they are a reflection of the concentrations of wealth in society in the days before mammon achieved complete ascendancy. Wren's half century in London is the product of taxation levied on a conurbation whose population even then was well into six figures, and was already drawing its wealth from far beyond the shores of this island. Norwich, on the other hand (and it may be regarded as typical, not exceptional) was blessed with one church per thousand souls at the start of the nineteenth century, thirty-six in all. Their placement within the city walls, themselves mediaeval, together with the Cathedral, is indicative of the wealth a regional centre could draw out of its hinterland aided by the horse and cart and sailing vessels. Norwich is still recognizably a mediaeval city, even though the city walls have been overridden by the twentieth century plague of the motor vehicle.

The architect then, is inextricably bound up with the growth of towns and cities, is in fact a product of urbanisation, part of the intellectual infrastructure needed to control and sustain the growth of densely packed communities. While towns existed on a modest scale pre 1600, the city, as we understand it today, then had only one representative on these shores; London. Cities in the sixteenth century were, to our eyes today, merely less modest towns, for we still think of Salisbury or York as town size, because the city has expanded to the point where many cities in England now hold more people than the whole country did in the first decade of the fourteenth century. To look at the domain of the architect we must draw distinction between the town and the city, and the distinction, while apparently being one of physical scale, is essentially one of wealth, at least as far as church architecture is concerned.

The town, typically a modest conurbation, though frequently walled, as the number of streets ending in 'gate' suggest, is rarely as well provided ecclesiastically as the city. Howden, as an example, is content with a single church serving a few thousand people. Devizes, like Beverley, is not content with one and needs must have three. The reason for this seeming paucity is that the general ratio of one church per thousand head of population applied not just to cities, but to the towns and villages as well, and many a mediaeval town considered itself well populated if a thousand souls sustained it. Towns relied on the trade of their hinterland and, across the length and breadth of lowland mediaeval England, were nowhere more than ten or fifteen miles apart. A thousand people relying on the agricultural produce of a hundred square miles is a fair burden for a subsistence economy to bear, and only the richer quarters of the landscape could cope with more.

To add interest to the urban scene, there are the occasional survivors in the shape of houses of religious orders, by some miracle lasting into the twentieth century after long ages of alternative use and disuse. Beverley's Friary suffered partial annihilation in the railway mania; what was left was derelict for much of the twentieth century, but is now restored, or partially so, and both a credit to the town and an unusual essay in brick and chalk.

The architect's arrival in the town is thus somewhat later than in the city, for the spread of the profession depended not on the church, but on the emergent middle classes, and when the Dissenters launched the second phase of church building at the close of the eighteenth century, the architect was there and touting for the commissions, many having already cut their teeth on church repairs and alterations. While architects as a genre thus spent much of the seventeenth and eighteenth centuries waiting in the wings for the church to send new commissions their way, the task of shoring up the fabric of what we now call our national treasures, fell to the principals, people like Wren, Hawksmoor and Wyatt, and what they did is in no small part a chapter in the history of the Church of England. The national treasures then, as now, were the cathedrals and the great collegiate churches. The humble, and the not so humble, parish church gains sustenance from a world remote for the most part from the great and the good, was ignored by the church hierarchy for virtually the whole of the last thousand years, and given similar treatment by the architectural profession until relatively recent times.

Cathedrals and Monastic Buildings

Lastly then, in terms of succession, we have the principal buildings, the cathedrals, abbeys and minsters, symbolic of the wealth, power and influence of the mediaeval Church that was their foundation; sustained them through centuries of development and growth to maturity, and remain a staff to the Church of England in the decline of its old age. Their numbers are relatively small; perhaps only twenty make the premier league alongside their continental brothers and sisters. They are not the tallest (that prize goes to Ulm), nor are they the most extravagant (there are a number of candidates for this, and Gaudi's as yet incomplete Sagrada Familia cannot be more than first among many equals). Their value is that on their own they represent the pinnacle of achievement that is English Church Architecture, a showcase for the many lesser churches that lie in their shadow, smaller maybe, but often better loved and cared for by their parishoners, both in the past, and down the ages to the present.

Many people will commence and conclude their architectural tour by viewing a cathedral. The Excursion. Even after several hours, the observer will only have scratched the surface, and most people will not even have sat down, unless it was to rest their legs. This is the surveying equivalent of driving past the job; at best you won't actually have collided with anything, and in half an hour you will not be entirely sure if you had been to see Acacia House in Lilac Grove or The Lilacs in Acacia Avenue. One edict then is more trustworthy than any French king's missive from Nantes; sit down, take your ease, rest your pins, avail yourself of the comfort of a pew and begin to see what you came to look at. To illustrate this point, remind yourself that the average surveyor will spend at least two hours on the visible bits of the smallest church, one you might comfortably fit into a modest suburban garden. Not a single one of those valuable minutes will have been frittered away in quiet enjoyment. The layman, lacking the whip of commerce and the staff of experience can easily double this timescale in quiet enjoyment. Perhaps even eternity is too short.

The reader will then understand the limitations of this book; to be comprehensive would stretch the timescale of mortality. Limits have been placed on the churches sketched, and it is thus impossible that every item of interest can have been covered. The message however is clear: interest, variety, enjoyment, puzzlement, wonder and understanding (perhaps!) await. If you wish to see a leaning tower, Puxton is a handy local alternative to Pisa (leaning spires like Chesterfield's, are almost ten a penny; finding a straight one, a bit more of a challenge). Wren is a splendid counterfoil to Brunelleschi. Your buildings are far less likely to have a severe attack of scaffolding in England than in Italy, and who would really want to exchange a really good bracing winter's day on the East Cliff at Whitby for all that horrible hot sun in Pienza?

Before we look in detail at the wealth that is church architecture, we need to understand the origin of that wealth. How did a subsistence rural economy generate an economic surplus sufficient to pour seemingly limitless resources into the Christian Church, and further, how the political and politico-religious forces at work in mediaeval England combined to fund a building programme a full five centuries in duration.

Chapter Two:
The Foundation of the Wealth of the Church

With the rebirth of the Christian faith in England during the Dark Ages, the English Church, its functions, procedures and liturgy demanded a particular form of building. A glance at St. Gregory's, Kirkdale, will give us the flavour (with a distinct Victorian odour) of the Saxon, or rather the pre-Norman church, with its massive rubble masonry walls with small openings, unpretentious proportions and simple beam and post trusses. Churches like St. Gregory continued to be built even into the last century, economizing in the expensive items of glass, lintels and arches, sporting only a single large window in the East or West end, where no great structural loads were being taken. This is not the church at the height of its wealth and power. The journey from these modest beginnings to immeasurable wealth and near supremacy, in matters both spiritual and political, and back again to a state pensioned old age, is one that takes church architecture for a ride through history to a point where the architecture is a large slice of the history, certainly the largest remaining.

England is a rich land. Picture it fifteen hundred years ago: vast swathes of virgin territory 'For Sale With Vacant Possession'. Population? At best a couple of million souls. It's too soon to think of England in terms of parishes, but of the villages that were to become the core of parish life nationwide, perhaps five or six thousand are already hard at work pushing back the wild. The villages are not very big; two or three hundred people at most, over half of them children. Perhaps only forty or fifty able-bodied males and half that number of women, owing to the rigours of child bearing. Between sixty and a hundred adults economically active in each community. This is the England that accepted the teachings of the early Christian missionaries. This too is the England that took the faith and housed it, first in the rude hovels of their own, and then in rapid succession, built and rebuilt churches on a scale and magnificence not seen since the departure of the Romans.

To build for the future requires a future, one that can both be seen and planned for. The first churches were modest structures because the village as an economic unit takes time to accumulate wealth, and that wealth is exactly what invaders are seeking to deprive your average villager of. Successive generations of invaders took possession of the land from the end of the fifth century onwards, settled down, tilled the ground, and were in their turn displaced or forced to surrender lands and livings to the newcomers almost as soon as they had beaten their swords into ploughshares.

Thus far plenty of fields, but not too many folk. Word on the richness of this land spread, and the departure of the hand of Rome left the door ajar for five centuries of migration and conquest that mitigated against a prosperous society. Change is the handmaiden of decay and the Church, when the spiritual reconquest of the land recommenced in the sixth century, cried out for stability and permanence, and for nigh on two centuries found it not.

Yet the waves of settlers and plunderers continued to fill the land, and fast, and as the land filled so room for each new band of settlers became less easy to find. From this chaos a new society was emerging: feudal England.

If in these early years the Church was unable to command the resources of the country to build for the second millennium, then the foundations that it was able to put down in the form of an unrivaled influence in the lives of ordinary people, stood it in good stead for the future. Almost from the first the Church was able to command a pivotal role, taking unto itself the rites of passage with an easy grace born of much practice elsewhere, planting its roots firmly in the heart of every community. Feudalism as a system was destined to provide the structure, organization and wealth that was to underpin mediaeval England and the Church, for the next eight hundred years. On its own though, merely to have a pivotal role in society is not to guarantee great wealth and success. So while the Church waxed fat in the century preceding 1066, it was yet to be the body politic that laid the golden eggs. What was needed was that little extra, and William of Normandy very kindly provided it.

A Crock of Gold

By the dawn of the eleventh century the estate agents' signs had long fallen in decay, and the immigration service was toying with legislation on repatriation. William could not do what his forbears had done, move in lock stock and barrel, and hope to find enough of the best land to sustain his followers. The Norman invasion was not so much that as an imposition of a new ruling class on a land well filled with folk. The Duke needed the Church as part of the tripartite plan for welding and ruling the new nation state, just as much as the Church needed him, and if the marriage was not made in Heaven, then it was certainly forged by Tubal Cain, and in solid gold on the Church's part.

Thus was made the pact that tied the throne of England to the Church of England, a pact that was to outlast the mediaeval England that gave birth and sustained it. England is a rich land, and to the Church accrued lands, tithes, livings, free or exclusive use of stone and timber, iron and lead. Nigh on five centuries of living off the fat of a fat land, underpinned by a system of semi-slavery that tied the producers of wealth to the land they tilled, systematically depriving them of the fruits of their labours.

The results of such a system are inevitably twofold; on the one hand a host of magnificent edifices that speak across the centuries of a glory that was God; on the other the repeated efforts, such as those of Bernard of Clairvaux, that tell only too clearly of the corruption of vast wealth and its effect on the Church's morals. When considering the one aspect of the mediaeval Church, and this work is nothing if not an appreciation of the magnificence of those centuries of labour, it is important to recall the other, and those, like Bernard, who fought against the corrupting tide of wealth.

The pact lasted almost five centuries and funded the emergence and growth to maturity of what we now call Gothic Architecture, even though the architect, both as architect, and butt of criticism (more usually the latter), was yet a century in the future, and 'Gothic' a term of abuse not yet invented, when Henry broke the pact and sued for divorce, several divorces to be precise. Not all the works of this half-millennium of sustained effort fell down, though many did, as in fact had been happening throughout the Middle Ages, and many more threatened to, a fact that in itself had given considerable momentum to the building programme. Today only a few of these churches survive almost as built, most are substantially altered, either during or after the Gothic Age. The great era of church construction was over by 1540; the future, uncertain.

In his divorce from the Church, Henry had pulled the rug from under an organization that was already tottering. What he wanted was the capital; lands, livings, rights to the resources of the countryside, that were the wealth of the Church. What the Church lost was the income from that capital, the means to continue as it had done for twenty generations. The effect was almost as spectacular as turning off a tap and finding that Lodore has run dry; you have difficulty in believing that the scale of the event is far beyond the realistic outcome of the action. This tableau, though enacted on the English stage, was driven by events elsewhere, and to understand this, we need to look at the wider Christian Union, on the mainland of Europe.

Schism

The Christian Church has never been united in its view of the world. In the first millennium, with the perils of persecution and the severe difficulty of travel within Europe, Asia Minor and the Middle East, it is not surprising that the Church displayed a tendency to diverge into various sects. Despite numbers of pilgrims and clerics almost continuously on the road, keeping all sections of the faith on the same path was a task beyond the means of the Church. Secondly, the tendency of individuals to assert their independence, means that if it takes a year to travel to Constantinople and back, no Pontiff is going to have a decisive say in what goes on in all corners of the faith.

Unity, then, is a relative thing, with the Eastern Orthodox Church going its own way after the great schism in 1054, and the Celtic Church diverging until the decision to swing into line behind Rome at the Synod of Whitby in 664. That the Western Church was, at the end of the eleventh century AD as unified (Cathars apart) as it appears to have been, and that the unity, despite the odd wobble or two, lasted over five centuries, is a matter of considerable surprise, and says much for the staying power of the Church. Quite why there were no major schisms is not clear, but in England at least, while there were disputes between the monarch and the Pope or his local Archbishop, and papal authority was on not infrequent thin ice, there were no effective challenges to the Church's authority until long after the power of the Church had started to wane.

If we consider the wealth and power of the Church in England, then from the unification of England under Edward the Elder at the start of the tenth century, the growth of that wealth and power was a steep curve, turning almost vertical after the Conquest. Reaching a high tide mark with the establishment of the Inquisition in 1231, the Church's power then declined, though absolute wealth continued to grow until it peaked in the first decades of the fourteenth century. At this date, probably a quarter of the total wealth of England was controlled, via the Church proper, and the various orders of monks and nuns. Henceforward, and it is probably due to opportunities that presented to survivors of the Black Death, and the body blow the disease gave to feudalism, the power and influence of the Church went into steep decline. There is nothing quite so tempting as kicking someone when they are down, and in this case as the Church went down, people started to queue up to kick, and the kicks turned out to be a mixture of pure greed, à la Henry, and philosophy. It is on the philosophy however that the Church's power broke, and it was more than a little of being hoisted by its own petard.

The Birth of Protestantism

The sound of Martin Luther's hammer pounding the door of the cathedral at Wittenberg in 1517 sounded the death knell of unity in the mediaeval Christian Church; his ninety-five theses were the wedge that split the union, paving the way to three hundred years of dissent, in which violence was on the surface much of the time. The Church's failure to lay its hands on the renegade, after excommunication failed to stop him, due to protection from the local aristocracy, was an error that led directly to establishment of the Lutheran Church, and the realization across the rest of the Christian world that Rome's grip was beginning to slip.

At this distance of time and place we are left to wonder as to what had so riled Luther that such drastic action was his chosen course. Five hundred years of absolute spiritual rule is half a millennium to accumulate bad habits, and the Church, which is only human after all, had landed itself with some first class habits, which were, when put under the philosophical and religious microscope, spiritually indefensible to say the least. If trade in relics and indulgences, and perceived massive wealth, caused some unease, it was the intolerance of the Church, as symbolised in the institution of the Inquisition, that caused most opposition.

We still argue today over the mediaeval deception of the Turin Shroud, simply because people want to believe, and to put their belief in something tangible. This is a defensible view, but it was this seeming religious hypocrisy combined with vast and corrupting wealth, that set the moralists to work demolishing the edifice from the outside, rather than reforming it from within. As feudalism dissolved in the fourteenth and fifteenth centuries in England, it did not do so, either in the rest of the parish of Rome, or in the realm of the Eastern Orthodox Church. It is useful then, to glance at the rest of the Christian sphere of influence, to see the whole view from the steps of St. Peter's, rather than from those of St. Paul's.

At the start of the fourteenth century, the Western Church, at the height of its power, could legitimately claim to be the only pan national institution in Europe. Pope Urban had 'cast his arms abroad', as the poet has it, to launch the first crusade in 1096. In reality he did not leave the Christian Union. The rules, in the Latin texts and language that the church in Rome laid down for the whole of the Church's sphere of influence, did not vary at the borders of those few states who could legitimately claim to have such artifacts. To the Church, the passing of a few princedoms, or the creation of a union of states, was of no more consequence than the march of time. True, the Church involved itself in serious politicking when it saw fit, an action that became almost continuous as the halo started to slip. The key to this internationalism though, was the binding universality of the creed as the foundation of the Church, and it was this that was to lead to a crusade in Europe, and eventually the parting of the Christian Church.

The European Crusade against the Cathars (the Albigensian Crusade) was launched in 1209, and counts as serious bloodletting of Christian against Christian, a taste of what was to become common in the sixteenth century. This led directly to the foundation of the Inquisition in 1231, and heralds the rise of papal intolerance. The Albigensian crusade was a thirty year act of bloody suppression, meant as a severe warning to all who sought to question papal authority in matters spiritual. From this point on monarchs took up the cudgels with their religious betters at their peril.

As an institution then, the Church was multi-national when monarchs generally thought only in terms of their own territoriality, and how much of another's they could grab; the people on the whole were tied to soil they didn't own. Institutions see no great need to change systems that have brought them great wealth and stability over hundreds of years, but the dynamism that is human existence, and the forces that cause change within societies, submit to no higher authority, on this earth at least. The Church could oppose change, and did so with all its considerable might, but the dies that cast the course of the Church of Rome were forged by Rome in the first three decades of the thirteenth century.

That course, from Wittenberg in 1517, through the launch by the Council of Trent of the Counter Reformation thirty years later, and for next three hundred years, was all downhill. While the Church could reform itself from within, once there was room enough outside for dissent to flourish, then there were

Dissenters a-plenty queuing up for a little space to worship God in their own way. The problem the Dissenters had, from 1517 onwards, was that the space they needed to thrive in kept shifting. Kings and queens loyal to Rome really had little choice but to suppress dissent; those of the Protestant persuasion, a little more latitude. One extreme begets another, and the wild swings of loyalty were a signal moving force in the migrations within Europe and ultimately the emigrations to the New World.

It would be a long time before Protestant monarchs felt secure enough to grant Catholics their religious freedom, and even longer in the reverse direction. If you are tempted to think that mere words were involved, then remember the bloody cast of the die in South West France in 1209. Remember too, that the marchers of Northern Ireland still celebrate the use of carts after victory on the Boyne, to kill, by driving over them, the wounded of the defeated Catholic army.

Internal reform of the Church had occurred intermittently over the half millennium prior to Martin Luther. The Pope had issued guidance to restrict the retinues of the more senior clerics; Bernard had reformed the monastic movement, but these reforms had been temporary, overall there was little change. The shadow of the Inquisition is still with us even as we enter the third millennium, and little flexibility was granted to those who wanted to sweep away the clutter and constraints surrounding the faith. Inevitably there comes a point where the critics feel strong enough to show their hand, or an individual throws a spark into the tinder. This is what Luther did, and the Church has not been the same since.

The schism that was to prove (so far, that is) permanent, generated such intense feelings on both sides that Christianity became a significant threat to life and limb, and the practice of making martyrs of your opponents became relatively commonplace. In troubled times such as those that took hold of Christianity after 1517, architecture took a back seat against a violent adjustment of philosophy. The split produced the Lutheran and Moravian churches and, eventually, the Church of England; The Calvinists and Presbyterians led to the establishment of the Presbyterian Church of the French Huguenots, closely followed by the Scots, Hungarian and Netherlands churches.

24

Of the Continental churches, all except the Netherlands fell to the forces of the Counter Reformation over the next century and a half, and today the Presbyterian Church is strongest in North America, whence the faithful fled to avoid persecution. The Church of England eventually split into three further Nonconformist groups; the Baptists, Congregationalists, and the Methodists, while within the Church of England itself, the 'broad church' encompassed a swathe of belief from Anglo-Catholic to evangelist.

In essence, all the Protestant churches eschewed any organizational form that resembled the Church of Rome and a single, all powerful leader, a state of affairs that was to persist until the rise of the 'fringe' Christian sects of the twentieth century. The effect of this independence is that you can find churches and chapels of all European nationalities and persuasions in all corners of the globe. The Church of England can be found in the far east, and independent Welsh chapels in Patagonia; the ends of the earth were avidly sought out by those escaping Rome's heavy hand.

Back, then, to England's relatively calmer shores.

The Dissolution of the monasteries, while symbolic of the tearing up of the agreement between church and state to rule together, was not so important as the establishment of the head of state as head of the Church, for this is what turned off the tap of funding. England was no longer ruled by lords and bishops, for while the monarch made a grab for the wealth of the Church, the people were asserting their independence by creating wealth untouched by the clammy hand of Feudalism. With this new found financial backbone, the people looked from church to state and from state to church, and decided that neither of them deserved the allegiances of old.

So it was that the official Church of England became estranged from the papacy. Those that decided to follow Rome became Catholic; it was to be almost two hundred years before the Catholics felt sufficiently free to build on their own part, and anti-Catholic riots in England were a feature of the nineteenth century, if not of this one. If the Catholics were oppressed, then it can hardly be concluded that the Protestants were united; at times they were united only in their wish to tear down what they regarded as evidence of a reprehensibly catholic past. Tearing down is not widely regarded as architecture, and at the one extreme any sort of imagery was regarded as blasphemous, while the other, what we might now call moderate, sought to preserve the works of the past; hiding glass and images from the smashers and hackers.

The Church wilted under this onslaught; for over a century Catholic and Protestant fought for control of the Church via the monarchy, while the various factions on the Protestant side fought each other as to the form that the church should take. The populace as a whole now counted enough scholars in its midst to demand that the Bible and the Book of Common Prayer be not only available to all, but the content thereof should be a matter of public debate. Demand for these two works in English was immediate upon publication in 1549, and the debate over their content continued for decades. Well before the conclusion of this turbulent period, various groups saw that their vision of the Christian faith was not to be visited on the population as a whole. There then commenced a slow emigration of the more radical elements, mostly but not exclusively to North America, until the Dissenters became the Nonconformists of the eighteenth century and started to build their own churches.

For two centuries, from 1550 to 1750, there was little by way of new work. Gaily-painted interiors gave way to bleak, austere whitewash. Windows lost their stained glass either by neglect or deliberate destruction. Bells could not be rung for fear of collapse. Sections of larger churches were abandoned, some parts were demolished while others fell down; rood screens were removed, services shifted from chancel to nave to choir and back again as one liturgical whim followed another; pews arrived, so did Carrarra marble tombs, and galleries just had to follow. The pipe organ reached maturity. Altar rails finally made it to the altar — well, the chancel arch, causing the downfall of an archbishop on the way. The master mason became an endangered species, leaving the way open for the architect.

By the middle of the eighteenth century, the pattern of Christianity in England was more or less stabilized. A largely apathetic Protestant majority, loosely tied to the established Church and adhering more or less to a somewhat watered-down liturgy. A severally divided, but very active Nonconformist movement, where reconciliation between fellow Christians foundered over what today seem relatively inconsequential differences. Finally, an oppressed Catholic minority, banned from political office, but seeking a way both to re-establish a physical presence and to gain public acceptance. Of these diverse groups, whose Christian charity towards each other was effectively nonexistent, the Nonconformists were putting together building programmes; small chapels that would bloom into magnificence to rival their older brethren, and wither over the next twenty decades. The established Church's property portfolio was larger than it wanted to handle; and the Catholics dare not risk a show in public.

A divide had been wrought, a divide in the hearts of those whose faith decried such division, the cries of their victims proclaiming the new era, the laughter of the faithless their reward. Would the ruin of their temples proclaim their end?

Decline and Fall

Two hundred years ago England abounded with churches and cathedrals that could be described as 'under construction'. In fact construction had ceased abruptly in the 1540s and was not recommenced. Many churches proceeded to deconstruct themselves faster than their builders had been able to erect. The proclamation of the monarch (Henry VIII) as the head of the Church of England heralded a period of severe recession, periodically racked by dissent, both internal and external. Worse was to come; there was no guarantee that all succeeding kings or queens would be Protestant, as in fact they were not. This succession was predictable; it was known who was next in line and worrying over the prospect of a new Catholic or Protestant monarch was both a reality and an important fact of life. One way of tying the next ruler's hands was to hedge bets by depriving the Church of livings. Anticipating the opposition assuming top dog status had a very real and negative influence on the finances of the Church. Churches rapidly became maintenance-free zones. Wise parishioners kept an eye on the roof during services to ensure they weren't carried off to heaven by default. An Archbishop was deposed because he championed altar rails to keep livestock out of the sanctuary. Towers and spires collapsed, naves and vaults bulged. Above all, nothing was done.

Well actually something *was* being done, or, rather, *undone*. Redundant churches, monasteries, abbeys, chantries and chapter houses were being sold for scrap, dismantled for the lead, timber, stone and glass they contained, or converted to other uses. The tally of losses runs well into four figures, and most of the conversions to alternative use were failures, resulting in dereliction and further demolition. Worse still, there was no shortage of takers for these materials; England was changing to a land dominated by towns, and running out of crown timber for house building as a result. Churches make good quarries, which is why most of our ruined abbeys and monasteries are out in the country; the town ones were quickly recycled. If indifference was not enough, then the move from Catholicism to (at times) radical Puritanism, was accompanied by a good round of iconoclasm. Thomas Cromwell, not to be confused with the Roundhead chap Oliver, set the theme by 'rooting out all the false images', a term that meant smashing everything that came within reach, not just icons.

By the middle of the seventeenth century, ten decades had elapsed, in which the whole of the skilled workforce that had assimilated, and was the product of, five hundred years of experience had simply ceased to exist. A hundred years is a long time for a church to stand out in the open air, *sans* maintenance, and frequently *sans* belief. Yet, while the Church suffered a crisis of philosophy and rocked on the very foundations of belief, while the English Civil War added to the tally of dereliction with a further round of church-bashing (stabling and housing prisoners of war were just two of the innovative uses for churches in this turbulent period) power passed from the country to the town, to the merchants and middle classes, to the emergent 'Middle England'. Appeals for funds to repair the fabric, a new experience in a society that clung quite determinedly to the concept of the abbot fat in purse and person, were a feature of the sixteenth century. Lessons of camels and needles fell on many a newly rich and conveniently deaf ear.

Enter Inigo Jones, First Architect.

Most famously - no, *infamously*, for it is important to set the scene by properly naming the event, an appeal was raised to repair Old St. Paul's, London, a cathedral of first rank (the largest in England) and typical of the Church as a whole in that it was in a decidedly wobbly condition. The job went to an Architect, one Inigo Jones. What he did, or caused to be done, deserves and receives further mention. It was an inglorious start for the architectural profession, but in those times, as now, the truth was what people wanted to believe. The Gothic Cathedral of St. Paul's, was showing signs of distress as the seventeenth century advanced; the vault was too much for the piers and buttresses, and was spreading, a fault that was almost invariably fatal. Whether Inigo was aware of this is uncertain, but, aware or not, his proposals to encase the Gothic work in Portland Stone and add a full-blown Classical facade across the west front was accepted, and completion was greeted with wide public acclaim. Acclaim or no, the fact that St. Paul's continued to tear itself apart could hardly be overlooked.

Inigo was lucky; a bonfire in a bun shop did for his work before it could self-destruct, and this cataclysmic event both saved and made the reputation of the next architect to try his luck on St. Paul's. Saved it, by burning down the building that Wren was trying, almost certainly without hope of success, to prevent from falling down. Made it, by placing him centre stage in the only sustained building programme of neo-classical churches this island has witnessed. That this programme only succeeded by dint of a tax on coal, shows how far England, in the tightening grip of the 'Little Ice Age', had depleted its timber resources, and how far the Church had depleted its spiritual and financial resources. Henceforth, fir from the Baltic, and further afield, can be found alongside English oak in church roofs. Henceforth also, the English Church was obliged to cut its coat to its cloth, no longer a cloth of gold.

A New Era

Wren had to depend on a coal tax, symptomatic of the depletion of natural resources that mediaeval England had depended upon. That he had to rely on taxation at all was a sure sign that the world had moved on, both spiritually and economically. Spiritually, the Church had passed through a turbulent patch; iconoclasm, at the hands of the two Cromwells; minimalistic Puritanism; a brief return to Catholicism under Mary; long and increasingly bitter arguments over the form of the Church and its position in the ecclesiastical spectrum. It is not surprising that the Church of England should emerge from this trauma, at the Restoration in 1660, as a staunchly conservative body, with the puritanical element in retreat. The Catholic-leaning clergy and laity had been appeased to a degree, and the Church was set to defend the remnants of its power and glory to the last chalice.

By the dawn of the eighteenth century, the Church of England might claim that it represented the religion of a nation. By that century's close, the claim had been fairly laid to rest. The Church still acted as if it were the sole religious authority in the land, and while pretending that business as usual prevailed, could not ignore the shower of masonry that was being regularly shed by a broad spectrum of ecclesiastical buildings. The Church of England lost buildings as it lost followers; more by default than any negative action.

In the shadow of the established Church, the other hues of the Christian spectrum were gathering. For obvious reasons (Catholic priests were still being martyred for their faith on this island in the first half of the eighteenth century), the adherents to Rome were estranged from the fold. While Catholics might be deterred from building their own places of worship by a sustained campaign of persecution, there was no chance that this substantial minority would put its hands in pockets and stump up building funds for the established Church.

Likewise the disaffected sections of the Protestant faith; the hardline elements had set sail to forge a new life in North America; and the Dissenters, typified by Wesley, made a point of preaching in the open air, a state of affairs that was not destined to last. Methodism and all the other 'isms' quickly decided that no matter how fine in theory worship at the mercy of the elements was, the strength of faith of lesser mortals was far more likely to be sustained by a modicum of protection greater than that offered by the greenwood tree. Faith, as ever, proved capable of raising funds to raise the roofs of a new series of buildings to the honour of God. By the end of the century the rate of church and chapel construction among the Dissenters was running at about one per thousand head of population, per generation. A dramatic illustration of the power of prayer. The Church of England could only watch as rival institutions sprang up all over the land, pouring the wealth of the peoples labours into coffers other than its own.

The established Church though, still had friends who were not prepared to see their local church fall down. A glance at the timelines of two contrasting churches (see chapter 11) Howden and Urchfont, shows that while the one was left to the ravages of time, surviving by perhaps the slenderest of margins, the other continued to receive the best of tender loving care that its parishioners could lavish upon it. This is the contrast between the two parts of the Church in the seventeenth and eighteenth centuries; the village church was dependent on the whim of its parishioners, as always, and those that wanted to stump up for repairs, did so provided they were not physically obstructed in their labour of love. Churches without a dedicated congregation were left to the mercy of the Church, and it was quite a long time before an architect was detailed for the repair project, if at all. We have, too, seen the early and horribly inept start that the architectural profession made to add expertise to the repair bill. So much flak has been lofted in this respect that the effect is to conceal the true effects.

Architects on the whole are unassuming fellows who just like spending someone else's money in designing and erecting monuments to themselves. They are not generally at their best when working on existing buildings, which have a tendency to get in the way of the real objective. Nonetheless, whilst the Church could not offer a great number of new commissions in the fifteen decades prior to the ascent of Victoria, it offered considerable scope for those who could partially control their primeval urges and lend a hand to keep the fabric up.

Enter 'The Destroyer'

The fame and infamy garnered by those brave souls who ventured into repair and restoration is something of a legend in itself. Top of the tree comes Mr. Wyatt, who for all the praise he received from his successors who bestowed his title 'The Destroyer' upon him, would have been better off as a transported criminal. Reality, when disengaged from the abuse, is somewhat more forgiving. James worked hard in difficult and frequently dangerous conditions on buildings that defied the structural knowledge of his times, with funds that rarely went beyond a partial solution. With architect and craftsmen alike guessing what had gone before, often it was necessary to decide what to save and what to demolish, lest all fall to an equal ruin.

To defend one architect of this period, is not to defend them all. The craze for the 'purity' of classical Greece and Rome led to all sorts of amazingly putrid schemes; Beverley Minster gained a set of classical columns in the inside. The culprit? Nikolaus Hawksmoor, who to add insult to injury, missed the fact that the Minster's south transept was parting company with the nave. By copying the west front towers, adding a few classical motifs, and transposing them onto Westminster Abbey as his own work, Hawksmoor endowed London with a modern copy of an East Riding masterpiece, built with West Riding stone. Perhaps it was to atone for his sins on the original.

Hawksmoor, unfortunately, was not alone, and the list of churches repaired in both Classical and Gothic copy idioms is both long and famous, with much infamy garnered and stored for the second generation restorers in the nineteenth century.

With the industrial revolution gathering pace in the last decades of the eighteenth century, the new wealth of the pits and furnaces, mills and sweatshops did not on the whole land on the offertory plate of the Church of England. Many of the leading lights of the new 'busyness' were Dissenters, whose generosity, and that of their employees was towards the roof over their own places of worship, not the 'official' one. As the Catholics emerged from under the beds and began their own building programme, so did the drift from the established Church accelerate. Closet Catholics no longer felt the need to conceal their true feelings, though Birmingham was to witness anti-Catholic riots only a little over a hundred years ago. The first of the migrants from elsewhere in the British Isles helped to swell the number of adherents to Rome, and their position at the bottom of the social heap proved no bar to their ability to build in honour of their God.

Nationalisation

As the nineteenth century advanced, England, once more a rich land and in world terms, the richest land, was beginning to look like a spiritual desert, especially so from the point of view of the Bishops at Westminster. Content to look on for decade after decade as the industrial towns of England turned themselves into cities, in stature if not in name, the Church at last woke up to the fact that a crash programme of new church building was needed to compete for the souls of industry.

There was just a small problem, a lack of money. No problem, though: Parliament, whether conscious or not of the irony of giving a church money that belonged to the people, people who had voted with their feet not to give the Church money, produced the proverbial rabbit out of the hat in the form of the Church Building Acts. A tidy seven figure sum was allocated to the Commissioners, who proceeded to build a mostly dreary series of brick and (if you were lucky) Bath Stone detailed churches. The slow decline of the official, now state-maintained, religion continued. Not so the rest of the Christian spectrum, however.

Where the official religion failed to win new converts, the Dissenters and the Catholics were thriving, and while their architectural contributions from the latter part of the eighteenth century are mostly modest buildings in the Georgian classical mould, there are some gems to be found. The Dissenters adopted for the most part a rectangular plan, occasionally a 'gothic' layout; were generally quite fond of galleries, then very much in vogue, and an organ, virtually obligatory for any pretensions to wealth, often placed centre stage to substitute for the altar. All this in an architecture that followed fashion, a fashion not led by the Church, but followed.

The Catholics were more remote from these, being torn between the desire to remain discreet and not make a target for bigotry to aim at, and to express the natural flamboyance of a faith that at the grassroots had lost none of the joy of living. Their churches up to the time of Pugin thus show a marked independence born of this dichotomy. The full blown neo-classical St. Francis Xavier at Hereford (1818), is both remarkable for its High Street site (Broad Street actually, literally a stone's throw from the semi-ruin that was the Anglican cathedral), its ostentation, and for the use of long span built up Warren type timber roof trusses, of which more anon.

With confidence soaring after emancipation, the Catholic faithful, aided in no small part by defections from the established Church, including intellectual giants such as Robert, Cardinal Newman, launched a sustained programme of town and city churches from the 1840s onwards. Mostly of Gothic or Romanesque form, with some very well set stonework, a variety of timber roof forms and a rebirth of the passion for coloured and stained glass, these churches, unlike their state-sponsored counterparts, are still comparatively well used and loved. The Dissenters' impressive tally has survived the heavy hand of time less well than they might have wished, despite the periodic revivals that saw large scale building booms, often proudly recorded on foundation, or key, stones.

Twenty and Finish?

To say that the Christian church entered the ultimate century of the second millennium in rude and robust health would be, superficially at least, true. The curate's egg, good in parts, is perhaps a better way of describing the overall picture. Both the Catholics and the Dissenters started the century in good form, and the Catholics have not stood still since. Some of this rosy glow rubbed off on the established Church, which had embarked on a couple of new cathedrals (Liverpool and Guildford), neither of which has a great deal to recommend itself to the student of architecture. If the future looked bright in 1900, then the First World War dealt a body-blow scarcely a decade later, with perhaps the single most vivid image, that of the Established Church blessing the weapons of mass destruction, still passing down the generations as folklore.

With fragmentation of the Christian faith gathering pace as the century progressed, churches have shrunk into the general fabric of society, no longer, apart from the exceptional few, exuberant and distinctive, proclaiming the faith to all from afar. Perhaps the decline of the Christian perspective is summed up in the last great place of worship to be completed in England in the second millennium since the birth of Christ, a Hindu Temple.

Twenty centuries is not the full span of the Christian Faith, but on the resultant architecture, this book is closing, not just a chapter, but perhaps the storyline itself, with only the soap remaining. To the historian and the student of architecture, this is a massive irony; for fifteen centuries the church knew what it wanted in terms of buildings, and for long periods knew how to build in quantity and quality unsurpassed. Three centuries after their invention, the architectural profession cast off its borrowed old clothes and proclaimed a new era in design, only to see one of its prime clients go into recession, a recession from which there is much debate as to whether it will emerge. The Church, having hitched its postern to the concept of design so late in the day (not that it was in any way alone in this), leaves the story of design in church architecture primarily as one of a missed opportunity. The Christian Church, having missed that opportunity for nineteen out of the twenty centuries of its existence, has been one of the major beneficiaries of design theory and practice over the last hundred years. How design operates is thus worthy of a more than cursory examination.

Chapter Three:
Design in theory and practice - A Plan Conceived in the Mind

The interrelationship between the theoretical and practical design of churches, and the actual course of history as far as the chronological sequence of buildings is concerned, indicates that the application of design theory, as we recognize it today, did not emerge until the latter part of the nineteenth century. This is, however, to take the cart before the horse, because few lay readers will be familiar with design theory as it applies to buildings, and many, while designers in their own field, may not be familiar with the philosophy that underpins architecture today.

The key to design freedom, and it applies to all design, is not to think of what you want, but to determine what you want to do *with*, or *in*, what you will eventually design (establish the functions without attempting to determine the form). Only when the functions are set out can the designer, step by step, establish how the building will perform, how the functions will interrelate, how much area and height you will need, and so on.

Then set them aside and forget about them, temporarily at least.

The next step is to conceive a form; organic, mechanistic, human; and the dominant and sub-dominant materials which will determine shape, texture and colour. This stage may also include decisions as to how the end result will operate as a structure, but that is not essential (virtually all successful designs are structurally thought out at this point, though).

This is the design concept. Welding the determined functions, into the form that has been conceived, to produce a building; a presidential palace in Brasilia, a museum in Bilbao, or a press box at Lord's, is to (hopefully) successfully navigate the design process. In design terms it avoids the abyss separated by the two phrases 'I want a house' and 'I want somewhere to live'; the one implies a three-bed semi in darkest Surbiton; already you have resigned yourself to some Norman Shaw mock timber on the front and pebbledash on the back; the other suggests that a rock dwelling in central Turkey, or a teepee in the Nevada desert might be on the agenda, or that you just need a few thousand square miles of the Australian outback to fulfill the needs of domesticity. Just how far the structural limitations of the past have dictated to builders throughout history is a moot point, but there is little doubt that what survives of our forbears' architectural efforts shows little integration of function and form beyond the tiresome necessity of producing a building that will not fall down too soon after completion.

Design, then, is about the manipulation of three-dimensional space within a three-dimensional envelope, and it is the space, not the envelope, that is the objective; the envelope is the means to that objective. Buildings are for people to use, and the envelope modifies the climate of the spaces it generates. People use space, not the building envelope, though that the envelope should enrich both the spaces within and without, is not necessarily a concept that has found universal adoption among schools of design. Where then, does the design of churches fit in this scheme of things? Until this century the answer is that very little design has been applied to the honour of God in the best part of two millennia. And the reasons? We shall see.

In the beginning, there were the Greeks, who, while perfecting the rules of classical architecture, also painted themselves into a design corner from which they were unable to escape; their buildings were dominated by the trilithon. From that point on classical architecture only refined the decoration or adjusted the proportions, until the Romans applied the arch and the vault to do things that a lintel could not. Whilst Roman buildings are almost inevitably poorly proportioned in a strictly classical sense, when compared to their Greek predecessors, they are better designed because they are not tied to a system that only allows one sort of building. The Greeks would never have built the Pantheon or the Coliseum.

When the Christian Church came to this island to try and put an end to the Dark Ages, the architecture it came with was already set firmly in pre-Romanesque mode. Experiment with other designs did not reach these shores and survive to grace even the not too recent past; it was an aisled church with arcades, or one of the many variations thereon, or nothing. As we shall see, the width of the nave was dictated by the size of the timber that could be found to span it, and the module size of the arcade bay was limited by the same factor. This did not change at all between the ninth and the sixteenth centuries; design changes in this period were restricted to the shape of the arch and the proportions of the space enclosed, notably the height.

True, the pointed arch allowed proportions to be refined and stronger, lighter structures to be developed, but in essence the spaces enclosed, while they might be a little higher or longer, were the same. A system was being evolved to its limits, primarily to tease out the many drawbacks of the buildings that had already been built. Of these drawbacks, the lighting of the generated spaces is the single item around which virtually all of the detail design changes rotate, and lighting deserves a section all to itself.

At the end of the Gothic period, a large number of monastic buildings were redundant, and as they had been evolving over the centuries, so too had they become specialized; they were religious buildings and there was virtually no other purpose to which these structures could be put. Hence the mass demolitions, and the abandonment of the rural sites; over-specialization makes buildings difficult, if not impossible, to adapt to new uses. When the new age of the architect hove into view in the seventeenth century, they (architects) were already hidebound to the concept of classical buildings; the reasons are not clear, but the most obvious one that springs to mind is the 'not Gothic' reason. Demand for new buildings in the late sixteenth and seventeenth centuries was not primarily ecclesiastical. As the Gothic style was difficult to adapt to any other use (Wyatt had a go, bless him, but Strawberry Hill survives only as a memory, and the later effort, at Fontwell, is mostly nightmare) hailing the Classical as the new motif is thus the easy option as, once again, the design theory has been done for you. If the delights of Paestum or Pergamun cannot be transplanted from the shore of the Mediterranean to this sceptered isle (visions of Vanburgh explaining to his client on a bracing January day why the walls of Castle Howard need only be a double row of columns for complete comfort and protection from the elements, occur here) then the architect, while reduced to sticking the decorated bits on the inside and outside, can still proclaim the new era, if only because everyone wants it.

One freedom had been gained, the design of long span roof trusses, attributed to Andrea Palladio, but these were not effectively utilized to produce anything in the way of new ecclesiastical design. Where the vault was used, the lessons of the Gothic were unlearned, relearned and the vault as a structural entity consigned to the dustbin of history. In the execution of the dome was there visible progress; Brunelleschi had shown that centering could be dispensed with and a dome built solely with interlocking brick or stone courses and ribs. Fourteen centuries for the church to get even with the pagans, and even then it is possible to nit-pick that Florence gained a rotated arc, not a hemisphere.

The classical facades of the seventeenth, eighteenth and early nineteenth centuries for the most part concealed little that was new. Trussed roofs generally allowed the aisle to be dispensed with, and a glance at the hefty piers Wren was obliged to put into his masterpiece, St. Paul's, explains why. St Paul's is host to Romanesque plus sized columns, and all the awkward little relationships between the elements of the building that just won't tie up, because of the constant span/rise ratio of the semi-circular arch. The two last major churches of the Gothic style, Guildford and Liverpool, are technically and in design terms no different from those of a thousand years previously. For all their influence on church architecture, the major structures of the nineteenth century might just as well have not been built.

In the twentieth century the Church and the architects appear to have emerged, like a dog from water, shaking the past from their portfolios, and saying 'what if?' Can we really believe that our forbears were so blinkered? We now have churches in the round, curves galore, wedge shapes, indeed anything so long as it is not rectangular. Architecture has come of age by ditching the past's motifs. In ditching too, much of the past's technology, some would say that the baby has been thrown out with the proverbial bathwater, but that is one of the consequences of change; you will not change the legal system while retaining the judiciary, and so it is also with buildings. Time is a good filter, and when our children come to judge the worth of the twentieth century, the enormity of both our successes and our failures will be there for all to see.

Design then is not supreme craftsmanship or carving or repetition of a style, it is thinking the unthinkable, conceiving the unconceived, making dreams come to reality. Design is manipulating the materials of the earth to create something at once imaginative, pleasing to the eye, and above all, and this applies especially to architecture, an object of great utility. To the designer, a church represents an almost ideal commission; there is a set pattern of worship, a number of fairly simple criteria over the disposition of the building elements, and relatively few functions to be catered for. Within reason, the more outlandish the proposal, budget notwithstanding, the more likely it is to receive an ecstatic reception. As few people will actually work in the end result, the design will probably not receive an excess of criticism, or be subject to the kind of ultimate trial by ordeal that is now the lot of an inner city secondary school.

Having thus disposed of the theory, a glimpse of the practical, architecture being a practical art, is definitely in order.

Design Practical

At the start of any design process, the designer in taking the client's brief cannot do so immediately, unless he is really unlucky. If the client already knows what he wants and has bolted and barred the door on ideas other than his own, or, worse still, the client has already drawn up a 'plan' that he is

41

determined to see built, then the designer is in real trouble. The story comes to mind at this point of the owner of a not very prosperous football league club, who decided that what he wanted was a new house to his own design. The site was superb, the potential obvious, and the client was used to having his own way. The result was not a home but a straggly unformed blot on the landscape. The reason? While most people think that they know what they want, as individuals they are almost invariably unable to subject their proposals to the sort of critical analysis that might at the end produce a workable scheme. The role of the designer therefore is at the first to discover what it is that is actually wanted. This is the most difficult task, and clients who accept the first scheme that is shown to them, are missing out in a manner they cannot possibly conceive. What they have missed is the 'feedback loop', a process that is essential for both the designer and the client to climb onto the same design bus, and drive it in only one direction, hopefully forward.

In the absence of scale drawings until the nineteenth century, the classic way of demonstrating a proposal was to build a model. Models don't solve your constructional headaches, but are an excellent way of explaining a three-dimensional object, and the designer is not too tied by the model if he finds that what has been proposed cannot actually be built. Professional model makers have been with us for several hundred years, and the trade continues to thrive, for the time being, in spite of severe competition from the 3D image makers.

The designer's second duty is to produce a scheme that works, and while that objective might sound self-evident, there are a number of high profile buildings built in the last fifty years that fail to meet this and a number of the other basic design criteria. These fundamentals have not changed down the ages and they are briefly; that the building can be built; will not cost more to maintain than the owner wishes to afford; will provide an acceptable internal climate; and permit the uses originally intended. These four horsemen sound straightforward enough, but there are many ways in which apocalypse can arrive unbidden at the church door. As concepts in design have flourished in the twentieth century, so too have failures, and by no means does every designer learn from those failures.

Let us then stroll back ten centuries or so to the gloom of the Dark Ages, and have a peek at the practical design that was all the rage then, how to make the church soar, when all it was doing was lumbering. Hang on a minute though, haven't we missed something, like, all of the conceptual design? Quite right, we have, and so did the clerk and mason. They already had their instructions, and in terms of the end product they were in order: oblong, two oblongs in line, cruciform, double cruciform, aisles if you want to go wider, choirs and apses are fine, towers and spires also.

Design of churches a millennium ago meant not design but detailing, how to make the spaces bigger, the arch and vaults hang together; how to manipulate the proportions of the space by the use of detail, creating emphasis with string courses or grouped shafts; where to add the carving. It is the fact that the design of the English church did not change for hundreds of years, only the detail did, that makes the whole so homogenous. This happy absence allows the late fourteenth century work to sit snugly alongside that of the twelfth, or on top of, as often as not. What changes were made were evolutionary, adding light to the nave by means of a clerestory; making piers appear less bulky by adding shafts to their perimeter; altering the proportions of windows and walls. All this was pushing the Gothic design to its limits, but leaving the concept unchanged.

To a degree, this lack of change is reflected in the work of the mason; the carved tympanum (Norman) at Kilpeck is just as well executed as the label stops of three hundred years later. What changes is the decoration and the way that it is used to refine form, rather than just being applied, displaying considerable maturity as the Middle Ages advanced. The structure it is applied to is taller and wider perhaps, pushing the material to the limit of the Gothic concept, but no more. Ten generations of craftsmen have moved on not at all from dog tooth moulding to ball flower keystones, and while their designs are just as wonderful a reflection of their craftsmanship in the fifteenth century as in the twelfth, they do not change the canvas.

Conceptual design, then, is effectively absent from the history of church architecture right down to the start of the twentieth century, as function and form are tied to a past that is, even at the very end of the Gothic period, visibly Roman in origin. The changes we see are evolutionary, but the effect is a transformation, a transformation primarily of light, and the discussion of the way light was handled and developed in the English church is justly an element to be discussed under the heading of design.

Light

There is a school of thought that maintains that to be successful, a building must handle light effectively. There is a further school that says that the driving force behind the development of churches from Saxon to Tudor is in the increasingly sophisticated way that natural light is used to light the interior spaces. In essence this comes down to two factors; quality and quantity, and as the latter appears to have been concentrated upon first, this is where we will start.

In the section on glass, note is made of the fact that the first of the English churches to grace the landscape did so without glass in the windows, and that Bede had to send to Gaul to import the all important technology. The practice of glazing windows up to the dawn of the tenth century had not been universal, quite the reverse in fact, and the point at which window glass became generally available at prices all could afford, is the point at which people stopped living in 'black houses'. This varies across the country, but 1750 would not be a bad date to hang your hat on. The importation of the Romanesque from the continent did not imply that glazing came with it, and until the start of the twelfth century, glass was a luxury and windows remained small to control wind and rain ingress.

The Saxon church was, then, a dark, at times stygian, place, but this would have been in keeping with the times as a whole; buildings were built without windows, and the cooking fire was usually the only light source when the door of house or hall was shut. People were used to the dark, even if they did not like it, and darkness inside buildings was normal. Glass enabled churches to become light inside by allowing windows to be both more numerous and wider. As we have no unaltered

Saxon churches, we can only speculate as to how many windows they had. The Romanesque use of paired, narrow windows of limited height minimised wind and rain ingress, and while this tended to minimise light as well, the advent of glass as a general fixture meant that there was no bar to taking the plunge and going for something a mite larger. Before we look at the 'mite larger', a brief analysis of the way light is handled by the Romanesque is in order.

There are essentially two forms of natural light; general illumination from a bright sky, and direct sunlight. The first gives light into an interior from all points of the compass, but is brighter in the quadrant in which the sun is lodged, a quadrant that migrates from east to south and round to west as the day progresses. North light is less variable and lacks the warmth that solar gain imparts elsewhere. The narrow paired windows of a Romanesque church admit only modest amounts of light, and whether glazed or not, interiors have a continuous air of gloom; cool and shaded in the summer, and downright chill in winter. Into this the direct sunlight blazes as a series of narrow wedges, sweeping the floor and walls in a path that depends upon the time of year. The effect can be dazzling, but equally the opportunity arises to use these beams to illuminate important objects at particular feast or holy days. The need for artificial light was not great, as only the clergy had books and could read; there were few prayer or hymn books; the choir learnt by rote as there was no written music. For services after dusk only enough light was needed to prevent people bumping into one another. This then, is the gloom that the Church set out to dispel.

The Early English style is, in lighting terms, a revolution; the windows are so large they quite simply have to be glazed. In fact from 1100 on, windows are designed on the presumption that glass will be available in quantity to fill the opening, irrespective as to whether or not the window would be glazed before the church was complete, or some time afterwards. That this objective was not at first realised is evident, because not only is the Early English style a change in the way that the building is structurally supported (from a shell wall carrying distributed loads in Saxon, and Norman/Romanesque work, to concentration of loads onto piers and columns) but also a significant expansion of the church sideways, lengthways, and upwards. Merely adding larger windows to the external walls does not guarantee more light if the church is wider and higher. We have the evidence of the first Early English church at Howden to confirm this, and as early stained glass was famed for its full hue colours, the light quality may have been good, but the quantity was certainly lacking. Again, without the need to do anything as complicated as read a prayer book, this did not particularly matter, but having seen the effect that good daylight could create, via a glazed (or open) clerestory, no church that was in funds was likely to spurn the trend of fashion.

Successive developments through the Middle Ages saw the thinning of the structural masonry in the Gothic church and the enlargement of the windows, to the point where there was barely enough masonry to hold up the roof. As the windows swelled to reflect the pride of the Church, and the stained glass in them became more tinted, so the light levels rose and the 'gloamin' dispersed to the corners. There were limits however, and the last of the Gothic churches dating from the mid sixteenth century are still, to our eyes at least, cool and dim. When the new generation of churches began to dot the townscape in the eighteenth century, that master of light, the architect, was on hand to ensure that the play was effectively stage-managed.

By the eighteenth century, the number of literate churchgoers had probably reached a majority over the illiterate. The Bible and the Book of Common Prayer were in full use, both being in English (the Bible in the Middle Ages was in latin, and Sarum Use, the equivalent of the prayer book, was also in latin). Likewise music; the organist had a script, recognizably musical, if not quite the sophisticated notes on staves that we know today. The choir probably still knew its words by heart, but as new hymns were written, they were circulated in manuscript, not by word of mouth. Light, then, was much in demand and if there is one thing that architects could provide, it was lots of natural light, and the glass it shone through was truly clear, even if a little wobbly still. As a commodity, light from the sun had a brief reign, due to the next technological leap, the gas lamp.

While Tetbury is an enlightened essay in the handling of light in quantitative terms, architecture generally does not hang onto a good thing once found, but needs must look for something new. The arrival of the gas lamp, in its filthy fishtailed format, *sans* incandescent mantle, was enough of a revolution (whatever happened outside, it was now possible to read inside at any hour of day or night) to take natural lighting maximization off its number one spot on the architect's shopping list. As a result too many nineteenth century churches were not so much underlit as undeveloped in their use of natural light, spurning the cheer and delight that lots of light brings, yet failing to exploit the air of mystery and surprise that effective use of natural light can generate. Electricity as a whole has not, despite being around for a hundred years, made the Church its home on the inside, though providing spectacular effects on the outside. The opportunity to make magic with lanterns seems too often to escape humanity's grasp. Finally, and while it is nothing to do with England, and there is nothing to compare on these shores, mention of the supreme use of natural light at Notre Dame du Haut, by Corbusier, just has to be made; too often examples of how not to do things spring first to mind. This is how to get it right.

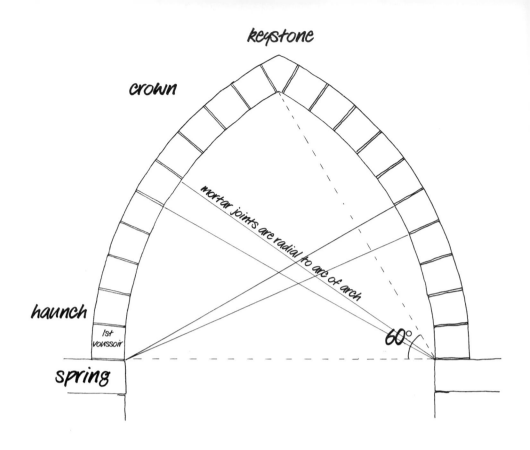

keystone

crown

mortar joints are radial to arc of arch

haunch

1st voussoir

spring

60°

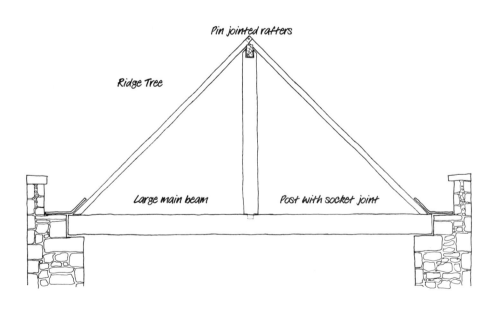

Pin jointed rafters

Ridge Tree

Large main beam

Post with socket joint

Chapter Four:
Structural Theory - In Defiance of Gravity

If the reader has gained the impression, by the perusal of this work, or by some fanciful vision, that the architect or mason trotted off to work each morning armed with a set of safe load tables and a slide rule, then firmly set that rosy vision aside now. As far as structural theory and church architecture is concerned, the Dark Ages lasted virtually to the dawn of the twentieth century. The development of the Gothic form is almost a denial of calculation, the substitution of the classical a structural step backwards, and the 'neo' revivals merely a further essay in structural ignorance. It appears that not even the simplest of calculations were performed to determine any aspect of structure, nor any effort made to establish the suitability of materials for their intended structural purpose. Until the nineteenth century then, all practical structural theory was empirical, a heady mix of experience, common sense (or lack of it) and a general belief that if it stayed up, all was well with the world.

There is some evidence to suggest that, when the basis of effective calculations came to be determined, the emergent architectural profession ignored the implication that mathematics could give them insight into their building problems. When structural engineers eventually forced their way onto the scene, their welcome was, to say the least, muted. Let us return then, to the bottom of the learning curve.

History does not record that Bede or St. Augustine added the letters 'C. ENG.' after their names at the foot of their letters, so we can take it that they were not the brilliant structures experts of their day. What we can take, however, is the notion that once the conversion of the English gained an unstoppable momentum in the ninth century, the full technological resources and expertise of the society were laid at the feet of the Church. In structural terms those resources were meagre to the point of absence. Expertise in building in stone was limited. No major buildings had been seen on this island since the departure of the Romans. Most structures were framed in wood. Roofs were made of thatch, walls infilled with wattle and daub. Foundations were non-existent. The nearest standing Roman buildings were a long way away in the south of Europe. While St. Augustine almost certainly had studied the works of the ancients at first hand, or could draw on the knowledge of those who had, the vast majority of the people who were to put together the first churches of the Saxon era, the masons and carpenters, would not have left these shores, much less be familiar with the actual methods of construction employed by the Romans.

Two Challenges

The Saxon church as first conceived did not present anything great by way of structural challenge, but two challenges on this front were met virtually from the start, modest though the first structures were. The principles of arch design and construction and the effective span of timber beams determined proportions of the early church, and their limits. Before we consider these, a brief look at a technology that was in use, the stone lintel, will prove instructive.

Timber beams were in common use in domestic construction in the ninth century, and with underwood poles and organic materials, spans of twenty or thirty feet were easily achievable. A simple stone lintel, requiring half a dozen men to lift it onto the top of a door opening, will only just span an opening wide enough to drive the cows through, and the cows that were available were somewhat on the small side, too. No one had any coherent theory as to why this should be, only that it was part of the natural order of things. What in fact is happening is that the stone is acting as a beam, with the top face placed in compression, and the bottom face in tension, and stone is very limited in its tensile strength.

Failure of a stone lintel, or beam, when it occurred was thus a failure in tension. What experience taught the ninth century structural engineer, was that a stone lintel on its own is not very strong; place it on the ground and jump on it and you are quite likely to have two lintels. Place the same lintel over an opening in a wall and pile as much masonry as you like on top of it, and, provided it's properly built, you can then do clog dances to your heart's content on top without causing any damage at all.

This was a lesson well learned, but hardly understood. What is actually happening is that the various components are joining forces and being interdependent. This phenomenon of interdependency is critical to the success of mediaeval masonry, and the Gothic arch depends on this no less than any other feature of church architecture.

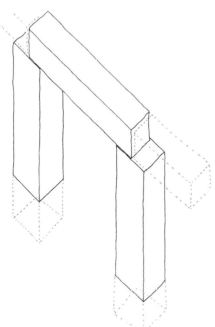

The Trilithon - I

The foundation of architecture is the raising of the lintel on two posts, as exemplified by the Eocene sarsens of Stonehenge. Proportions are dictated by the size of the stones and the span of the lintel, the span being limited by the tensile strength of the stone.
This arrangement is very stable - Stonehenge is a ruin primarily owing to it being used as a quarry

When a lintel is placed over an opening, it is longer than the opening by the length of the bearings at either end. As the wall is built up on top of the lintel two things occur; firstly there is load placed not only on the span of the lintel but on the section over the bearings as well. This load on the bearings has the effect of pre-stressing the lintel (by jacking down the ends) reducing the tension in the bottom face that will cause failure if excessive.

Secondly, and crucially, the stones above the lintel, even if they are not bedded stretcher bond like bricks, will cantilever out from the bearing. If there is enough masonry above the lintel the masonry will cantilever over the opening, leaving the lintel only supporting a triangle of masonry immediately above it. That this was not understood is obvious by the relieving arches that have been commonly inserted over stone lintels right down to the twentieth century. When we look at the arch, the one thing that is missing in a wall with arches in lieu of lintels, is the triangle of masonry over the opening. So what is the arch actually supporting?

The Arch

The principle of the arch is that a number of individual shaped blocks of stone or brick interlock to form a single unit where all components are in compression. The components, called voussoirs, rely on the line of thrust of the arch passing through the joints perpendicular, or nearly perpendicular, to the plane of the joint, friction within the joint allowing for some modest divergence from this rule. This rule for a stable arch is not obvious, and failures due to divergence occurred until the nineteenth century, when one famous engineer refused to strike the centering for fear that what he had designed would not stand up on its own. In the ninth century though, there was trouble enough in mastering the semi circular masonry arch without need to worry about flat elliptical brick ones. What was driven home very quickly was that if you wanted to escape from a technology that allowed the construction of small arches for doorways, and little else, then you had to move away from rough rubble masonry and thin tilestones for voussoirs, and get seriously into dimension stone, and accurate dimension stone at that.

You also need a little bit of luck, and the luck, as we have seen with our deliberations on the lintel, is that the masonry arch isn't actually doing a great deal apart from holding itself up. To increase the span of a masonry arch involves changes in the arches proportions. The ratio between the thickness of the arch ring and the span of the arch determines the slenderness of the structure, so increasing the span while keeping the voussoirs the same general dimensions increases the slenderness ratio. This in its turn increases the accuracy demanded to ensure that all the forces acting on the arch ring remain within that ring. Walls that are not straight cannot be supported by an arch that has a kink in the middle.

All this had to be learnt the hard way.

Learnt, these lessons were and the churches of the tenth century began to soar, as the right stone was quarried and accurately shaped to perform the more onerous duties these structures demanded. This was the first technological gear shift of the mediaeval Church, and once launched on an upward trajectory along the learning curve, the spirit of competition kept the engine of progress in full forward gear.

Romanesque

The Romanesque style is dependent on the large span masonry arch to free the insides of the church from the numerous columns that would otherwise fill the space and blot out the view; it is the arches chief advantage over the stone lintel. Small spans are little use, due to the necessary minimum dimensions of the columns that proffer the support. Imagine Tewksbury Abbey with the column centres reduced by half; there would just be room enough to squeeze between the columns when passing from the nave to the aisles. Of view, there would be none. The Romanesque style is conceived around the semi-circular arch, and, as a single slim ring of masonry, such an arch is completely unstable. Removal of the centering will cause collapse due to the weight of the crown pushing out the haunches.

This arch form is thus mostly, but not entirely, decorative, generating lateral thrusts along the line of the arch or arcade that must be buttressed at the ends, with quantities of masonry that are quite inappropriate to a church. The arch in church architecture is in fact mostly decorative; to fill the space between the loadbearing columns, link the elements of the structure together so that they act monolithically, and receive the, hopefully modest, lateral forces generated by the non axial loads. As we have seen, the infill masonry above the spring of the arch will cantilever quite happily most of the distance between column centres, and that masonry provides the loads on the haunches of the arch to counter the lateral thrusts. The arch really only has to sit there and smile, no hard labour required.

Architecturally the semi-circular arch is a bit of a handicap, not due to its lack of potential muscle, but due to the constant span/rise proportions of 2:1. That ratio is actually better than is demanded purely for reasons of internal space and sightlines, and it was only when the next fashion fad, the vault, came along that the limitations of the semi-circle were exposed.

Barrels and Vaults

The Pantheon has lot to answer for. It was a constant reminder to the many pilgrims to Rome that no matter how superior their religion might be, the heathens were one up when it came to matters of architecture. If flattery is the best form of praise, then the Roman gods must have spent most of the middle ages laughing their insides out at the attempts to copy this most enigmatic of structures. The problem was one of lateral thrust, and how the Romans had solved it could not be guessed. The one Christian church with a dome, Hagia Sofia in Constantinople, gave its owners incessant nightmares as it spread and was repaired, and spread again. When a simple barrel vault was tried in England, no one actually succeeded in making the semi-circular form stand up. Was a true dome ever attempted?

The trouble with barrels and domes is that they distribute their loads equally about their base, and to make matters worse, they shed their lateral thrust in an equally indiscriminate manner. As we have seen, the arcade-supported wall is really only a series of columns with a bit of pretty stone in between. While this exercise in fashion could be beefed up to take the vertical loads, there was no way that the lateral thrusts could be accommodated, short of making the walls thirty or forty feet thick. And then there was the little problem of adding more masonry to the haunches of the barrel to prevent the weight of the crown pulling the plug on the whole edifice. To work, such an arrangement wouldn't so much have lumbered as lurked, threatening to crush all who entered its grim portals, beneath ton upon ton of masonry. An entirely impractical proposition in a building.

Not to be outdone, the solution that evolved was the pointed arch, and from this one piece of structural sleight of hand evolved a whole series of churches that dominated the architecture of northern Europe for nearly half a millennium.

Pointed Arches

It will probably never be known who first thought up the idea of altering the span/rise ratio of an arch by chopping out the top third and leaning the two remaining segments together. The coincidence of the emergence of this form with the launch of the Crusades, may be just a coincidence, or may point, as has been suggested, to the idea having being pinched from the opposition. The fact that it worked and was structurally very stable owes nothing to the structural knowledge of the day. The freedom that it brought to the designers of the twelfth century is everywhere reflected in their achievements. The problem that it solved, the concentration of the thrusts and loads of a vault onto piers, where they could be supported and buttressed, was relatively insignificant when compared to the fashion statements that sprang up to honour the new technique.

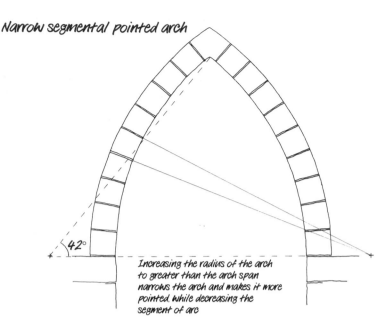

Narrow segmental pointed arch

42°

Increasing the radius of the arch
to greater than the arch span
narrows the arch and makes it more
pointed, while decreasing the
segment of arc

The problem of the vault is this; to divert the load onto piers requires that arches span from pier to pier along and across the nave of a church. This produces an intersecting, or quadripartite, barrel vault, with half of the masonry forming an arch at right angles to the axis of the nave. This requires, using a semi-circular arch, that the nave width is the same as the arcade spans. Tewksbury Abbey was probably planned with this system in mind, with enormous stone piers to take the loads. This still leaves the barrel too thick for comfort on the haunches, because the thrust line of this shape of arch threatens to leave the masonry at the haunch, and has to be held in by brute force, like an ageing midriff.

This problem gets worse as the span increases, producing a practical limit for this arrangement that is not large enough for the typical mediaeval church. If however you can substitute the solid with ribs, then the infill between the ribs can be much lighter, but only if the ribs dissect the space into areas small enough. This can be achieved by putting ribs across the diagonals of a bay, but if the ring of masonry is semi-circular then its rise will be 1.414 times that of the arches that span along and across. In other words the six arches won't intersect to form a decent vault.

This is the problem the pointed arch solves.

Three dimensionally the object of vaulting is to span (usually) the nave and display a single level internal ridge line. The pointed ribs will achieve this, and by dropping the apex of the ribs that span between adjacent piers, an effect akin to a barrel vault can be attained. The beauty of the rib is that it is only the rib that needs centering while it is erected, not the infill masonry. Careful sequencing of the stone infill, coupled with some timber struts and shuttering, allow a comprehensive 3-D centering arrangement to be avoided, together with all the attendant support.

If the pointed arch only achieved this, then success would have been assured, but not glorious. Pointing the arch did one other, vital thing, reducing the bursting forces on the haunches, and allowing the lateral thrusts to be taken down below roof level and buttressed. Gothic structural system complete. All the rest is just fancy masonry.

Hold on a minute, all the rest is *not* just fancy masonry, there's some pretty fancy woodwork, and structural woodwork at that, to consider before we relax and say 'that will last for a thousand years'.

The transverse arch ribs and the diagonal arch ribs are built first on centering. The tiercerons and liernes, and the ridge ribs are then built to subdivide the vault, avoiding the need for centering to support the infill, which accounts for 70-80% of the load. After removal of the scaffold, all rooof loads are taken on the piers and their buttresses

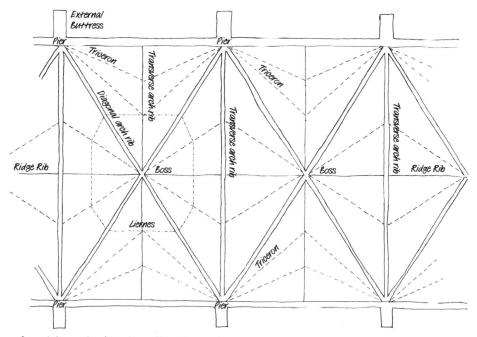

Quadripartite Vault - Plan Layout

Timber

The structural contortions that turned the semi-circular arch into a pointed one can be identified as the root of the Gothic system. The structural limitations of timber beams can with reason claim to determine the proportions of the mediaeval Church. The pointed arch solved a structural problem; how to perch a vault on top of masonry, whose scale and proportions were determined by the ability of timber to span the spaces generated. Timber determined the proportions of the mediaeval church, because timber was there first, was needed to form the centering for masonry arches and vaults, and outnumbers the fancy vault ten to one in the churches of England, and more.

The first churches were probably no different structurally from the domestic buildings that surrounded them in the seventh, eighth and ninth centuries. That happy conjunction was not destined to last, for the Church determined to distance itself from the domestic and become a power in the land. Circular churches have made something of a comeback this century, but they appear to have been *verboten* a thousand years ago. By denying people the ability to enclose a circular space for worship, and demanding that the structure and materials distance church construction from the common, the stage is set for an adventure in timber structures that began with the beam and ended, well, we shall see.

Ridge Trees

The chosen form for the Saxon church was a rectangle, or two rectangles, the smaller one housing the chancel. Roofing such a space is easy; fix a beam to span the length of the ridge and then tie your rafters to it. The rafters will span half the width of the building and support the tiles, thatch or slates to keep the rain out. No need for any purlins or ties, and the inside is clear to the underside of the roof. Only one snag. A straight(ish) tree is needed to form the ridge tree that must span the long side of the rectangle, and it has to carry half the weight of the roof. This is a pretty big snag. For reasons to be explained, the most appropriate form for a Saxon timber beam is rectangular, basically a squared log.

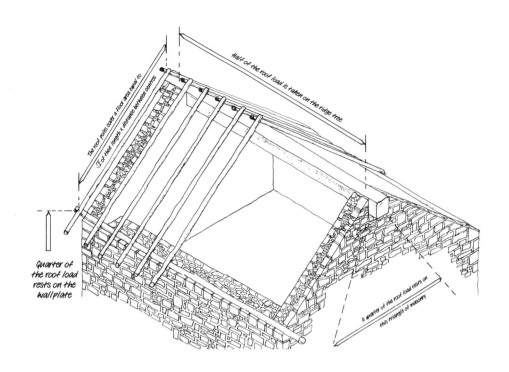

Quarter of the roof load rests on the wallplate

The roof poles cover a floor area equal to 1/3 of their length x distance between centres

Half of the roof load is taken on the ridge tree

A quarter of the roof load rests on this triangle of masonry

There are limits to the size, both length and girth, that you can obtain oak logs in. True, you can force grow a stand of timber to give you a log eighty feet long, but you then have to wait two hundred and fifty years to put the roof on the church. Practically, ridge trees could not be obtained longer than about forty feet, and a foot to eighteen inches side when squared. This is not really large enough for anything but the smallest church. The problem this presents was solved by a bit of lateral, or rather transverse, thinking.

Trusses

The length of a church need not be limited by the longest span of a timber beam, if that beam can be supported at mid span, or at two or three places along its length. It is in fact quite feasible to place arches across the width of the nave to provide that support. An arch the width of the nave was no mean feat in the ninth century, and the solution arrived at was a timber solution; secondary beams supporting posts that held up the ridge tree at the necessary intervals. These are not trusses, but simple beams taking a point load in the middle

59

of the span. There is not really a *worse* way of carrying a load, and the size of the timber needed for this arrangement, and the limited spans that could be bridged, demanded something better.

The problem the ridge tree, beam, and post generates is that half of all the roof load rests on the middle of a beam, which has to perform like the proverbial Atlas as a result. If some of that load could be shifted onto the walls, or onto the beam closer to the walls, then the workload would be reduced. Longer spans were only possible if the carpenter put his brain in gear and came up with something different, and over the centuries lots of carpenters had lots of ideas on how to achieve this, and all of them can be loosely described as timber trusses. There is no particular order of development of trusses, only that the 'King Post', a direct development from the beam and post, probably came first and has certainly stayed longest. Not that the ridge tree is dead, for the author spotted one being built into a house in Shropshire in 1998. The advent of the truss meant that the ridge subsided in importance to a relatively modest chunk of timber, particularly as moderately efficient trusses could be spaced at reasonable intervals without laying waste to every mature oak in the English lowlands, just most of them.

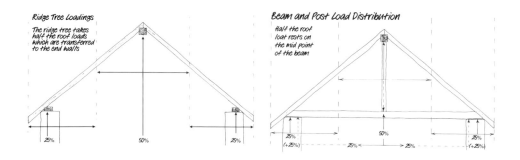

King Post

Most people will recognise a king post truss. Not one in a hundred will twig the advance over a beam and post, because superficially they look similar, and with the limited technology of the Middle Ages the full capacity of the king post, which requires a full tension joint at the mid point, could not be achieved. Nonetheless, the king post dramatically redistributed loads away from the middle of the beam, and it did it by allowing the purlin to sneak in and hold up the rafters. The way the king post works is this; the truss is an 'A' frame, in which the raking members are housed into the ends of the horizontal beam to make two compression joints. Two similar joints near the apex house the rakers into the king post, which is slotted to take the ridge. The loads of the ridge are thus distributed into three timbers, two of which transmit their loads directly to the side walls, their lateral thrust being taken by tension in the main tie beam. If this was all that the truss achieved, then the central point load would be one third (approximately) that of the load on a beam and post system

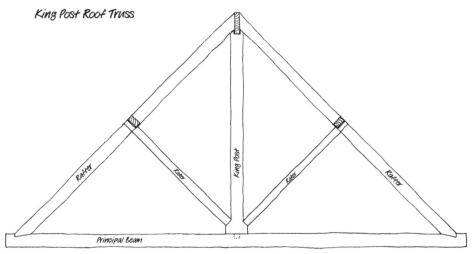

King Post Roof Truss

Rafter Raker King Post Raker Rafter

Principal Beam

The king post is one of the most efficient traditional truss forms owing to the fact that no load is transferred onto the principal beam by the king post. The principal beam takes only its self weight and tensile loads from the rafters

But what about the purlins? The presence of the rakers in the truss allows purlins to support the rafters at mid span. These purlins now take one half of the roof loads, leaving the ridge with a quarter and the walls one eighth each. So the point load on the middle of the beam is now only one quarter, rather than the third it had been. But the truss has to support the purlins, and it does this via the two struts that rake out from the king post base. These struts also have housed compression joints to the king post, not the beam, and the effect of the purlin loads is to place the king post in tension, the socket in the beam merely acting as a location point for the truss. All of the purlin loads are thus taken either as tensile or compression loads in the truss and transmitted to the wall bearings, eliminating the point load at the middle of the beam. A brilliant piece of timber engineering, achieved without a single calculation, and more to the point without actually knowing anything about compression, tension and bending.

The king post truss then, reduces the point load on a roof beam from one half of the load on a simple beam and post, to effectively nil, and allows for smaller roof timbers to be used in the ridge and in the rafters. A virtuous circle of lighter construction and more efficient use of timber. The reason why evaded the mediaeval carpenter, but is easily explained today. Timber is strong in both tension and compression along the grain, and in compression across the grain.

Timber is, however, poor in tension across the grain, and timber beams fail at modest loads owing to rupture of the wood fibres, caused by the tensile failure of the bonds between the fibres perpendicular to the plane of tension/compression, the failure usually occurring at a defect such as a knot. By using timber subject to tensile or compressive forces but avoiding excessive bending force, the carpenter was able to get more useful work out of the timber. All the main players in a king post truss are in either tension or compression, not bending. The main cross beam is reduced to a bit part player, useful for getting the thing up and running, and good looking to boot, but seriously overrated in terms of actual muscle.

Queen Post

Not so good looking and a bit of a weakling (that's not pure misogyny, just nearly so), but it sums up the relative merits of kings and queens, in roof construction at least. As an alternative to a king post (the system is basically three king posts in one truss), the queen post truss suffers from an excess of complication and, while it has the merit of taking load off two purlins, against the king post's one per side, it is at the added expense of a second hefty post. The load is then split in two and moved to positions one third of span from the supporting walls. With the use of purlins the loading of the truss is actually increased, the main beam supporting five sixths of the total roof load (five twelfths per side), instead of half with the beam and post. The difference is that the principal members are either in tension or compression, with the exception of the tie beam. The queen post nonetheless allowed for a modest increase in the spans of church roofs, or an increased load, from tiles, for example, and is about as effective as the Middle Ages could produce. Not efficient, but it worked, and didn't demand miracles from timber or craftsman.

Trusses Galore

Because there was no real understanding of the forces and loads being taken on the timber in a roof truss, trusses developed in a number of ways that had no particular structural logic, and we must look for the driving force of change elsewhere. To do this, it is worthwhile to consider the roof as a whole, for the whole is dependent on the sum of its parts. Trusses were not the only item in a roof that changed as the Saxons lost top dog status to the Normans and the Romanesque gave way to the Gothic. Prime among those changes was the waterproof layer, which can only have been thatch in the beginning, and thatch is a wonderfully all embracing covering that needs little by way of support, and is usually tied on to a woven undercloak.

Thatch, prior to its stockbroker renaissance, was very much the poor man's roof, and while thatch is still to be found on churches today, it quickly received short shrift from the better class of church in the tenth century. Like many 'improvements', thatch's successors were more demanding in terms of support, and less efficient in the discharge of their duties, but they were longer lasting.

Thatch was superceded by lead and tilestones. Both demanded a complete rethink of the roof structure. Firstly they were heavy, very heavy, and needed virtually continuous support. This demanded the use of close boarding for lead, and either closely set rafters and battens or close boarding again, for tilestones. These boards could not be sawn, but had to be split from tree trunks and were usually between one and a half and two inches thick, spanning from ridge to purlin, and purlin to wallplate. Such construction can still be found today, though it has probably not seen serious use this century past.

Cast lead sheet, up to 10mm thick (today's milled sheet code 4 is, well, *thin* in comparison), was mechanically fixed to the roof boards. There was at least little chance of the roof blowing off. If the underside of the boarded roof was unsatisfactory, then it could be painted, the paint at least, was not a very heavy burden to add to the truss loadings.

Hand in hand with the increase in the weight of roof coverings came a shortage of timber. Split a two hundred year old oak into boards two inches thick and what you *don't* get is a lot of boards. To make matters more difficult, only trees with a sufficiently straight grain and free of major defects will split easily; the rest have to be sawn, and sawing was not a practical option until saws became the double-handled pit saws that still find occasional use today.

If you are going to saw timber then you can make the resulting wood stretch further by using joists and thin boards, or, better still, you can substitute underwood in the form of split poles or wattle for the boards, and plaster the underside to make it look good. There's no saving in weight, but a good saving in precious timber. Having to saw the timber needed to form a roof placed limits on what could be achieved and the sections that could be used, and this fact, rather than any structural design considerations, dictated the development of the timber roof.

Sawn green timber in small sections, as opposed to squared tree trunks, that is, has a marked tendency to twist, cup, bow and warp, and all of these mean that what was sawn straight, didn't stay straight for long. The only way to ensure a reasonably useful section of timber in the Middle Ages, was to saw, or more normally adze or axe it into a square section, or as near square as was practicable. This is fine for struts for king posts, but not desperately efficient for beams, purlins and rafters. To assist beams in their duties, where there is frequently an excess of timber, but in the wrong shape, it became custom to add straight or curved braces, adding greatly to many a churches charms. Possibly this led to the development of the hammer beam, but it is more likely that this was an experimental exuberant model that just happened to work.

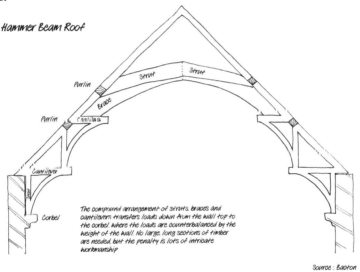

Hammer Beam Roof

Strut
Strut
Purlin
Brace
Purlin
Cantilever
Cantilever
Corbel

The compound arrangement of struts, braces and cantilevers transfers loads down from the wall top to the corbel, where the loads are counterbalanced by the weight of the wall. No large, long sections of timber are needed, but the penalty is lots of intricate workmanship

Source : Bacton

Strip out the embellishments and it becomes clear that hammer beams are beams, that is, the principal rafters are acting as beams. The edifice is really a series of cantilevers where the roof loads counterbalance the turning moments of the loads from further up the roof, with the two sides leaning together at the top, and the point of load transfer moved down the walls to where the masonry can add counterbalance. The whole structure is, as usual, an excuse for some fancy detail carving. As with all mediaeval timber design, the joints are in compression. The really brilliant aspect of this structure is that while the concept of a king post or a tied rafter is fairly obvious, even if you cannot appreciate the ideas of tension and compression, stress and strain; the hammer beam actually looks as if it shouldn't work, even to the point where the sheer arrogance of the carving and the curved work appear to mock all structural sensibility.

Rafters

For the sake of structural convenience we have been too free with our use of this word so far, but as an element of structure the rafter is a name in common parlance, and conveys the idea of roof loads being transmitted to purlins, that are in their turn supported by the roof trusses; a system of load transference. Rafters as we know them are modern; the product of the saw pit and the rack saw, a reflection of the need to produce timber that could do more with less. Yet the concept is age old; underwood poles used in the round to support straw, thatch or turf. You can still see the tradition of round wood for building in the more remote parts of the Mediterranean today.

As a structural element the typical rafter is square or slightly oblong in section, not because it is the best structural shape, but because that was the most stable shape that could be sawn by hand or machine and remain reasonably true as it seasoned. Only since World War Two has this traditional shape demised in the face of truly engineered timber. The advent of the power saw in the nineteenth century certainly revolutionised timber production; its effect on conservative timber sections was almost nil. The presence of quantities of easily converted imported softwood enabled the Victorians to modernise the timber church roofs of England, and most of the rafters to be seen now are machine sawn softwood, though many of the larger timbers survive from an earlier age. The hybrid roof is the norm; old oak throughout exceptional.

Modern Trusses

This is a bit of a misnomer; timber trusses with tension joints are illustrated on Trajan's column in Rome, and the King Post can be persuaded to act as an efficient truss even if it isn't designed like one. Likewise that church favourite, the scissors truss. The modern truss is not so much an actuality as an idea; the product of someone sitting down and working out why timber behaves as it does; what is happening in the various components of a composite beam, and designing a structure that uses that knowledge to advantage. The principal is simple; in order to design a tension joint in timber, the material for all trusses until the mid eighteenth century, you need to understand what tension is. All conventional timber joints have only limited tensile strength, but many are excellent in compression.

In truss design the bottom boom is in tension on a simple span, and without an efficient tension joint the longest span is that of the largest tree, about eighty feet. The theory was both understood and practical designs built, by the architect Andrea Palladio in Italy in the mid sixteenth century, who managed to span over a hundred feet, a distance considerably in excess of the demand in building, and remaining so for a further three hundred years. The key to Palladio's success was the use of wrought iron straps and pins, and while the mathematics that underpin the idea were understood, and used in later centuries to design much larger structures, architects then, as today, were quite happy to use the idea without bothering to brush up on the maths.

Long Span Timber Truss

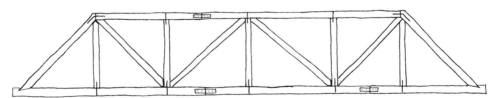

The long span timber truss made the post rennaisance classical church an essay in light and space by spanning where beams and arches could not. The key is use of wrought iron straps to form tension joints. Sophisticated trusses like the one above could sport span : depth rations of 1 : 5 or so, against 1 : 10 or more for a simple beam. and pro rata were both lighter and stronger. and less likely to sag

Source : St Francis Xavier

The idea that the new style of church could dispense with the high vault (the barrel vault was just as difficult to put on a neo-classical church as it was on the Gothic), avoid the steeply pitched roof of the conventional Gothic form, and hide the roof completely behind a false parapet, became a reality with the adoption of the modern timber truss. Typically the truss was a forerunner of the classic iron trusses of the nineteenth century, still in widespread use on rail systems worldwide; top and bottom parallel booms separated by vertical and diagonal braces, with sloping ends (that at St Francis Xavier, is technically more advanced than the iron truss used by the Stockton and Darlington Railway to span the river Gaunless seven years later, and while the latter is in a museum, the former is still performing its duties in Hereford). The ends of these new trusses were clad in slate, and the top received a lead roof. A hefty parapet hid the whole from the viewer at ground level, and was designed in the idiom of the past with the intent of disguising the present. Later designs made use of iron, reverting to the traditional triangular truss form, and frequently the bottom boom was reduced to a thin iron bar, in complete contrast to the massive beams of their predecessors.

Today we have complex structures in steel and concrete that are as often hidden as exposed, frequently covered by details that look structural but aren't. There are however some beautifully detailed churches using curved timber as portal frames (a modern version of the mediaeval cruck, still to be seen in timber framed buildings), the latter day crucks being in glued laminated timber, one of the delights of the twentieth century. Mass concrete, despite the opportunity of infinitely curvaceous walls and roofs, beyond the odd headline commission, has not caught on, in England at least, and while plastics and other metals, particularly aluminium, have a small presence, their structural use, like that of glass, remains modest.

Mastery of structures meant, until the advent of the twentieth century, mastery of the properties of timber and stone, with a little assistance from iron. Whilst essentially a structural problem, the provision of foundations was not approached in any sort of analytical manner; what a church received in this department was pot luck, if anything. Foundation provision is thus an 'art' in its own right, and is discussed under its own heading, along with the basics of the geometry needed to set out the larger buildings with a degree of accuracy sufficient to defy gravity, at least for a little while.

Chapter Five:
Foundations and Setting Out -
The Essentials of Substance and
Accuracy

If there was one element of construction technology that had to be learnt the hard way then foundations, their design and the actual need for them tops the list. Until the end of the ninth century most buildings had been built in wood, stone only being used where it was readily available and in convenient sizes. Foundations for wooden structures consisted of little more than digging a post hole and dropping the log in. Pointing the end and bashing it in with a hammer was the sharp end of technology. If the building sagged or leaned then it could be propped, or if it was far gone, taken down and rebuilt. Stone proved to be just a little more recalcitrant.

Learning from the past was in the main unhelpful, because the only Roman structure left standing above ground in Britain by AD 800 was Hadrian's Wall, and the stone bits of that are founded on the rock that was used to build it. Even more unhelpful is the surface geology of this island, an issue well beyond the ken of ninth century man. Almost no two sites present the same subsoil or rock to act as a loadbearing strata. Many churches, and this is particularly true for those of the larger size, have a number of different subsoils to rest on, and those subsoils are in their turn often underlain by material that can vary between rock and quicksand. A veritable mediaeval minefield for the inexperienced and the unwary. If this weren't bad enough, groundwater and its infinite variability added its spoke to the wheel as well.

Trouble that could not have been foreseen lay in store for the builders of stone churches, and it duly arrived, not always at the first, but usually as the priest and his mason were toying with something a mite more ambitious than the Anglo-Saxons had run to.

Central to the problem is the concept that it is the natural ground that supports a building, a philosophy not expounded until the end of the eighteenth century, not understood at all at the start of the mediaeval period, and comprehended only dimly as the centuries progressed. The idea that soils and rock have a limit load capacity, which if exceeded will result in plastic deformation or compressive failure, was not appreciated. Nor was the variability of that load capacity in nominally similar soils, or the effect of the rise and fall of the water table, or the drying and recharging of clays due to seasonal rainfall variations. Worse still no one bothered to estimate, let alone calculate, the loads that were going to result from adding a triforium or altering the roof to include a vault.

Success first, then failure

In the beginning, the Anglo-Saxon Church could, and almost always did, choose a greenfield site for a new church. If there had been a building on the site previously then it would be demolished down to ground level and built over, a process shown to classic effect in the excavation of Troy, where the process was repeated so often that the city rose above the plain it stood on, but equally applicable to many city sites in England. The effect of such action is to form a platform of rubble, a foundation of sorts, and much better than no foundation at all, though very much a double-edged sword. The tendency of our forbears not to dig down below the surface of the soil they stood on when building something new is a boon to archaeologists, but the process is aided by two natural effects that cause the relative positions of the land surface and buildings to shift. Firstly there is the compressive effect of the weight of the building upon the subsoil, which can be squeezed, allowing the building to sink slowly over time. Secondly, there is the rubbish, vegetative growth and deliberately placed rubble, stone flags, dirt or other material that is used to keep land around buildings passable to foot and vehicles. Buildings have the tendency therefore to sink relative to their surroundings.

All of this is very well when the ambition of the age is not to build higher than you can punt an inflated pig's bladder over. The trouble starts in earnest when the tower of Babel has lodged permanently in the mind's eye.

The realisation that substructures were necessary to support above ground superstructures took root slowly, but as the twelfth century advanced and churches started to reach for the sky and spread significantly beyond the footprint of their predecessors, wise clerks and masons set about ensuring that before the building started to go up, some sort of foundation went down. The really difficult question was, what to put down? To this there were basically four answers: Do nothing, dig for victory, pile in, or go for a raft.

Doing nothing is an inherently defendable stance. To some extent it is still used today in this country, and even the casual observer will not have to leave the shores of Europe to find this method of foundation design alive and flourishing. In an age where animals could be tried for sins, there was little likelihood of a conviction of a church builder who had, after all, just put his faith in God, and could rely on a divine defence. With an almost total absence of insurance assessors, loss adjusters, articulate barristers and all the modern appurtenances that make apprehension of felons possible; what would now constitute criminal negligence, was in the twelfth century little impediment to further employment. Having made a small mistake, it was relatively easy to go on and make a really big howler.

Deciding to forego the foundation option is not an instant death wish, just a moderately risky decision. On the plus side it is cheap, and even with the best masonry, if the ground starts to give as the work proceeds, the courses can be adjusted to keep the work in trim. Pisa's tower is the classic case of the mason trying to accommodate such movement, though the dipping masonry course with adjusted work above it is almost

71

common enough to be unremarkable. With rubble work it is difficult to spot such tinkering, and soft lime mortars are equally amenable. Even if splits and fissures open up after the church is complete, so long as movement is not excessive, then recutting of string courses and arch ribs can be used to fool the eye with almost complete success.

Many people will spot the slight subsidence of the tower piers at Howden. The relative movement at high level where the nave arcade abuts is effectively invisible. On top of all this is the fact that life generally was fairly short, and many parsons and masons did not live to see their work completed, let alone live long enough to witness what, when failure did occur, was usually an event prolonged over several years, if not decades. With apprenticeships starting in the early teens and lasting for seven years, to be followed by several further years as a journeyman, masons could not expect to be masters until their late twenties, and most would not live to see forty. Only the lucky, or unfortunate few, could expect to see their buildings mature, or not, as the case may be.

Dig For Victory

Digging down through the top layers of the earth's crust is one of those fascinating activities that all of us have had a go at in childhood, and the Victorians built a whole leisure industry on this basic human need (the seaside resort). Delving in search of a crock of gold, with or without the Swaffham Pedlar's driving vision, pays dividends if your particular crock is firm foundations. That the ground gets harder as you descend through the topsoil and subsoil to the undisturbed strata beneath, proved an attractive concept to masons, with a load to shift off their minds and onto something with a trifle more backbone.

On thick clays, gravels and rock, good foundations were effectively guaranteed by digging down two or three feet, a distance that took the plane of load transfer down below the zone of climatic and vegetative influence. Only the really unlucky folk who dug down to, but didn't quite meet, a lower layer of peat, running sand or other nasty, were caught out when adopting this strategy. The really enthusiastic diggers, and there is ample evidence that there were plenty of these, would not content themselves with just a few trenches and pits for the walls and piers, but would clear the whole site, or a good part of it, and be rewarded with the space for an undercroft.

Piling and Rafting

While digging is both an attractive proposition and a successful means of ensuring good foundations for a new church, there are many sites, perhaps no better illustrated than at Winchester, where if you dig a hole you get a duckpond. There is no evidence that the use of coffer dams and efficient dewatering techniques was part of the mediaeval mason's art. The hand-powered archimedian screw appears to have had a place in mediaeval construction, but its effective head was limited by the power available.

The *shaduf* is inherently more efficient, but evidence of its use scant. Accordingly, driven piles and rafts were used support churches where the water table proved too high for comfort. While these two techniques are different in the way that they transmit and support loads, they both relied on timber to do the job.

Rafts are the low-tech solution, used to form the prehistoric trackways on the Somerset levels, with woven mats of brushwood, small section timber, heather or any other readily available resilient material. This method works in wet ground because the anaerobic conditions help prevent the decay of the woody fibres. In use throughout history, the technique was only superceded when reinforced concrete and steel piles came into general use a hundred years ago. Crown timber, that is large section trunks of trees can also be used, but is much more efficient when used as piles.

Piling, if not invented by the Romans, was certainly developed by them to an impressive art. Driving a post into the ground with a hammer is undoubtedly an ancient activity. Whether it was used before about 500BC to support buildings is another matter. What is certain is that the Romans developed piling to build coffer dams so that they could build in the dry below both the water table and sea level. The technique was also used to support masonry bridges.

Driving a pile involves the use of an impact force, usually applied by dropping a weight through a height onto the top end of the post to be driven. The rigs used until the steam age comprised a frame supported by outriggers, containing the pile and the driving weight, the latter attached to a rope that passed over a pulley. Typically, in a man-powered rig, the rope split into ten or a dozen ends, each one hauled upon by a labourer. Repeated hauling and dropping drove the pile into the ground. While this sounds good in theory, the practice was somewhat more exhausting.

What the Romans did not know, any more than the mediaeval monks did in their turn, was actually how a pile works. To drive a pile with an impact force requires that the force be larger than the resistance opposing it. To assist in the driving, piles were pointed at the business end, which, if you think about it, means that the load that the pile will ultimately have to bear, will only act on a very small area. Piles, however, take very large loads, and they do it because of friction between the sides of the pile and the surrounding ground. That friction acts to prevent the pile being driven, and it is the local liquefaction of the surrounding soil, caused by the vibration of the pile when it is struck, that allows the pile to enter the ground.

As the pile is driven further into the ground, the friction increases, and if the piling is stopped for any length of time, the soil sets round the pile, which will not then go further into the ground. This remains a not uncommon event, even with today's powerful rigs, when piles are left part driven overnight. Once begun, therefore, piling had to continue until the post was fully sunk, for with hand power there was no surplus of available force, only a bare sufficiency.

In spite of all the efforts of the mediaeval mason to ensure a firm foundation for his work, the fact that there was a total lack of calculation and basic understanding of the principles of bearing capacities, meant that here, below ground, more than anywhere else, where it was not possible to see what was going on as the church went up, the risk of failure was greatest. That risk did not change, as each generation had to make its own decisions on foundations with no effective information as to the reasons for success or failure in times past. Only with a systematic and scientific approach could reliable church foundations be designed, and this is an event that only the twentieth century has witnessed, and only after the structural engineer showed the way (and provided the calculations).

If foundation design then was an expression of faith in the absence of mathematics, then the process of determining the position of those foundations, Setting Out, was, and still is, a cunningly simple application of geometry, but without Pythagoras.

Setting Out

Understanding, or to be more precise, lack of understanding of the principles of setting out, has given those in the know, as it were, much amusement; a whole pseudo-science has been built up around the idea that *Homo Sapiens* are not capable of accurate setting out. But I take the cart before the horse in assuming that the reader knows what setting out is. So let's begin with an easy first lesson: how do you build a nice pyramidal pyramid, where all the sides are the same length, each corner is a right angle, and all the sides slope to the top, which is exactly over the centre of the ground plan square: oh, and the sides are a hundred feet long at the base or ground level. As many folk ascribe the accuracy of the pyramids in Egypt which we will be copying to aliens from outer space, let me assure the reader at this point that the author was born in North Ferriby, truly the very heart of Western Civilisation.

To achieve this wonder we need to do two things; firstly form a level base or platform (earth curvature will do, but it is easier to make it flat), and secondly establish on that flat surface the position of the four corners. For equipment we need a few rods, say straight(ish) ash or hazel poles six feet long or thereabouts, and some heavy string or light rope. If we are going to make the sides of our pyramid a set length in feet or metres we will need a measure as well, but if the sides are just going to be equal lengths, then we are fully equipped. In order to succeed we first have to level the site, and for this we need one rod of a set length, to which is attached at the top a sighting rod or board (the work is a lot easier if you attach a plumb line to this, but it is not essential). The site datum level is then established and marked, usually with a short stake driven into the ground. This level is protected from damage during the subsequent muckshift. Using the sighting board, other stakes are driven in round the site so that their tops line up with the top of the sighting board.

The finished level is then marked on the lower section of the stakes by comparing them with the rod of set length. Once the approximate four corners have been levelled in this manner the rest of the site can be brought to the same datum by sighting across two fixed stake tops to the moveable sighting board. Bring on the slaves and in a twinkle the base is as flat as you could wish for, indeed flatter than you need, as you can achieve accuracy to within half an inch without exceptional effort. In contrast, concrete floor technology today accepts an overall 20mm variation (10mm above and below datum) and laser levelling is used to achieve this. Now comes the real crafty bit.

Just by chance you have never heard of Pythagoras, but you know that the pyramid needs a square base, not a parallelogram. You have tied a couple of knots in your light rope, as far apart as you wish the length of the sides to be, and by waiting for the sun to hove into the due south spot, aligned your first side due North/South. Two rods now mark those corners, with the rope pulled taut to delineate the first side. The rope is laid out beyond both corners in a continuation of the straight line of the first side. On either side of each corner two marks are made on the rope equidistant from the corner. From these marks two further ropes of equal length are used to determine points on the second and third sides. The knotted rope is then used to locate the remaining two corners. A check with the rope on the fourth side tells you if you've gotten it right, and a check of the diagonals, which should be of equal length, will tell you that it's square. Job done. No Pythagoras, no tape measure, no set squares, accurate to a few millimetres, self checking, and you have the position of the top set out on the ground, which a plumb line will easily transfer to the top as the work is raised.

Who needs aliens?

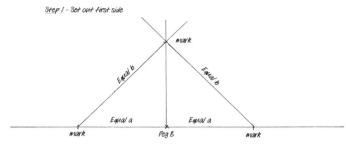

Step 1 - Set out first side

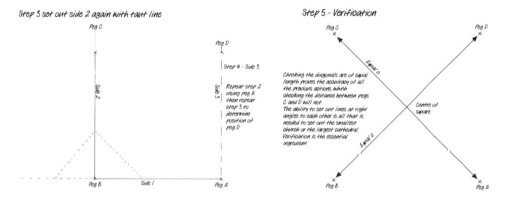

Step 2 - Set out right angle

Step 3 set out side 2 again with taut line

Step 5 - Verification

Step 4 - Side 3

Repeat step 2 using peg A then repeat step 5 to determine position of peg D

Checking the diagonals are of equal length proves the accuracy of all the previous actions, which checking the distance between pegs C and D will not

The ability to set out lines at right angles to each other is all that is needed to set out the smallest church or the largest cathedral. Verification is the essential ingredient

This, then, is setting out, not exactly as practiced by the ancient Egyptians, but the fundamentals are all there, and the principles are still the same today, whether you're setting out the bottomless pit for the Royal Opera House bank account, or having a pleasant evening making crop circles.

Before the ninth century church needed anything as accurate as a pyramid, the Romans had perfected the art of surveying, and it was on the writings of the likes of Vitruvius and Frontius that the mediaeval Church relied to provide technical support. The earliest churches did not need any sophisticated setting out. Masons had inherited the try square and the plumb line and level (a try square with a plumb line built in), and these were good enough for most early structures. Setting out the centres of piers for long nave arcades, checking that transepts were at right angles, that the centre of a pier, or the centre of a tower or spire remained plumb to the work required a little more effort and application of basic principles, but no more. This ensured that the large canvas on which the masonry and decoration was to be hung, was sufficiently accurate for the opposite sides of a church to meet eighty feet in the air, without having to put too much of a kink in the work. Without this basic engineering, mere skilled masonry would have not been enough.

All done with simple tools, steady hands and the human eye.

Chapter Five:
Mastery of Materials I - Timber and Glass

The use of wood in the English church is comprehensive; wood was the first material that was used, and it is still with us today. In the intervening fourteen centuries wood has seen use in just about every possible manner, though by no means all species have found either a temporary or a permanent place in English church architecture.

Wood is utilized in a number of different ways; as withies, specially grown wands of one or two years growth ten or more feet long (the author has recorded a withy of a single seasons growth at ten feet in length, and high rates of growth and neighbour annoyance are not just the preserve of cupressus leylandii); underwood poles as rafters or battens, or split to form laths; sapwood and heartwood for the best structural timber and the finest furniture and carved work; and finally as processed timber, plywood, paper, veneers, sawdust, and fibre and chip boards.

While not strictly an architectural use, the bark of trees (and other much more revolting substances which will not be mentioned here) has been used in the preparation of leather, the preferred material for binding books down the ages, of whose production the Church once held a virtual monopoly. Handsomely bound bibles and parish record books still form an important part of the history of the English church.

The key to understanding the place of wood in society until the end of the seventeenth century, is to realise its absolutely crucial role to the survival of every person; England was uninhabitable without it. Wood housed, cooked, ploughed, heated, smelted all metals, and was the major material component in almost all tools, furniture, transport and farming implements. To make matters worse, wood competed directly for land that was needed for food production, and at the time of the Norman conquest the land that produced timber had been whittled down, probably to below that capable of producing society's needs.

The inevitable consequence of such action was the development of a sophisticated timber growing industry; as the price of timber rose it became worth someone's while to grow it. Whilst this is an easy solution when the product takes only a short while to produce, the growing of crown timber took up to five or six generations to yield a mature tree, well beyond the lifespan of even the longest lived person. While William's first and most enduring act after Hastings was the declaration of the Royal Forests, an act history records as being for the preservation of the beasts of the chase, the reality is that this was in effect putting under royal ownership much of the remaining crown timber (hence the name), that England possessed. There is little doubt that William was fully aware of this.

From the conquest then, the timber resources were split; Crown timber became the property of the king and the nobles who were rewarded for their efforts in battle with hegemony over large tracts of countryside; and timber that was produced as a crop from withy bed and coppice remained part of the feudal administration, governed by such laws as were necessary to the production and exploitation of what was a vital subsistence resource. Whilst prior to the conquest, the Church had been just one competitor for timber, among many, afterwards it had a prior claim as part of the Norman settlement. The strain on the timber resources of England, that began to show in the thirteenth and fourteenth centuries did not have any serious impact on church building, which if anything tended to benefit from the pressure to economise by the increasing sophistication and ingenuity of the carpenter.

The impact of the population reduction of the plague years 1349-50 was to give the hard-pressed trees of England a break from ruthless exploitation. Only minimal effects on church timber supplies were felt until long after the Reformation, when the landscape was no longer a feudal one, and the towns, where population growth was relentlessly channelled, were already being powered by a different fuel, coal. By the time the religio-political climate had stabilised sufficiently for the Church to be concerned about the roof over its collective head, the lack of maintenance had made history of a goodly number of churches.

The restorers of the eighteenth century were by then scouring Europe for timber, not just England, for without the great wealth and privileges granted under the Norman settlement, there were just too many demands on too small a supply for the Church to secure the lion's share. Times and traditions had changed from the mid sixteenth century, and as new materials came onto the market, so the form the church roof adapted followed the lead of others, rather than leading as it had been so used to do in times past. Softwood from the Baltic was now available, but only as crown timber; it may be possible to grow softwood withies and underwood, but it has never been the practice in England, and as England could still supply these items when needed, imports were not required.

With the dawn of the nineteenth century, the repair movement discovered to its dismay that the treadmill to which it was hitched, far from slowing in response to the efforts of the previous ten decades, moved up a gear. The numbers of distressed churches was everywhere on the increase and, with few exceptions, this spelled the end of the use of withies and underwood, except as plaster laths. New roofs by the tens of scores were almost formulaically constructed in imported softwood, retaining the original principal oak beams from a previous age, adding machine sawn, planed and moulded rafters to the new interiors.

Almost invariably these rafters were paired with thin sawn softwood close boarding, boarding that could only be mass produced with power saws. Church roofs would never be the same again, with the rare survivors of the age past, such as that at Peterborough Cathedral, attracting intensive and expensive conservation programmes in the twentieth century. The budding aircraft industry added plywood to the timber repertoire, in the decade after the First War, and since then

81

has been added sheets and boards of all sorts, and one new wonder, the glued, laminated, softwood beam or portal almost infinitely curvable, if curves are what you want, and fit to be seen anywhere.

Today we use wood either as paper or board (frequently the only difference between the two is in the glue and thickness, and you can be forgiven for thinking that paper is the thicker when it comes to some building materials), or as crown timber from mature trees. Withies and underwood are of the past, and just possibly the future, definitely not the present.

Variety Show

Timber is one of those areas where the action of *Homo Sapiens* has actually increased the number of species of timber available in England. Some of the trees that we now regard as our own, particularly chestnut, plane and sycamore, are relatively recent imports. The London Plane, for example has been here long enough to have been singed in the Great Fire, but only just, and hybrids such as the Leyland Cypress are so young that we do not have a single specimen that we can say has 'topped out'.

Nonetheless, twelve centuries ago our ancestors had a good choice, and as the need to plant and cultivate trees arose, they chose a number of trees for their particular qualities. The pecking order for use in church construction meant oak first and the rest, including ash, willow, alder, beech, cherry, elm, walnut and chestnut, a long way behind. This is a somewhat simplistic view, as not all trees grow everywhere in England, and it ignores the type of wood that trees yielded in various areas, the competing demands of other industries, of which there were many, and the convenient sizes that could be obtained for a given species, which of course varied from place to place. What it does do however is give a clear indication of the primacy due to oak, a primacy not evident in the host of other uses for wood in the middle ages, apart from church buildings, that is. Oak, then, is due the lion's share of attention, and for good reason.

Oak

By the middle of the nineteenth century, when the Victorian obsession for measuring and tabulating everything, reached trees that yielded timber (crown timber, that is), the average length of felled oak trunks in English timber yards was recorded as forty two feet, with a mean diameter of thirty two inches. A tree of these 'average' dimensions would be not less than one hundred years old, and probably nearer a hundred and fifty. As oaks do not willingly form trunks more than the length necessary to keep their leaves above the height of browsing animals (even the tallest horse cannot manage to reach up more than about ten feet), then this was timber, as you would expect in the nineteenth century, from a managed plantation.

In such a forest, where the trees had been grown together to prevent the low crown forming, there would be little in the way of underwood, and the prospect would have been one of many trunks set in a cool twilight. The trees that yielded the trunks had been planted in the years either side of the '15', at the start of the eighteenth century, and the most that the optimist who planted them could have expected would have been some thinnings towards the end of his very long life, and an expression of the anticipated future value in a land sale or will.

In an unmanaged forest twelve hundred years ago such an average tree would have been rare, far outnumbered by older and stouter colleagues. The author, in felling a hedgerow thinning, was only able to secure a six foot trunk for conversion into a dining table, nothing approaching church proportions. Forty two feet is not a great length, but as the width of the nave of the English church or cathedral, you will only find it exceeded in the largest of them all, York, and then not by much.

To build what we can still see today, there must have been a supply of larger (length) timber, as even stone vaults need timber centering, and diagonals in the quadripartite vault are nearly one and a half times longer than the width of the nave they span. There are no prizes for guessing the width of the nave of St. Paul's Cathedral, as it is, surprise, surprise, forty two feet, determined in exactly the same way as its Gothic predecessors. Plus ça change!

The supplies of oak structural timber, be it for the Victorians, or the mediaeval or renaissance carpenter and builder, can only have come from planted and managed trees. When Henry III's Justiciar of Forests, Geoffrey de Langley, was supplying oaks for church building in the middle of the thirteenth century, the timber he was disposing of had been planted within a few years of the Conquest.

The royal forests, it is quite clear, were being managed for timber right from the start, and that beasts of the chase were, literally, a pastime, timber being the real prize. The size of the available timber, and in this context timber means oak, determined the proportions of the mediaeval church, in direct obeyance of the law that states that you cannot build beyond the means of your materials. It is logical to conclude therefore that not only did William I not invent the management of the English lowland forest, only made a grab for its wealth in a more public manner than most monarchs have found seemly since, but that the management of crown timber, primarily oak, was already a feature of feudal England, and a well established one at that.

To take this issue to its logical conclusion, the existence of churches with large span arches and naves from the late tenth century onwards, implies the establishment of a sophisticated timber growing industry at least one hundred and fifty years earlier, for without the grist, the mill could not have been built. As such an industry cannot have had the Church sitting on its doorstep as a potential customer champing at the bit while it waited for the trees to grow, it is reasonable to conclude that there was a ready market for this kind of wood, long before the Church came along and cornered it.

Having established oak's credentials in terms of its primacy in determining proportions, we can now look at the material itself. Oak's claim to be the lead structural material is well founded, and not just because, of all the large trees with strong timber, oak is the most widely distributed. Oak as a tree is almost legendary for its long life; two hundred years growing; two hundred years standing still; two hundred years dying. Even today there are old oaks that first put out leaf in mediaeval England, and the felling of trees and counting their rings must have told the settlers in the dark ages that this was indeed a long lived species.

In contrast the two other large timber trees that are, or were, widely distributed, ash and elm, have habits that would give any carpenter second thoughts when searching for the best that nature could offer. Ash is a tree with habits similar to oak, in that it is slow to start but vigorous when established, producing a hard timber that was ideal for tools and other small items. As a forest or hedgerow tree though, it is relatively short lived, falling apart due to rot in the heartwood, and being fairly hazardous when planted near dwellings as a consequence. Likewise elm, which has, or rather had, the habit, since there are no mature elms in England today, of dropping its branches without warning in old age.

Oak, then, was the best candidate, obviously long lived, with a good-sized trunk and branches. Closely growing stands of the tree produced long trunks, so it could be 'forced' to abandon its spreading crown and grow tall and slim. Unlike elm and ash it does not have the tendency to bifurcate when given the order to grow straight and true. When the timber grown in this fashion was harvested, it could be split, rather than sawn, so the tree could produce beams by simple squaring of the trunk with an adze or side axe, or fairly thick wide boards for roofing, flooring or joinery, by being split using seasoned oak wedges driven into the end grain. Split, curved branches, or even whole trees (crucks) could be used for a variety of purposes, of which the most common survivor today is the curved purlin brace.

Oak is fairly soft and workable when green, but like all timber has a tendency to twist out of shape as it dries (seasons). This distortion was accepted when the timber is used for structural purposes; a squared log will season happily for a decade and remain reasonably true if the 'boxed heart' is more or less in the middle of the section.

Oak used in this manner was used green because human lifespans are too short, and the wood hardens as it seasons, becoming progressively more difficult to work. Not many clerics were happy to wait ten years before the roof went on the church, so all large structural timbers of oak are not completely true, and most have splits and shakes from seasoning *in situ*, that give them added character. Where the wood was used in the walls of a church, to form a timber frame, then this tendency to twist could be controlled by the use of cross members (nogging). This is a feature of old timber framing, where the nogging tends to be the same size as the frames, and of not so old framing, where a degree of economy can often be found.

When seasoned, oak is both hard and stiff, and ceases to split easily or 'cleave' evenly. If kept dry it is exceptionally durable, darkening slowly as the surface gathers dirt and oxidises. In this state it is almost immune to insect attack; that old friend and cohabitee of the Church, the Death Watch Beetle, prefers its wood sweetened with the sugars released, and the fibres loosened, by a suitable wood rotting fungus. When young the polished surface of a 'quarter sawn' plank shows fine silvery markings known as medullary rays, making oak the most readily identifiable hardwood.

In the English church oak is common in roof timbers, especially the larger ones; misericords are almost exclusively in oak; less common in pews and choir stalls, favoured material for doors and the older lych gates. What you will be very lucky to see today is oak's use in the form of underwood.

Underwood

Due to its wide distribution, oak was a favoured tree to be cultivated by coppicing, the system of tree cultivation that underpinned feudalism, providing the wood supplies for much of society's many needs. At first glance this is quite surprising, for oak is a slow tree to grow by most standards, but if measured by weight and not volume, then oak coppice, once established, gives excellent value for the time and effort expended.

Coppicing takes advantage of the fact that many trees, if cut down to ground level during the early years of their existence, do not die but grow with some vigour not one but many shoots from the stump, which is called a stool. As the stool ages, and the shoots are usually cut on a rotation that can vary, depending on use and species, between one and ten or more years, the stool becomes more vigorous as its root system expands, and more shoots grow and the productivity of the woodland increases. Oak coppicing produces poles that can be used for roofing, smaller rods for tile or slate hanging, split rods for wattle or plaster laths, or small timber for turning and furniture.

The oak pegs that hung slates and tiles, and fixed the mortice and tenon joints in structural work, were also sourced from coppice wood. The real crafty part about coppicing was the fact that, while the timber tree, if uncut, will eventually grow old and die, and ash, for example, will not normally live more than about two hundred years, trees that were coppiced remained youthful, putting forth fresh growth as the centuries rolled by. While a similar effect was noticed with pollarded trees, decay of the trunk often meant demise by collapse rather than old age, and if left uncut for a few decades pollarded trees such as ash or willow went downhill rapidly.

Softwood

Scots Pine apart, there is no native softwood in England, and when the first of the restorers came to replace the sagging church roofs of the late seventeenth century, and found the supplies of large section structural timber needed to be lacking on these shores, overseas supplies had to be sought. The closest places where timber was available at reasonable cost proved to be the conifers that surrounded the Baltic Sea, in Norway, Sweden, Finland and what is now Latvia, Estonia and Lithuania, then part of the Russian Empire. The timber was named after its source, with Memel Fir, Riga Fir, Dantzic (*sic*) Oak (not a softwood, that one!), and Norway Spruce, all featuring on importers' lists, along with the more exotic oak from Quebec, and mahogany from West Africa.

Up to this point in history the idea of sawing up structural timbers was not one that could be seriously applied to the everyday use of hardwood, because the smaller sections would twist, and it was a lot more effort than splitting and adzing. With softwood, splitting and adzing just wasted timber that was soft enough to be sawn for everyday structural use, not just for special work as was oak. At the same time iron technology had produced the double handled pit saw, that could be pushed as well as pulled, and the idea of sawing up a seventy five foot trunk of Riga Fir (the average length imported in the nineteenth century) no longer seemed utterly crazy, so long as you were not the bottom sawyer, that is.

Softwood had the added advantage of seasoning quickly, arriving at the east coast ports semi-seasoned due to the long river and sea voyage from the forest of origin, and needing only to be converted (to beams, joists, etc.) sticked and stacked (piled in a heap with small cross sections to allow air to circulate) for a short period before being fit for use.

This new wood was immediately adopted for new construction, as it was the ideal material for the large truss spans that the new breed of neo-classical church demanded, and its use became, by degrees, almost universal in the roof renewal programmes that the later Victorians put in hand. One of the reasons for this softwood gaining the upper hand in the nineteenth century was the fact that it was one of the few exports that the Russian Empire could sell to pay for the imports it needed to kick start its own industrial revolution.

To suggest that England obtained the timber for free would be untrue, but it certainly came very cheap. The effect of a new lighter wood that could be sawn into small sections was to make the small 'jack rafter' the standard roof member, though purlins and boarding survived well into the nineteenth century. Thin sawn softwood boards were available for roofs and floors, and thin deep sections could be sawn for floor joists. Oak could not compete, not even when power rack saws made the top and bottom sawyers redundant. Oak's transition to a luxury timber was virtually complete, as a structural material it was history. Almost.

Glass

As we look at the materials which supplied the needs of the Church down the centuries, there is a recurring theme; where the mediaeval craftsmen wrestled to overcome the technical hurdles to work metals and composite materials, the Romans handled them with comparative ease. This is the case with glass; the Romans were every whit the masters of the material as the Anglo Saxons and their later masters, the Normans, were not. Yet it is the very lack of mastery of the medium that produced the flowering of English stained glass from the twelfth to the fourteenth century. We have seen that the form of the early church moved swiftly (for feudal England at any rate) from the Saxon form, with its small windows, through the Romanesque, with its reliance on massive masonry walls with modest window openings, to Early English, the first of the Gothic styles.

That transition was primarily one from darkness to light, as the window expanded to fill the whole of the bay between what was to become the masonry structural frame, and with light also came the draughts and the need for something better than shutters. Glass was the obvious answer, indeed without glass there could not have been an Early English or any of the later styles, but as with many things Roman, the mastery of glassworking had faded in the gloom of the Dark Ages. The craft of glass making and working was reintroduced to Britain by the infant church in 675, and when Bede needed skilled glass workers he was obliged to send to Gaul for them.

Glass as made a millennium ago was a mixture of three natural resources; silica, in the form of sand; lime, usually as crushed shells; and soda, in the form of wood ash. None of these materials will immediately strike the prospective glassmaker as being either consistent in terms of their chemical composition, or free from a myriad of potential or actual contaminants. Striking the right combination of materials that will produce a clear glass, is obviously not easy.

To the mediaeval glassmaker the concept of consistently producing a clear glass in melt after melt, was the stuff of dreams, very far removed from reality. Reality was that the glass produced was on the whole translucent, but it was not clear, and what was worse was the fact that the product was full of streaks and blemishes, and, while it is this that gives glass its depth and brilliance, the end product was far from pristine, even after the worst bits had been cut out. The solution was beyond the meagre technical resources of the times, but not beyond the imagination. Experimentation produced a superb, if restricted, series of coloured glasses, and onto these the artist could, with genius driving his minds eye, paint parts of scenes that could then be fired onto the glass surface. The sum of the (often very odd-shaped) parts, could then be ssembled to form a complete window, where the variations in colour and texture of the original glass added to the beauty of the creation.

For over two centuries the struggle to produce glass at all produced probably the best stained glass this country has ever seen, for glass making was one of those technologies where, like iron making, the material did not melt *per se*, only softened. Glass was only workable at temperatures that were difficult to achieve, and sustain for long periods. That threshold is about 700 degrees centigrade, but the fact that the fuel and the raw materials cannot be mixed (a reverberatory furnace is required, where the fuel burns on a hearth separate from the crucible that holds the glass, which is indirectly heated) meant that in addition to being difficult to sustain, the process also needed lots of fuel.

Like iron working, the glass industry's voracious appetite for fuel was probably the factor, rather than lack of skills, that led to the widespread use of imported glass to meet demand. There appears to have been no major homespun glass industry prior to the establishment of the Wealden glassmakers of the early thirteenth century, at Chiddingfold, between Haslemere and Godalming in Surrey. The record of this community is illustrative of the rise and fall of glassmaking for windows; by the end of the thirteenth century the industry had secured a royal charter; twenty years after Henry's smash and grab raid no window glass was being made at all. Much glass, having a very high value/weight ratio, was thus imported from northern Europe, primarily France, but some coming all the way from Venice, the intellectual heart of glassmaking throughout the Middle Ages.

Later demand for glass was not fuelled by the Church, but by the demand for domestic glass, and glassware, and once again the issue of fuel came hot on the heels of the industry, with a royal proclamation forbidding the use of wood as fuel in 1615. This was followed by the granting of patents for the use of coal, and the suppression of the small glassmaker at whom these actions were aimed. Thenceforth the manufacture of glass began to leave behind the small scale woodland enterprise that had characterised the industry since its inception, with the economics of scale and the thermal economics of larger furnaces combining with the rudiments of quality control to produce clear sheet and crown glass.

The technological great leap forward of the eighteenth century was the manufacture of polished plate, laboriously ground out of cast plate at the Ravenhead works in St. Helens. Glass could now be heated well beyond the 'just workable' stage and could be poured onto sand beds like lead and iron, and at this point in history is described as a 'metal'.

The nineteenth century saw the mass production of sheet glass started by Robert Chance at Spon Lane, Birmingham, and this left the production of church glass in a backwater, with specialist suppliers, such as Hartley Wood in Sunderland, hand blowing antique and 'Norman' glass for church and stained glass use into the twentieth century. One glass, designed specifically for church use is 'Cathedral Glass', a rolled sheet glass where rollers imprint a pattern on the glass, first produced by James Hartley in 1847, and still in use today.

Producing Glass and Windows

Unlike iron, the process of fusing the materials together is not exothermic, necessitating the use of indirect heating in the reverberatory furnace. The net result of this was that until the eighteenth century, long after glass could be heated to melting point and beyond, glass was worked as a bloom, a roughly spherical loop manipulated on the end of a hollow iron bar (the blowing iron) in a small furnace. On the other end of the bar the glassmaker would twist and puff to produce a disc of glass by blowing the loop into a hollow globe and then flattening it (crown glass) or blowing and rolling to make a cylinder that could have the ends cut off and then be opened out into a sheet (cylinder or sheet glass). This entirely manual process governed the size of the glass; crown glass could only be spun to about five feet in diameter, and the bullion or bulls eye in the middle was deemed useless for most practical purposes (there are bulls eyes in the clerestory of St. Martins Le Grand, York, so it was perhaps not entirely useless).

These two production methods are readily identifiable by virtue of the path of the irregularities, bubbles, streaks, etc; crown glass has them in a curved pattern, sheet glass has a

91

parallel 'grain'. From this basic sheet material would be cut a number of small sections (dictating pane sizes and window proportions until the middle of the nineteenth century).

In the case of stained glass, after painting and firing, these small, irregularly shaped sections could be made up with lead strip into a large stained glass window depicting a scene or a number of scenes or figures. Larger windows would be made up of several individual panels, and assembled finally by fixing into the stonework of the window and securing to bronze saddle bars with soldered on copper ties. Before we move on, it is instructive to take a peep at the method of production of an actual window.

In order to design a stained glass window, the first step today is to produce a coloured sketch of the proposal. Whether this was the case six hundred years ago is a matter of debate, though the technique is so obvious that it is probable that the artists had a series of prepared sketches of all the favoured scenes and saints, and a pretty good idea as to what glass would be used in the individual panes as well. Once the window was approved, the artist would have to take a pattern of the window in wood and lay it out on a suitable table. On this pattern, or on the table itself, the surface is painted with whiteing (a mix of ground chalk and water), the design set out, as a mono or polychrome sketch, complete with hatching for the shadows. The actual colours of the various parts are then identified and the glass chosen to cover each area of different colour. On each glass section, after cutting to size, the detail is then painted and the shadow added, the techniques for this changing with the passing centuries. The glass is then fired and is ready for assembly.

Technological improvements fed through on a regular basis; in the thirteenth century the glass available was primarily the brilliant-hued red, blue, green and violet, with an enamel of white, which could be left on or ground off as needed. From the fifteenth century came silver nitrate to give a golden yellow, and the rapidly increasing colour palette available for painting pushed the deep hued base colour glasses out if favour. In parallel, the introduction of the forced draught furnace driven by the waterwheel, pushed the achievable and sustainable temperatures of the glass furnace well beyond the point at which earlier craftsmen had struggled to make glass, and by allowing a technically superior, and consistent glass to be made, put an end to the golden age of stained glass.

A little later Thomas Cromwell and friends put an end to much the golden age had produced, though due to poor quality control much mediaeval glass may well have been of limited durability (use the materials in the wrong proportions and the resulting glass is porous and erodable, or *in extremis*, soluble in water). Very little church glass appears to have been made in the century after 1540, but the puritan zeal for plain glass could be met from those suppliers who were setting up to supply the domestic market. The production of stained glass has probably not ceased in over nine centuries, owing to its inate attractiveness; no church seems complete without it.

With good clear glass came the opportunity to make coloured glass, that is plain glass that is pigmented but otherwise undecorated, but attractive in its own right because it is not full of the defects and blemishes that plagued the twelfth century producers. Control of the melt and the ability to make larger batches meant that large areas of consistent colour could be achieved, though the size of the glass panes remained small due to there being no advance in production of crown and sheet glass until the 1830s. This fulfilled a need, particularly where congregations could not bring themselves to admit that what they really wanted was stained glass, by introducing colour into what had often become quite austere buildings, liberally coated inside with whitewash, to eradicate the wall paintings. In the nineteenth century the coloured diamond leaded window became almost an 'industry standard'.

In the nineteenth century also the glass industry changed to that of a scientifically controlled mass production process, making glass that was optically flat, clear and blemish free, in sheet sizes and thicknesses that could meet virtually any demand. Church glass, stained glass at least, retained the technology to keep, or to put back in, the colour variation and defects that had always been its trademark, and while there are modern churches with modern glass used to effect, they fly in the face of both history and tradition.

Finally, there is the use of glass in lighting and chandeliers, and this stems primarily from the addition of lead to form lead crystal glass, a glass that can be given facets to reflect light and takes grinding and polishing to a high degree. First made in England in the mid sixteenth century, it has been the preferred material for this work for four centuries, and still finds a place in top quality light fittings, alongside all manner of modern heat resistant and toughened glasses.

Windows - Tracing History

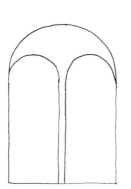

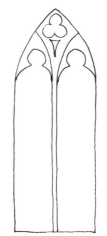

Romanesque: Simple Semi Circular arch paired windows

No tracery - originally without glass

Early English - window taller but not wider - again paired openings separated by central mullion - Simple head tracery

Mature Gothic - window as wide as the structural bay permits - multiple mullions supported by transoms - riot of decorative tracery

Chapter Six:
Warming the Heart and the Soul
- Music and Heating

The history of western music is effectively the same as the history of church music; from the laying of the first foundation stone of the first Saxon church, to the emergence of popular music at the end of the sixteenth century, and so far as 'classical' music is concerned, for a further two centuries or so after that. If this appears to overestimate the utterly dominant position of the church in matters musical for a period not far short of a thousand years, then let your mind be put at rest, for this was exactly the position.

The importance of music as a window onto the soul, so obvious in its origins in courtship and lovemaking, and the bond of love and trust between parent and infant, was not missed for a single minute by the Christian Church. The Church accordingly allocated time, energy and money down the centuries to both developing, and when it did not seem to be taking the right direction, suppressing the art. Despite this seeming ambivalence, without the resources of the Church, much of the music that we enjoy today would not exist. Effectively all of the last four hundred years' developments in music rest on the work of the Church; all the basics of scales, notation, harmony and instrumentation were thrashed out under church patronage.

'Well', says you,' what has this to do with the development of church architecture?' In terms of the design of Gothic churches the evidence that the clergy driving the process of change were aware of the basics of sound technology is scant, yet it is clear that as the internal spaces in church, chapel and cathedral grew, appreciation of the acoustic qualities grew also. The musical qualities of the generated space were, to say the least, variable, but from the earliest days of the Christian Church, architecture for the delivery and enhancement of music has been an 'add on' rather than integral.

The reason for this is almost certainly ignorance; there was no appreciation of the mechanics of sound. The real problem down the ages has been change; the Church always knew what it liked, and by and large preferred composers who were not inconveniently alive. So it was that when chants and plainsong were corrupted by the introduction of counterpoint and harmony, the Church agonised over acceptance of the new. Our old friend, the Council of Trent, duly tried to put down these unseemly inventions, but this was a normal reaction and only really reflected the staunch conservatism that has always underpinned the wider church.

The two major architectural items influenced by music are the choir and the organ, though for a period after the reformation, church orchestras were a popular part of church life, and an architectural form, the gallery, developed partially in honour thereof.

The Choir

To avoid confusion, the choir we are talking about is the human one, not the section of the church betwixt altar and rood screen. From the start singing has been part of the service and until the advent of written music (notes, staves, etc.) the choir was essential to lead chants, and the choir has its own seats in the form of Choir Stalls. These carved benches with bookrests and high backs, tiered on either side of the main axis of the church and occupying either part of the chancel or a choir (the place) of their own, have been the site of a peculiar flourishing of the woodcarver's art.

The choir stalls in even a small parish church can be a positive riot of ornamentation, with carved testers (the overhanging bit at the top, like a tester bed), backrests, front panelling and armrests, but the real fun is in the misericords.

The misericord is a marvelous device that enables the chorister to rest on his or, increasingly these days, her laurels, even when they stand up to sing. The idea is very simple; form each choir seat individually and arrange for it to tip up. On the underside is a ledge that is just at the right height to perform as a sort of shooting stick. As the seat is usually carved out of a single piece of wood, generally oak, the opportunity presented for the woodcarver to have a bit of fun in a location where, unless you actually go and look, there is nothing normally to be seen.

There are some brilliant sets still extant, with, in numerical terms at least, the sixty eight at Beverley Minster leading the field. While the carving seen elsewhere in a church is usually but by no means exclusively exuberant but restrained, carved scenes on misericords are a riot of tableaux, portraying rural life, the clergy (frequently the object of thinly disguised ridicule) local people and armorial bearings, scenes from fables and mythical beasts, to name but a few. The choir stalls that we see today are usually an amalgam of original work and restoration; few master carpenters could resist the temptation to add their contribution. Who could possibly blame them?

With the choir happily ensconced in their stalls by, at the very latest, the end of the fourteenth century, music had to await both the development of the organ, and the Church's acceptance of counterpoint and harmony, before the next major changes could be wrought, by the installation of what we would now regard as the fully developed organ. In strict musical terms the Church has always remained very active, maintaining both the choir schools and the paid choirs themselves as music developed into the western music we recognise today.

The organ in principle is an ancient instrument; blowing down a tube to produce a sound, I hesitate to call it a note at this stage, and is both an ancient craft and a very effective, in fact the most effective, way of producing volume. Blowing has its drawbacks in that lungs are unable to expel and draw in air continuously, doing one or the other but not both. Once bellows had been invented it was a simple step to working them in pairs and connecting to an air reservoir, which could then supply air to a tube continuously.

This is the principle of the organ, though with a large enough reservoir and a non return valve one air pump is enough. Controlling the air and the note with valves and adding more pipes to give more sounds is to turn the instrument into an organ. To get to the point where we have a recognizably modern organ took over a thousand years of development, and by the Norman conquest the organ was still a relatively crude beast; no pedal board and valve actuators that had to be hit with the fist. Being a musician on this sort of organ was no sinecure.

The modern organ

So many church organs dominate the spaces into which they have all too frequently been squeezed, that a brief description of the working mechanism is appropriate; they are an architecture in themselves, an architecture driven by the practical necessity of producing an instrument that works, above all therefore an honest architecture. There are basically four components to an organ; the console, where the organist sits; the action, which connects the stops, keyboards and pedal boards to the third component, the windchest; and the pipes and their frequently ornate case.

It is rare to find a hand-pumped organ these days, as electric blowers are almost universal, but this air feeder is connected to the heart of the instrument which is the windchest. Mounted above the windchest are the pipes (the larger organs have many banks of pipes) and each pipe is controlled by both a stop and a key. The key controls only one pipe in any one rank of pipes, and the stop controls all the pipes in a single rank. Each rank has a particular tone assigned to it and pulling out a stop allows that rank of pipes to play. Pulling out all the stops gives the organ full voice from all ranks, hence the term.

The hand keyboard is called the manual, and the larger organs have more than one manual to operate the various ranks, keeping the connections (called stickers, trackers and pallets) that operate the valves in the windchest as uncomplicated as possible. Some of the ranks of the organ are connected to a pedal board, operated by the organist's feet, and as a consequence the organ seat is a shiny but very hard wooden one, allowing the derriere to wiggle about to reach the foot pedals.

Where the organ is manually controlled, the console is close to the windchest, and this direct connection has its adherents. Organs are still evolving, though, and electrical and electronic control are to be found in both old and new instruments. Organ building and rebuilding is one of those obscure specialist professions that continues to thrive long after its late nineteenth century heyday.

The organ has been the subject of many outbursts of megalomania, culminating in vast instruments at the start of the twentieth century, though by the early eighteenth century the five manual (five separate keyboards) had been made, and the number of stops was well into three figures. The pipes are grouped into stops (controlled by the stops or pull knobs on the console) and are named after the length of the pipe that sounds the lowest note on the keyboard, the eight foot stop sounding a note of the same pitch as the same key on the piano.

The organ then has sixteen foot and thirty two foot stops (sixty four foot stops have been made) which sound one and two (and three) octaves below respectively. On the upper side there are four foot and two foot stops, sounding one and two octaves above (I expect there are one foot, and six inch stops somewhere, and someone has undoubtedly gone the whole hog down to fractions of an inch at the upper end of a stop).

The tonal range possible is thus equal to the full range audible to the human ear. Then there are stops to introduce intervals of thirds, fifths and sevenths (not all such intervals would appear to be sweet music perhaps, but beauty is always in the ear of the beholder). If this is not enough, the whole gamut is repeated to produce different tone colours, with voices to imitate the flute, oboe, clarinet, trumpet etc, and then there are devices to cross link the manuals in order that several tone colours can be played at once, and the tremulant to give a vibrato effect, and so on. Even angels have their own stop!

Some people obviously do not know when to stop. The organ however stops here, and if religion failed by means of ever more complex organs to warm the cockles of the congregation, then it wasn't for want of trying. Batting on more than one wicket is always a good idea though, and if the soul could not be warmed by the power of prayer and song, then the body might be a little less chilled if a modicum of physical warmth were available.

Heating

Heating buildings is one thing we regard as essential, part of the nuts and bolts that secure our continued existence, yet the deliberate heating of the inside of buildings is modern, a trend started in the little ice age of the seventeenth and eighteenth centuries. Prior to this, people in England used buildings as shelter from the excesses of the climate, not as envelopes within which to create a sub-tropical zone. You can guess, then, that churches had no form of heating whatever, until the advent of pew rents made space for the footwarmer and cast iron stove.

That this is a mite surprising is true, for there are many parts of the world where heated homes are essential for survival; England just doesn't happen to be one of them. A brief look at the resources of feudal England will illustrate the impossibility of heating buildings; an open fire run for six months of the year on a hearth big enough to hold a six foot log (to economise on cutting) will burn ten or more tons of wood. For your sins and effort, this is enough to heat a single room twenty feet by twelve (average hovel size). Four acres of coppice are needed just to supply this one need, more land per household than was available to grow food. Fires were needed to cook on, any heat gains were incidental; when not in use for cooking, fires were either banked up or out. English architecture paid no account to heat loss until the middle of the twentieth century, and has paid little enough attention since then.

The concept of indoors and outdoors is one we have assiduously cultivated; we put on special clothes to go out; the serf of the Middle Ages, and most working people to the middle of the nineteenth century, only possessed the clothes they stood in, and wore them everywhere, not excluding bed, if they had one. Going out meant putting on your hat, at most, a tradition not extinct today.

The Saxon, Norman and Gothic church then was not heated, nor was the Georgian, though some parishioners brought their own heating from the middle of the seventeenth century onwards. These were in the form of cast iron stoves, stoves that will warm up in ten or fifteen minutes, and radiate a comfortable glow over the half dozen lucky souls that can get within range. That comfort is relative; given the miserable state of repair of the church fabric in this period, draughts, water and at times, snow, must have been regular companions, and while the heat from the fire would have been welcome, the resulting cold air convection current at ankle level would have been less cheerfully received.

The reason for the arrival of the stove in church however is not due to the inhospitality of the church due to its poor state of repair, but to the fact that the wealthier members of the congregation were now using fires to heat their homes, wearing indoor clothes and indulging in occupations that did not require them to exert themselves physically. The better off were adopting lifestyles that meant lower heart rates and circulation that eased up on sitting down, to a point where they felt cold if not in a heated space. For most people though, life continued to be physically hard, and it was not until the technology of the nineteenth century provided the means, that churches began to install heating proper.

By 1850, the means to heat a large space, such as a church, were to hand, and the origins of the system owe more to developments in engineering than to architecture, for the coal fired boiler, cast iron pipes and thermo-syphon circulation are a radical departure from anything that had gone before, and churches shared the technology with the gentleman's mansion and the ocean going steamship.

The science that underpins this 'wet gravity' heat distribution arrangement is simple in principle, but subtle in execution; to work the boiler had to be below ground level, within reason the further below ground the better, and those churches with a crypt soon converted a part to the comforts of the living rather than the dead. The boiler, a large multi-section lump of cast iron, was hand fired from a bunker, and the hot water rose up to floor level, where pipes were threaded through the pews to warm the congregation.

Churches thus gained a boiler house, a coal chute and bunker, and a chimney, this latter item often cunningly concealed among the parapets and finials. As this method of heating was really the only practical method in the nineteenth century, it was not perhaps ideal, and as imperfections are always a lot more interesting than perfection, a brief look is in order.

The heating boiler was not invented to heat churches, what it was actually developed for is not clear, but the most likely first is heating large homes, where the laying and tending of fires in perhaps twenty or more grates was both time consuming, and, even in an age of cheap coal, expensive in both materials and labour. The boiler of the nineteenth century quickly adopted the form that persists today; a series of hollow cast iron sections in the shape of a squashed 'O', bolted together with a fire hole at one end, a grate in the bottom and a flue at the other end.

The sides and top of the iron sections are hollow and filled with water. From the top of the boiler leads a pipe, perhaps six inches in diameter, the 'flow' pipe or riser, which must rise continuously to a high point. From this pipe smaller pipes supply the radiators and the pipes under the pews, the used water returning either to the same pipe (a 'one pipe' system) or to the return header (a 'two pipe' system). On completion of the job of transferring heat from the boiler to the church, the cooled water returns to the boiler. The whole system works on the pressure difference between the water in the flow and return pipes; hot water being less dense than cold, and the pipes have to be large to cut down the resistance to the circulating water caused by friction on the internal pipe surfaces. The heating pump as we know it today played no part in this system, which was entirely self acting; if the fire went out, the circulation stopped.

While circulating hot water raised the temperature in church, it had one other less desirable effect, which was that the thermo-syphonic action was not confined to the water, but started a second set of convection currents in the air in the church. This air movement, comprising rising warm air currents at the side and a descending cold air current in the middle of the nave (the higher the nave the more vigorous the

102

circulation), on its own did little to offend the congregation, but for the fact that the cycle was completed by a draught of cold air across the pews at foot level. To mitigate this penance, pipes have to be threaded through the pews, though there are still churches where it is the order of the day to kneel in a draught and to cry 'turn up the heat, it's not cold enough!'

Cast iron pipes with massive screwed joint and bends are not the thing of beauty that all might wish, and the wish not to visit these modern appurtenances on the church interior led to the development of the modern hypocaust. The pipes were installed in ducts in the floor, and covered with openwork cast iron gratings, a much neater solution and an excuse for some fancy ironwork, even if the pipes gave off a little less heat as a result.

Despite their lack of grace, the advent of radiant heaters, electric and infra-red heating, the large iron pipe still maintains a strong presence, though today the fuel is oil or gas rather than coal, and the boilerman has gone the way of many manual occupations, replaced by a multi-function valve, a couple of pumps, and a chip-powered timeclock.

Chapter Seven:
Mastery of Materials II -
Masonry Walls, the Oldest
Technology

Walls built out of masonry, that is brick and stone set in a mortar matrix, lend support to the vast majority of the structures that exist today and surround our daily lives. An obvious statement? Between the fall of the Roman Empire and the start of the eighteenth century, timber was the preferred building medium of well-wooded lowland Britain, and would probably still be if well-wooded lowland Britain still existed.

However there is no point in crying over spilt milk, and while the storyline could quite easily be taken forward from this point it is relevant, and a bit of fun, to go back a few thousand years to the start of building proper. This gives us the opportunity to have a brief look at the development of the masonry wall in the cradle of civilization, and sorry, all you anglophiles, that means the Mediterranean and the Middle East, not Rickmansworth.

The techniques of piling stones one upon the other in such a manner as they interlock, don't immediately fall down, and are capable of withstanding large imposed loads, goes back some eight thousand years, possibly more, to the civilizations of the Middle East and the eastern Mediterranean. The first walls that we know about are the brick walls of Jericho, and these were followed, possibly copied, by the civilizations in the valley of the twin rivers, Tigris and Euphrates.

In true direct lineal descent we have to fast forward five thousand years from the time of Jericho to the point, a thousand years before the birth of Christ, when the Greeks learnt from the Minoans the techniques of masonry construction and the principles of the pier and lintel, the Trilithon. Cutting stone into regular shapes is dealt with elsewhere, but the Minoans had either developed it from scratch themselves or, more likely, learnt from Egypt. The Minoans passed the torch of progress to the Greeks. In their own time the Greeks, blessed with a land full of fine limestones and tractable marbles, brought the craft and the art of stone working to a pitch that the world still seeks to equal, let alone surpass.

Nonetheless the influence of the Greeks remained local in world terms, not straying beyond the trade routes of the Mediterranean, primarily because the stone that they used was not widely available. Prior to the onset of the Iron Age proper, the effort required in less amenable rocks, with bronze, and emery embedded copper tools, to produce the same result was too great for the wealth of their immediate neighbours to sustain.

Proportion, Line and Rule

What the Greeks learnt from the Minoans were the basics. What they gave the world was perfection. They invented proportion, weight, massing, order, entasis, style, and slenderness. In short they created architecture. Where a simple stone section of a column of the correct size and load bearing capacity could consist of a series of squared blocks (for various reasons, to be explained, a cube of stone or a similar six sided lump is the most easily-won shape) the Greeks not only made the column circular in section, but in addition to the fluting designed to minimise the mass and create texture in the form of light and shadow, made the column swell along its length in order to further deceive the eye and emphasize the diminishing effect of the perspective as seen from the position of the spectator. Contrast that with today's crass parodies on out of town megastores, in real precast concrete blocks.

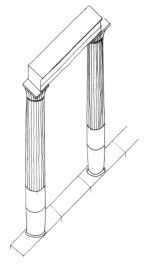

The initial span is no greater than Stonehenge, but this Roman example is fully carved; the columns are plain drums at low level, are slightly 'fat' with modest entasis, and are fluted to give texture. A string course forms the base and there is a minimal rim to the bottom drum.

The columns are as slender as can be achieved, and the opening to solid ratio at a maximum - the limit of classical architecture. These general proportions have been unchanged for over two millennia

Source : Pergamon

Perhaps no other single event in the history of stone working is more significant than the perfection that the Greeks gave to the world, a measure to measure all others.

Pax Romana

Being top dog in the Mediterranean in 500BC did not depend on the stonemason but on the warrior, and in this respect the Romans were very definitely in the ascendance. The Romans knew good work when they saw it, and were content to copy all that they fancied, adding to the store of knowledge by their relentless conquest of new lands to which they brought their peace. The Romans were also able to innovate when the necessary raw materials were not at hand, making extensive use of painted render over brick as a substitute for limestone and marble. With slave labour a plenty, the use of massive stones, weighing in at several tons apiece, was often employed in defensive or marine work. The Romans also made extensive use of the masonry arch and its rotated form, the dome, in manners that left their distant descendants, and much of the intellectual elite of post mediaeval Europe scratching their heads as to how it was done.

While the number of classical monuments that the Greeks left posterity is relatively few, if of incomparable quality, not so their conquerors. The legacy that was, and is, spread across the south of Europe and western Turkey, contains sufficient works of such impressive quality and engineering genius that the Renaissance can be judged as commencing when the works of Rome stopped being a convenient quarry and started to be a tourist attraction.

Technologists First

The Romans contribution to the history of the masonry wall is mainly technological. The spread of burnt clay brick; the use of hydraulic cement, albeit based upon volcanic raw materials not universally available; the systematic exploration and exploitation of the natural resources of Europe that included the stone, marls, clays and sands needed for wall construction; the use of metallurgical or mining waste products as fill or components for mortars. Wherever we have been since, the Romans were there first.

In the warmth of the Mediterranean the use of mortar was optional in many circumstances. Not so in the less temperate climes and with less than ideal stone. The widespread sea transport of Pozzuolan, the essential ingredient for Roman Hydraulic Cement (that sets under water) while practical, was expensive and the use of lime mortars as a cheap alternative accordingly essential.

By empiricism the Romans worked out the correct combination of clay, burnt lime and the fillers to bulk out the expensive end product, but empiricism could not tell them that the only essential difference between a hydraulic and a non hydraulic cement is the temperature at which the material is fired in the kiln, a discovery made (by empiricism interacting with a Yorkshireman) in the nineteenth century. The Romans found that a finely-gauged mortar could be used to substitute for expensive carved work, or as a render to face up poor stone or brick, and their inventiveness more than made up for their lack of ultimate craftsmanship.

In England, time's heavy hand in the form of a western maritime climate, meant the speedy demise of most things Roman, and within a few decades of their departure in the fifth century AD, the knowledge and skills cultivated over centuries had degraded to the point where they had to be learnt all over again. The reason for the decline in skills in masonry work is quite simple; why bother with stone when there is plenty of timber?

Back, then, to the tale.

The reasons for timber's dominance down the ages are fairly obvious; ease of working, availability, and strength in tension and compression. Where timber is still in plentiful supply; on the mainland of Europe, in parts of Austria and Switzerland, for example, it continues to be the favourite material, in sections and lengths that make our domestic floor and roof timbers look like a product designed to the specification of Ebenezer Scrooge on a particularly mean day.

Why then did first stone, and then its cheap and cheerful cousin, brick, win the hearts and minds of our forbears?

The key to the emergence of masonry as a preferred construction material, lies in its durability. Seasoned oak crown timber properly used, is a material that will give any stone, bar granite, a run for its money. Underwood however, that is the coppice timber used in the round or split, while in itself durable, had to be augmented with plaster (real hairy, dungy stuff, not the fancy pink icing we see today), and coated regularly with lime wash and tallow to keep out the rain. Timber as a system thus needed more and regular 'hands on' attention than stone, and in past ages when zero maintenance was part of life's rich pageant, timber came a poor second in the longevity stakes.

Stone, properly won, prepared and laid, matures, adding to it's beauty with each passing season, becoming a home for various small forms of wildlife, weathering in an assortment of unplanned and surprising shapes. The sandstone tombs, wind and water carved, in the churchyard at the top of the hundred and ninety nine steps, are at least as fascinating, possibly more so, than the followers of Mr. Stoker's fantasy who gather there on Halloween. An abbey, a church with a gallery, and a ruined mansion, all within stone's throw. Don't miss it. You can even cast a glance at the view.

Fashion

In the use of stone, it is important not to underestimate the part played by fashion, and if you are tempted to scoff, just consider how the motor industry stays in business, and it is most certainly not by producing efficient modern forms of transport. So too has it been the case with stone. The development of the masonry wall as a construction form, parallels the emergence of the Christian Church in an England shadowed first by the Dark Ages and then by the system of organisation and government that is known as feudalism.

As a building material, stone was, and is, a no hoper when the bottom of the garden is just brimming with healthy two hundred year old oaks looking forward to a contented middle ages. One of the consequences of the land filling with folk in the eighth, ninth and tenth centuries was an absolute decline in the acreage of virgin forest, forest that supplied the crown timber needed for new buildings, particularly large buildings.

The first action of the Normans after the conquest, was the imposition of forest law to large areas of the country, law that included the protection of the trees as well as the game. Sections of these laws still survive, though the language is now jargonese rather than Norman French or Latin. Gifts of oaks from the Royal Forests thenceforth became common, a sure sign of the value of such a gift, which would have been of little worth if the recipients had a ready supply on their doorsteps.

With the emergence of a unified (more or less) and stable (comparatively at least) England under Edgar at the start of the tenth century, the villages of the lowland shires were able to satiate their need for timber by coppicing, and to substitute to a degree for crown timber by the use of stone. Having mined the country's timber resources, the Anglo Saxons had to resort to mining, or rather quarrying, stone as a replacement.

Making virtue out of a necessity is an essential human trait, and not too many officials of the Saxon Church can have been overly dismayed to find that virtually every church that was to become a cathedral in later years, proved to be a maddeningly lengthy haul from the nearest decent quarry. A stern test of faith, when the decision to rebuild in stone was eventually made. York and Salisbury, to name but two, are over ten miles from their source quarries. The craftier monks of Rievaulx and Fountains looked for greenfield sites with extra stone supplies at a stone's throw, and found them.

While it was thus technically feasible to use timber, and there was probably just about enough timber to supply the demand, fashion dictated that, from the start of the eleventh century, the effort to build in stone, no matter how great, had to be made. Fashion made it impossible to consider the use of 'common' materials such as timber studs, wattle or rammed earth in God's house, unless the parish was too poor and lacked any sort of a benefactor.

Fashion's hand then, played its part, and almost certainly led to the use, first of stone, then brick, to distance the Church from the hovels that sustained it, and keep up with the Benedictines next door. Timber, due to its strength and versatility could not be completely or safely ditched from the supporting role in the masonry wall and is to be found, both as the structural frame and as reinforcement, at least until the appearance of cheap cast and wrought iron in the nineteenth century.

Celts and Saxons

The Romans, and I make no apologies for repeatedly dragging them into the text, were good masons. Their masons had a deliberate and systematic approach to finding, winning and working the best stone, and England, as was soon realised, proved a land positively stuffed with the best stone. More of this anon. The departure of the Romans in the fifth century left the land to the Celts, who were unable to sustain the Romans' lifestyle, and as a consequence were soon unable to carve a decent arise, and soon returned to living in circular mud huts.

Over the next six hundred years, many people took pity on the Celts, usually as they were taking the Celts' land, and while the land was not too full, timber could supply the needs of the people for construction. Progress, insofar as the development, or redevelopment of the technology of winning and working stone, remained slow. By the ninth century stone walls were once more in vogue, but in a form that would have given the Romans plenty to look down the length of their noses at. The rubble masonry wall had been reinvented, as a basic shell to enclose a space and hold up the roof. Had the Celts and their Anglo Saxon successors been left to themselves, it is quite possible that further developments would have taken a different turn.

The England of the Saxons in the first half of the eleventh century was a land of plenty, and the Church was flexing its muscles to build bigger and better than it had done before, and the way to do that was on the back of the mason and his skills. Almost before the Saxon mason had a chance to show his skills, events overtook them with the arrival of the last round (to date) of invaders by conquest, the Normans.

Normans

This invasion of new people and ideas led directly to the wider use of stone, initially as homes, usually fortified castles and manors, for the new ruling elite, but the Church, as a part of the tripartite arrangement to rule, was not more than a step or two behind. The Romanesque style, itself being little more than an application, a low level display of technical skill, of detail to a masonry shell, was hinting that the mason had served his apprenticeship, and was now master of his tools and his material.

The time had arrived for the for the masonry shell to be transformed into the Gothic frame and bay construction form that is the epitome of the English church. The technical break point arrived when the Church demanded equality with the pagans (the Pantheon problem) and determined that a solution be found to the structural problems posed by vaulting. Before we do that, a glance at the shell walls favoured by the Saxon mason will prove instructive, for when a solution to the vault was found, it was founded in the techniques that had been proved by the builders of the Romanesque.

Shell Walls

Shell walls are typically from eighteen inches to three feet thick, with an average of about two feet. Thicker walls may be found in exposed or coastal sites. The wall comprises three distinct sections; an outer skin of facing work, usually

112

the best stone; a rubble and mortar core; and an inner skin which can be as well built as the outer, or, if the wall is to be plastered, may present an appearance little better than the core roughly faced up.

The outer skin can be just that, an imported epidermis a couple of inches (50mm) thick, secured to the core with cramps or dowels. Portland stone is frequently used in this manner, particularly where the wall core is in solid brickwork or a less costly stone. More typically, the outer facing work will be sufficiently thick to support the core during construction, and be bonded to it solely by the surface roughness of the stone and the adhesive qualities of the mortar.

The tripartite shell wall was developed by the Saxon and Norman masons as a means of delivering adequate strength, durability and weather resistance to buildings that were significantly larger than their predecessors. This type of masonry work survived to the twentieth century as an acceptable form for new construction, but the key to its successful use in the Middle Ages lies in the quality of the finished work.

Quality Work

The essence of the development of the masonry wall lies in the word 'quality'. The better the quality of the work the less likely it is to fall down, the more slender the wall and the lighter the structure is as a whole. In terms of quality there are a number of important, but not immediately obvious features that need to be examined, and it is fairly clear that prior to the start of the nineteenth century there was little appreciation as to what were the essential quality attributes of masonry work. To be economical a wall must fulfil a number of criteria, and the unfortunate fact is that there are several sorts of 'economy', and most of them are mutually contradictory.

It is fairly obvious that a wall that contains the minimum of stone to do the job of bearing the imposed loads, keeping out the weather, resisting wind forces, and not falling down after the first hard frost, is economical in the quantity of material used. That same wall may also have cost twice as much as a wall built twice as thick that needed only half the skilled labour and half the amount of fully dressed stone. Appropriate quality is thus an appropriate term to use; matching the structural and environmental demands placed on the structure with a carefully judged essay in the use of labour and materials. Empiricism is all about careful judgment, and the history of the masonry wall from the close of the ninth century to the middle of the sixteenth, is all about treading ever closer to the fine line that separates success from failure.

Three examples will suffice to show how extreme caution moved the first generation of Romanesque work, was replaced by cautious confidence, itself in its turn overtaken by exuberant over-confidence. For this exercise we need to look at three of the larger churches: Tewksbury Abbey, Howden Minster and Salisbury Cathedral, and for ease of comprehension we can use that modified and overloaded piece of wall, the column or pier.

Dominating the nave at Tewksbury are a series of fine Romanesque columns more akin to the works of ancient Egypt than Rome or Greece. A family, provided they are of the surname Quiverful, is required to link arms round these massive drums, and they do what they ought not to do, obstruct the view of the altar, very well. They also hold up the roof, and would not fail in this task even if a herd of brontosaurus was to take up residence on the ridge.

Despite their solid appearance these columns are solid only on the outside: the core is almost certainly an unconsolidated mass of rubble and mortar. Nonetheless they are very robust and their low slenderness ratio and vast cross-section mean that they have not caused their caretakers a single night's lost sleep down the centuries, nor will they for ages to come.

Not so our next port of call, Howden. Here the nave piers are all that they appear to be: fragile, delicate, slender drums of solid stone holding up far more clerestory and triforium than they were designed for, if designed is an appropriate word. You can't quite put your hands round them, but you can give a pier and your loved one a hug at the same time and not feel that three constitutes a crowd. This is masonry at the practical safe limit: it looks good, has stood the test of time, including more than its fair share of neglect, and doesn't obstruct the internal views more than is absolutely necessary.

Lost sleep certainly featured in their builders' night lives, especially when the nave was raised, and the tower top section caused the foundations to give, even though the arcades held firm, but since completion they have stood straight and disturbed no canon's peaceful slumber.

Finally we overstep the mark at the tower crossing of Salisbury Cathedral. In proportion these piers are not too slender, not too tall, and neither are they too badly built. They are just hopelessly overloaded. Since completion of the spire virtually every generation has had its worries about those four piers, which have gained counterforts and underpins over the centuries, much as skin gathers wrinkles. To carry the analogy further they are bent under the burden carried into old age, an old age likely to be prolonged only by yet more wonders of masonry medicine. Yet, like Tewksbury, the masonry is only skin deep, but the loads are not truly axial, the core not pulling its weight, and it shows.

Piers and columns are in some ways microcosms of walls, and these three examples show just how much solid masonry will take (at Howden) and how much larger a shell and core (Tewksbury and Salisbury) need to be to do the same job, or to struggle to do it, as the case may be. In wall technology Howden is the exception: there are virtually no truly solid stone walls in the churches of England. Shell and rubble are what you get, irrespective of what was paid for.

Most economical in terms of material is not then the norm, and to progress we have to ask the question, Why not?

To answer that conundrum we need to step back again to the ancients of Greece and Rome, who certainly built solid walls, both as single skins of stone and as interlocked double skins. Troy and Hierapolis have examples of this art, but it is even there in the minority alongside shell and rubble cored walls, and the reason lies in the way that a stone is won, and the labour that is expended thereon to stack it on top of its neighbour. Squaring up a lump of sand or limestone involves sawing or splitting to produce the face that will be seen. The bed (top and bottom faces) will normally be reasonably flat. If you want true and flat sides then you will have to saw or split these also, likewise the back. By the time the job is finished the lump of stone you had in the first place will be half the size, plus a lot of chips and stone dust. If you have no use for the waste then it must be carted away or otherwise disposed of on site, and you will need to cart and quarry twice the amount of stone than is actually installed in the wall. Worse, you will have to double handle the spoil to get rid of it, doubling your transport costs into the bargain.

Solid walls have one further drawback. They are not waterproof. Water is drawn through those joints that are continuous from one side of the wall to the other. They have a similar tendency to be draughty, even when mortar is used in those joints.

Shell and core walls are a natural solution to the need to utilise waste and to avoid unnecessary labour. A rectangular looking stone can be produced merely by working the face and making the visible arises straight and perpendicular. The waste can then fill the gaps and economise on the mortar. This becomes an even more attractive proposition when you have the rubble remains of the previous church to dispose of. The result is a thick wall that is both wind and waterproof, ideal for England's balmy climate.

Ideal in that respect, yes, but not universally so, because in with the rubble core has been thrown the human fallibility factor. What the eye can't see, surely God won't notice?

On your voyage of exploration many wonders of carved stone will be seen. Just occasionally, when you peer into a dark corner or round the back of a column, you will find that the work on the back is as good as that on the front. Occasionally. Just occasionally, the wall core is as good as the enclosing shells, and when a wall is subject to trial by ordeal, it is always the weakest link that determines ultimate strength, and that weakest link is usually the core. Loadbearing capacity is however dependant upon a number of factors, and the most intellectually difficult of those to conceive is the concept of slenderness.

Slenderness

How thick a wall needs to be is dictated by two factors. Firstly, the slenderness ratio (height to thickness) of the wall when it reaches its full height, and secondly, how much load it will need to carry. Both are interdependent and seemingly beyond the wit of the mediaeval master mason, if not the mathematics of the time, to calculate. Therefore empiricism rules. How thin a wall can be is dictated by the stone it is made of. The inner and the outer skins can overlap, but only occasionally, and the minimum thickness is thus generally slightly more than twice the depth of the facing stones, rarely less than fifteen inches and usually more than eighteen. The larger the stones the thicker the wall needs to be to accommodate the individual stones.

To illustrate the next point we can fast forward to the jerry builders of the nineteenth and twentieth centuries, where a nine inch brick wall, tapering to four inches at first floor, was deemed sufficient for those who were perforce obliged to rent what we must describe as a home, however much the article mocks the title. In strict structural terms such a wall is adequate to hold up both itself and the roof loads of quite a moderate-sized church. Many church walls are not as high as a two storey house due to the sweep of the roof, and if four inches of masonry will do the job, then a wall that cannot reasonably be built to less than four times that thickness, stands a good chance of being a success. Slenderness and ultimate load capacity are clearly not issues, and certainly not with all those virile bulging biceps of buttresses that adorn almost every outside wall.

Good old human fallibility!

What economy of effort produced, in the form of the standard design of masonry wall, proved to be effective in terms of weather resistance, and structurally stable in its original, modest, Anglo-Saxon usage. As two skins of rubble or ragstone masonry with a core of waste and lime mortar, no ninth century church approached the limits of these design methods. With the dawn of the Romanesque and the filling of church coffers with gold from the Norman settlement, the use of larger blocks of accurately cut stone was an obvious way forward to beef up the wall to meet the demands of the new vision.

The advantages were obvious; walls could be built taller, faster and more accurately with less effort if the stone facings had at least three flat sides at right angles to each other (two beds and a face) and two perpendicular arises. Less mortar was needed, always an expensive commodity as lots of wood, peat or later, coal were needed to fire the kilns, and the stuff was a pain to transport. Here we come to the unfortunate bit!

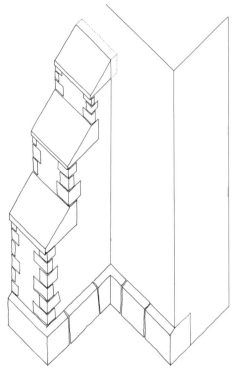

Buttress - this models steps inward by means of weathered (sloping) capstones that throw rain off. The front capstone edge projects to form a drip, and is grooved on the underside (throated). Well designed and effective.

If a rubble masonry wall is successful as a short thick structure, you don't get any feedback as to why it is a success. Such a wall may actually only just be capable of doing the job, because the inner wall core that of course not even God sees, may be so badly formed that it is only standing up with the assistance of the inner and outer skins. The core may in fact be adding its weight to the loads the outer skins are shouldering, not sharing the loads of the roof or vault.

Making the wall thicker to improve its load capacity, may make the wall weaker because the core will be that much more substantial. Ultimately such a construction can fall down under the pressure of an unconsolidated core, even before the church is complete. Dangerous ground indeed. And the very item you need lots of top quality of, lime mortar, is the one thing that is hard to come by and expensive. And its only going where no one will see it, so it doesn't really matter if it's skimped, does it?

Failure to properly construct the cores of masonry walls ultimately results in the collapse of the building. The thicker the wall, the greater the danger due to the bursting forces generated. The taller the wall, the greater the pressure the core can exert. Going for sheer size, as at Tewksbury, was no guarantee of success, and hard lessons were repeatedly learnt throughout the Middle Ages that skimping on quality would bring the house down around your ears. At the penultimate gasp of the Gothic in the last century this lesson not learned did bring the house down at Fontwell Abbey (Fontwell was a rich man's folly, not a religious house, but the crash was still due to poor work in the walls).

Quality, quality, quality...hmm. A mantra for the last millennium? Or for this one?

The Skills Evolution

As a society that has effectively consigned the skills of the mason to the recycle bin of a living history museum, we might well be near to the state of relative ignorance that prevailed when the need for the first churches arose. Building a rubble wall using stone gathered rather than won, placed unworked, bedded in a good mortar, faced up both sides, reasonably plumb and with square quoins is not a difficult task provided you're not too critical of the result.

Doing it so well that it is regarded as a work of art many centuries in the future is an achievement that cannot be underestimated. Could we, in the penultimate year of the second millennium, equal, or even surpass the work of the mediaeval mason, let alone set new standards that would put the Ancient Greeks in the shade? We do not, and therefore we can only judge our society inferior to both in this aspect. The stone for the last great religious house of England in the twentieth century came from, and was carved in, India.

Returning, then to the dawn of the twelfth century, we have a culture and technology that has seen the future of the masonry wall as representing an opportunity, in the shape of dimension stone. The winning, shaping and placing of quality

119

stonework will transform the Anglo Saxon Norman Romanesque church from a modest essay, to unrivalled splendour. An opportunity yes, that the opportunity was not an immediate success, perhaps goes without saying.

A number of hurdles had to be overcome, not least finding, winning and transporting the stone; producing simple (to us at least) hoists and cranes to lift the stone into position; making sure adequate supplies of mortar were available; developing building designs that would work. The first time round, at Howden, to quote just one example, the conceptual design of a church without a clerestory obviously didn't meet the bill. Developing a self-perpetuating elite of craftsman masons and their skills took time. Realising the necessity of foundations to accept the higher loads produced by taller, slimmer walls did not occur overnight. All lessons to be learnt the hard way, forgotten, and learned the hard way again by future generations.

This constant round of construction punctuated by failures, of extensions and rebuildings, by degrees boosted the confidence of both the clergy and their workmen. Competition to have the tallest spire or the longest nave meant that the limits of skill and material were always being tested, often to destruction, but a large scale collapse was often the only way of clearing a suspect structure and making a fresh start. Failure is also good way of learning, though it has a tendency to be expensive.

The skill of the mason to fashion stone to the whim of fashion was fed by the wealth of the mediaeval Church, and as wealth and confidence grew, Early English was followed by the more exotic variations of the Gothic. The decoration that was applied to the masonry wall and its other structural components, to some extent hid the true quality of the work.

While the lines of the arcades, buttresses and horizontal subdivisions deceived the eye, and the pinnacles and crenellations added beauty, it is in the accuracy and the quality of the solid work that we see the masons true skill; masonry pulling its weight; loads carefully balanced; the right amount of stone and no more exactly positioned to deflect a lateral thrust; the building of a wall as two thin solid skins to relieve stresses on older work lower down. In comparison the working of shafts and ribs to intersect is merely having a bit of fun after the real work has been done, the decoration a little light relief.

All of this took time, and the real joy of mediaeval churches is, that no matter from which period or periods a particular church hails, there is always the feeling that the design and construction was approached as an essay in limit state design, with joy, apprehension and terror balanced with a good dose of faith in the minds of the builders.

The end of the Gothic age in the mid sixteenth century meant also an end to the skill honing of twenty generations of craftsmen (women had the real drudge jobs such as sawing stone, and no, they didn't have power disc cutters, just iron tension frame saws that only cut on the pull, not on the push as we do today). Where the quality of masonry had not been up to scratch, the next hundred years were to prove to be the ultimate test as the church went on a maintenance holiday.

When the holidaymakers came back from the beach in the mid seventeen hundreds, it was to mend, or demolish what could not be mended, rather than build new. What new work was to emerge was not a jot different from the old in terms of its basic design, but the modern brick had emerged in the interregnum, and truly solid walls, either in brick, or brick with a masonry face, were now a practicality. With no demand for exotic carved work much of the flat facework of the neo-classical could be cut to standard dimensions at the quarry and site waste avoided.

Coursed and interlocking brick backing meant no place for stone waste in the finished wall except as fillers in the lime mortar, for which purpose the waste had to be crushed. Yet the twin skin and rubble core wall was not dead, indeed it would be three hundred years before it would be laid to rest. But the magic had gone, only the prosaic remained to be churned out as part of the neo this, or neo that. No risks, little excitement, and no challenge to the technological limits. The Church threw off the mantle of progress and became a little conservative. The emergence of the true solid wall in the seventeenth century, gave the creators of the post-Gothic church an opportunity to create something new. As we shall see, history turned out a trifle different.

121

Truly Solid

Solid walls are an entirely different entity from stone and rubble tripartiteism. They are a lot stronger because they are monolithic, acting as a single unit with no discernable core or skin. It will come as no surprise though to note that the solid brick walls of the eighteenth century were no slimmer than their stone predecessors of two centuries earlier. In their understanding of the structural nature of the masonry wall, the Georgians were no further advanced than the Anglo Saxons of the previous millennia.

The solid brick walls of St. Francis Xavier, Hereford, suitably reinforced with horizontal squared oak baulks in their thickness, are as thick as their mediaeval counterparts, yet were built in the second decade of the nineteenth century. Not until the middle of the Victorian era did the true strength of slim solid walls come to be appreciated, and wall thicknesses shrink to eighteen, thirteen and then nine inches, at which point they could not keep the weather out properly, and the cavity wall was substituted. Today solid brick, or stone faced solid brick, walls are a thing of the past, their fall from grace total, and no prospect of a revival can be anticipated.

Surface finishes – Ashlar, Rockface and Rubble

When a new masonry wall is being considered, prime, alongside the choice of the stone itself will come the surface finish, and top of the tree in cost terms is the smooth face of ashlar. Ashlar is facing stonework, with a smooth or 'boasted' face formed by sawing, dressing, scappling or rubbing, or a combination of the four depending on the stone being worked. The stones are either coursed or random blocks depending on the stone being used and the form of finish being applied to the joints, openings and quoins.

With ashlar, the stones are laid to break joint, as in brickwork, and will frequently use false jointing or projecting quoins to give articulation to the wall face. Without this face variety ashlar has the tendency to look rather flat, a feature of many lesser buildings that are either not very old and do not have the scars of time, or are formed in a stone where there is very little surface character. This is a particular risk with Bath Stone or Portland Stone, to use just two examples.

Some stones are harder than is desirable for easy working, and 'rockfacing' is one way of finishing the stone without the excessive labour that would be needed to produce the smooth flat face of ashlar work. The front face of the stone is hacked back to leave the centre proud. This technique is used on the harder sandstones, such as the Pennant Grit, a stone that does not split cleanly enough to present a smooth face, is too hard to be rubbed down to a flat surface, and needs must be sawn or subject to prodigious effort with a boaster if ashlar is needed.

There are distinct similarities between stone that is rockfaced and stone that is 'Rag'. The difference is primarily that ragstone is usually not worked to any appreciable extent, but is used virtually as it is won from the quarry face. Ragstone is a term applied to the Jurassic and Cretaceous stone of eastern and southern England, notably Kentish Rag and Ancaster Rag, but the principle of using a particular stone 'neat' as it were, applies in full to the next variety, rubble. Ragstone tends to have poorly defined arises, and is frequently defined by quoins, etc., of more tractable stone.

Most walls that are, or were, plastered internally, have faced or unfaced rubble masonry. The walls can be coursed, the individual stones roughly squared, or they can be 'ex source', which may be the local beach or river bed. The stones can be split to give a fair face, split twice to provide a quoin, or laid as they are. With some stones, such as flint or the thinner bedded limestones, the walls can be laid in patterns, 'Chequers' or herringbone, for example. Actual sizes of individual stones can vary from a couple of pounds to a ton or more in weight, larger stones generally being fairly close to the ground.

Corners, tops and openings

The corners of a building are defined by their quoin stones, and are the most important feature of a wall, since they impart a major amount of the wall strength, and their accuracy determines the appearance of the rest of the wall. Because of their key role, quoins are frequently composed of better quality materials and display the best workmanship. Features include the use of contrast materials, false jointing, chiselled arises, and projection beyond the wall faces.

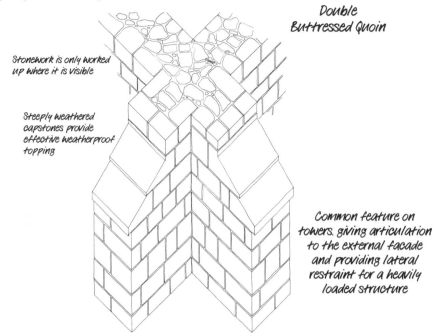

Double Buttressed Quoin

Stonework is only worked up where it is visible

Steeply weathered capstones provide effective weatherproof topping

Common feature on towers, giving articulation to the external facade and providing lateral restraint for a heavily loaded structure

String courses serve two basic purposes; to change the proportions of an elevation, or the whole of one side of a building; or to allow for a change in wall thickness, to support a gutter or other detail, or add reinforcement to otherwise minimal quality masonry. These two functions, architectural/aesthetic and constructional are complementary. Which came first, or begat the other, is a matter for debate.

For various reasons, not all walls are protected by the roofs they support. Weatherproofing and decoration are then provided by the use of capstones or coping stones, the two terms being effectively synonymous. Because they are exposed to the weather, top quality is the order of the day, though the visual impact of a decorated wall top frequently means that the material chosen is more malleable than durable. Typically the individual stones are quite large, half a ton being unexceptional, and old stones can be quite severely worn. Some copings incorporate drip moulds (see below), but most do not, even though they would perform better with them.

This coping stone has a level rather than a sloping bed to stop the copings above it sliding down the gable wall. The top face of the coping slopes to one side, as well as down, to prevent water running into the mortar joint between it and the next stone below on the wall top

This is a single stone, worked up to act as a horizontal stop at the base of a 'gable' or 'pine end' sloping coping. The stone is 'weathered', cut to slope on the top to throw off water, and 'throated', with a groove beneath the overhang to throw water away from the wall below

Whilst their construction is different, drips and drip mouldings have a common purpose; to throw off the wall face water running down it. In its simplest form a drip may consist of a row of projecting thin stone slabs or even brick tiles. More fanciful designs are moulded, have turned down ends (over windows, for example) or project further than necessary to create shadow or other visual features.

Buttresses and counterforts perform the same function: propping up walls; buttresses on the outside, counterforts on the inside. Because of their bulk, counterforts have tended to be unpopular with church builders, as they take up valuable internal space. Life, however, is about making a virtue out of necessity, and the buttress, necessary or not, as an art form thrives all over the land. As briefly touched upon, the development of the frame and bay enabled the vault to become a permanent feature in church architecture.

Many components of the frame are in fact buttresses, including the famous flying ones. Most true buttresses, those that lend support to shell walls, serve solely to allow a thick wall to be slimmed down, or, not infrequently to support a thin wall that should have been thicker, and started to show signs of distress as a result. Spotting those that are original as opposed to the later additions, is not an easy task, but many a spire sits on a buttressed tower (including the biggest of them all!) that was originally built without the necessary add ons.

While parapets appear to serve primarily as decoration, and can themselves be heavily carved, they are in the first instance functional. Walls need to be stabilized at the top, and the best way to achieve this is to make the top stone a 'biggie'. Likewise, large stones are frequently not found in many quarries and needs must be imported.

An imported stone is an expensive stone, and to have it carved as well will add little to the cost. Secondly, arches need to have loads distributed around their segments if they are to be stable. A hefty parapet helps do this.

Parapets then can be minimal, just large enough to accommodate the back gutter leadwork, or they can be two or three feet high, crenellated, capped with ornate copings, even stub pinnacles. At their extreme a parapet can be raised to form a false wall, between two towers, for example, purely for architectural effect, or as an additional wallspace to hang more carvings or statuary upon.

Kickers and kneelers are special stones, found in the line of capstones or coping stones on the top of a gable or pine end wall. The kicker is the bottom stone, frequently ornamented, in which the stonework is translated from the horizontal to the inclined plane of the roof adjacent. At intervals up the gable, are kneelers, stones cut to the profile of the capstones but having a wedge section, frequently disguised by a false joint that gives the stone a horizontal bed. This arrangement stabilizes the capstones, preventing them from sliding off the top of the wall.

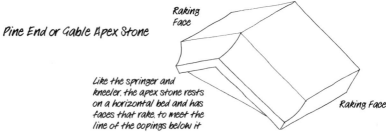

Pine End or Gable Apex Stone

Raking Face

Like the springer and kneeler, the apex stone rests on a horizontal bed and has faces that rake, to meet the line of the copings below it

Raking Face

Unlike most other wall components, the triumvirate of column, pier and pilaster, and pilaster aside, are usually solid masonry of the very best kind. Only in the larger columns is there room for a core of rubble. To draw distinction between each is not to split hairs, only nearly so.

Columns can be any shape (well almost); round, square, with piers or shafts attached. 'Pier' is a useful term that can be applied to any column! Shafts that are attached to columns are known as engaged, and a single column can be engaged many times. Shafts attract the best stone, not infrequently marble, even in relatively modest churches, and their purpose is both to decorate and to deceive the eye, for they rarely have a major structural role to play.

Pilasters are the engaged columns of classical buildings, typically being attached to the facade, and displaying a half or three-quarter section. Many pilasters are actually formed in render and brick, Roman fashion, rather than stone. With classical columns comes also the ultimate in eye deception - entasis.

Not content with the appearance of a parallel sided or tapering column, the ancients made their supports swell slightly to improve the perspective. When done well the effect is to dull the angularity of a facade or elevation, overdone gives a somewhat bloated appearance. Needless to say, the architects of the seventeenth century onwards adopted the lessons of the three p's (Paestum, Parthenon, Pergamon) without criticism. Not a few restorations of the nineteenth century included stripping out these pagan emblems from Gothic churches.

What's in a Wall?

The short answer to this is, almost anything, *except* perhaps ears, though the odd bone or two should not be ruled out. The classic tripartite solid masonry wall of outer face, core and inner face is an object lesson in recycling; until this century virtually nothing that could be re-used was discarded.

In middle-aged churches (1100 to 1550) most of the building to be seen, with a few notable exceptions, is not the first to occupy the site, and in respect of the Romanesque, most original material is going to be on the inside. The site will be original in most cases, because once a reservoir of stone has been established on site, its inertia will preclude relocation, even if dogma didn't. Into the foundations go large boulders, if available, glacial erratics, grey wethers, field clearance material, in fact anything suitable but not fit to be seen.

To these lowly goods is given the task of supporting the loads from the superstructure. On the second, third and fourth time round stone from further up the wall no longer fit for visible work would be recycled to reinforce the foundations, forming a platform. Whilst not being there to prove it, foundation failure probably ranks alongside wall core erosion in responsibility for failures.

New stone is brought to site for facing work, and to make up the numbers elswhere. Sound stone from the previous building, or from adjacent structures can also be used as facings (robbing stone from derelict structures has been systematic down the ages, most monasteries 'dissolved' in this way, and large chunks of Hadrian's Wall have been recycled many times). Depending on the stone, the facing work will be, in order of merit (and cost) ashlar; sawn squared blocks, either random or coursed; split or rockfaced squared blocks; split faced coursed rubble, or uncoursed random rubble.

The Portland, and Bath Oolites, and the Magnesian Limestone of northern England are the favoured stones, along with the permo-triassic sandstones, for ashlar work, and much else besides, and the stone is usually given a sawn and rubbed, or a boasted face. In important work projecting faces are used, with false joints, chiseled arises and repeat motif carving.

Sawing stone is hard work and many stones are sufficiently hard to resist this method of working, making it uneconomic except for the most important pieces. Split faces, either plain or tooled are thus commonly seen, for this is the method (splitting with wedges, crowbars, feathers and sledges) that stone is won from the quarry face, even today when compressed air tools have eased the task. Split faced stone can be squared, and coursed with scappled or tooled surfaces, or they can be rockfaced, or left unworked as rubble masonry.

Moving down the pecking order, we come to the thin bedded tilestones, so called because they are, or more usually, were, used to make roof and floor tiles. Tilestones are used where other more suitable stone is not available, and are generally too thin to receive a worked face. To add interest tilestones have been lain in herringbone or zig zag patterns, a sign of old work (not a sure sign - beware of imitations!)

Most humble of stone is rubble work, either split faced or 'as found' on the local beach or river bed, or recovered from tilled fields. Into this category falls such local specialties as flint, where the small size of individual stones led to the development of decorative 'chequerboard' patterns.

Brickwork, used as fill, repair or backing to stone, while not normally visible, is fairly common. As a base for render and stucco, brickwork is very common. The thin bricks of the Middle Ages were fired Roman fashion, in brickfield clamps (a method still to be seen in Turkey today, though with coal as the fuel). The modern brick, nine by four by two and a bit, is a kiln product. The development of the modern brick brought about the demise of stone and the end of the tripartite wall. The brick solid wall is completely different animal from the walls discussed here, and has no room for anything except the bricks and mortar.

Finally, in the wall core you can expect to find old, worn facing stone, fragments of carved work, quarry and bank waste, the larger river gravels, field stone, chalk blocks, in fact anything durable to reduce the need for mortar. None of this is readily visible under normal circumstances, though wall cores can be seen among ruined church buildings, and occasionally glimpsed during renovation work.

The poor state of the wall core was frequently a source of concern to restorers in the last century, and Scott's report on St. Albans, recording large voids and blaming the original builders, is not untypical. In retrospect voids in wall cores are more likely to result from settlement and erosion caused by water penetration, rather than careless work. It should be remembered also that we now look back with the benefit of two centuries of experience in repairing old structures. Where the reports of the pioneers, from Wren to Wyatt, speak primarily of their ignorance of structural design, the real message is one of courage, in tackling buildings that in some cases threatened to collapse upon them.

Where some movement was to be expected, horizontal baulks of timber were sometimes set into the wall core; perhaps not the wisest form of reinforcement, but well ahead of the iron and steel used a century ago, and causing so much trouble today.

Bonding all these disparate materials together is the mortar. Until the last century this meant lime mortar, for the Romans had sneaked off in the fifth century without telling anyone about their formula for cement. To be fair to the Romans, their hydraulic cement (which sets under water) relied upon reasonably fresh volcanic supplies, not to be found on these shores. The name Pozzolan cement (from Pozzuoli in the Phlegrian Fields near Naples) survives as a trade name for a hydraulic cement today.

Lime mortar, as burnt slaked lime plus fillers (sand, gravel, shells, crushed slags, coal dust - again, anything goes) forms the wall matrix, binding the parts together to make it act as a monolith. Lime mortar makes the tripartite wall possible, allowing uneven stones to be bedded, and filling most of the voids, though there are still plenty of these even if they're not three feet deep. Without mortar, stones would have to interlock. Merely cutting a stone to the accuracy needed to make two faces have more than occasional contact when placed together is a significant feat. Building out of stones that precise and making them interlock in a wall that is plumb and true needs labour on a scale not witnessed in Britain since departure of the Romans.

The Rise and Rise of the Brick

The brick effectively predates the use of stone for building, first as a dried mud block, but very quickly as a fired clay true terracotta brick. With the advent of this form, the lack of durability of the mud variety was transformed into a material that has lasted as long as cities have graced the earth. As with stone, the brick found favour because of the lack of timber. While the skills of brickmaking vanished with the Romans in the fifth century, they made a swift return in the twelfth, and though initially despised for the best work, bricks quickly found favour in the more mundane supporting roles.

Brickmaking is dependent on the right combination of raw materials; while it is possible to make bricks out of all manner of weird substances, in the twelfth century bricks were made out of clay. Where the stones of this land are not sticking out of the ground, like as not it is because there is a goodly covering of boulder clay, courtesy of the last Ice Age. Where there are large tracts of country in the south of England that are devoid of good stone, and where also the glaciers feared to tread, geology has been kind in providing large deposits of clay from earlier epochs. England took to brickmaking like the proverbial duck to water, and while the brickfield and the clay pit of rural England has vanished in the last fifty years, their products are as durable as those fashioned by the doomed brick moulders of Pompeii.

The role played by brick in mediaeval churches is a modest one; indeed you could visit a thousand churches and not see a single slim, pre-1600 brick. Yet they are there, behind the plaster, or forming the innards of the tower; their shyness is due to the undeveloped state of the technology of moulding and firing. Where they are to be seen, as in the hotchpotch walls of stone and flint at Clare, in the valley of the Stour in Suffolk, the brick is in two forms, mediaeval and modern(ish).

The true mediaeval brick is present as a series of thin bands running through the flint and mortar, so thin we would describe them as tiles rather than brick. Visually commanding more attention is the later brickwork; relieving arches over doorways, spot repairs among the flints and replacements for stonework around the windows. These bricks are again much thinner than today's chubbies, less than two inches thick, and anything but square and straight. This lack of dimensional stability is the real reason why so little brickwork is used as facings, and the cause of this is to be found in the clay pit and the firing regime.

With the rediscovery of brickmaking in England in the twelfth century came also the realisation that there was a lot more to making a brick than slapping clay into a mould and firing it. The only way that a brickmaker could refine his product was by experimentation, and this focused on two areas; the make up of the clay itself, and the way in which heat was applied to turn the raw clay into brick. The clay was always going to be a problem because the material is nowhere of a consistent composition over a wide area or depth, and this led to the use of specific bands of clay to the exclusion of other material that did not appear to meet the necessary criteria. Secondly, clay is notorious in its ability to change consistency depending on how wet it is; a clay can require the attention of a pick to excavate it, and an hour later, after a heavy shower be ladled as a soup. Various quantities of organic matter and stones are often present, which again affect the finished product.

When the clay had been pressed into a mould and turned out as a 'green' brick, it has to be dried, and this was achieved in the open air, with shelter from the rain. Thin bricks dried more quickly, and these were the first successes. Once dried there are two ways that they can be fired; the clamp and the kiln. Temperature control is critical to the finished product, to the extent that if you get it wrong, then you won't have a product at all, just a mess. While the pottery kiln was already ancient history in the twelfth century, firing a thousand bricks at a time required something just a mite larger. To add to the fun, the only fuel to hand was usually wood, even though peat and coal, with much slower combustion rates and lower ultimate temperatures, were already supplementing coppicewood by the start of the thirteenth century.

Clamp firing, then, was very much a trial and error business, with wastage rates varying wildly. The clamp is basically a pile of fuel and dried bricks. Fire is allowed to progress through the clamp and burn itself out. With minimal temperature control much of the end product would be either over or under burnt, a proportion cracked and/or broken, and large numbers curved into banana shapes. Clare has lots of these.

The end product was thus very variable, with shape, colour, texture and porosity all being unpredictable. When you are not trying to build what we now define as a brick wall, that is a series of regular courses with quoins and beds and perpends all running true horizontally and vertically, then the ultimate shape, size and colour of the end product is not critical. The bricks that can be seen at Clare, the later ones at least, are good enough to lay in a proper fashion; they have an even colour and texture; their length is equal, more or less, to twice their width plus one joint thickness, and their curvature is not more than the thickness of the mortar bed that they are set in. That said, they would not pass a quality control test of any brickworks operating today.

132

The learning curve of the clay pit and brickyard can thus be seen to be a long one; in fact the modern brick we use today did not emerge until the late sixteenth century, over four centuries after the reintroduction of brickmaking to this island, and the reason is the slow march of technology along the learning curve. That the march was slow was due for the most part to the lack of control in the firing process, control achieved by the adoption of the brick kiln, an insatiable monster that could only be adequately fed by the use of coal. Thereafter the brick is tied to the industrial revolution as surely as if it had been invented by it.

When identifying brickwork used in a church, we have an added difficulty over and above that of stone, for where stone is of a particular type from a particular quarry, bricks from the same source two hundred years apart may be identical or so different as to appear to be from a different planet. While we can therefore log the chancel at Holy Cross, Basildon as been constructed in brickwork and dating from the last decade of the sixteenth century, and be reasonably sure that much of what we see is original; where brick is used in a non structural fashion, to fill in the frame of a timber framed church, or to act as the plinth as at Greensted-Juxta-Ongar, you are left to ruminate as to when the brickwork that you can now see was put in. At Greensted the bricks *look* Victorian, but are they?

Brick identification is an unrewarding task: as with stone, the basic inertia law applies - bricks don't travel far unless someone else is carrying them, and most pre-nineteenth century bricks are thus local, unless there is river access or the bricks are few in number and have been imported as a feature. The net result is that with one major exception, all the local brickwork to be seen is red, or nearly red, in colour, and if the bricks in a church are not red, then the chances are they are under two centuries old.

The reason for this goes back to the problem of firing; clays that make good easy to fire bricks also have the tedious habit of producing red bricks, the exception being the clays of the London basin where the brick turns out yellow. Red brick is thus the industry standard, and while the colour variation and surface texture are very local, the widespread use of brick over the last three centuries has led to the subsuming of local variety in a welter of imported 'near miss' colour matches.

We may occasionally go to the extent of reopening a long abandoned quarry for fresh stone, but the prospect of true reproduction local made bricks is a concept that has yet to hit the market, long dominated by the self firing clays (owing to their oil content) of the East Midlands. All it needs it a little sleight of planning.

Brick, whole brick, and (almost) nothing but brick

As we have seen at Clare, the first use of brick, as a thin, minimalistic statement of a string course, was not followed by the wholesale adoption of the material as a structural material in its own right. Clare's string courses are decoration, the material is not to be trusted with the man's job of sharing the load, not even with flint gleaned off the parish fields. The idea that the material will take the place of quarry stone, is in the fourteenth century, a true flight of fancy. The inbuilt conservatism of both the church and the craftsmen needed both a long period when the material could be 'on trial', and to see technological developments improve both the consistency of the product and reduce the cost.

This latter item was critical in the later Middle Ages, because the one item that brickmaking required lots of was fuel, and in the regions where stone was scarce and brick potentially an attractive option, there was, naturally enough, no local fossil fuel supply. To a degree this want of a suitable fuel came to be satiated by the development of the sea coal trade of Eastern England, a trade that made the expansion of London feasible, and with the flooding of the peat diggings that are now the Norfolk Broads towards the end of the thirteenth century, coals from Newcastle made up for the lack of wood as domestic fuel, and enabled brick to be substituted for wood in buildings. A treadmill of fossil fuel dependency we remain hitched to today.

Until the end of mediaeval England, then, brick remained a curiosity, though you will find it today in the towers of both Holy Trinity, Hull, and Beverley Minster, and doubtless in many another church that hails from this period. While the church as a whole remained rich, brick was destined only for a bit part. Come the Reformation and the religious recession of the late sixteenth and seventeenth centuries, the maturing technology of the brickworks, produced a standard product that could be used as a loadbearing material in its own right. Bricks offered substantial economy of mortar use, and the writing was *on* the wall for stone and the tripartite masonry wall.

Building new four hundred years ago, for the most part did not mean ecclesiastical but domestic, and it is with domestic construction that the brick achieved both maturity and respectability in this period. Key to this maturity is the use of brick as facing brick, and the recognition that in order to be good enough to be seen, bricks had to be classified according to their regularity of shape, colour and evenness of firing. This led to the classification of bricks either as facings or commons, with the quality control for the former much more rigorous than the latter. With the cautious rebirth of the church building programme at the end of the seventeenth century, brick was very firmly among the options, now as a material of strength and beauty in its own right, and very competitively priced.

At last then, brick was on an even footing with stone, considered both as a thing of beauty and a joy forever. With brick, the bricklayer, patently a less skilled craftsman than the mason, could build walls that were as thin or as thick as the work demanded, in multiples of four and a half inches, or thereabouts (there were no British standards and brickworks made their bricks to their own patterns right down to the twentieth century). By the start of the eighteenth century, detailing using special bricks to form flat arches, string courses, cants, bullnoses, squints, cills, corbels and many other details besides, had been developed to mirror the stonemasons craft with chisel and boaster. Terracotta, a fine red fired clay, was available for decorated string courses, cills and other fine detail work, and tiles were being perfected, first for the roof and then for decorating walls.

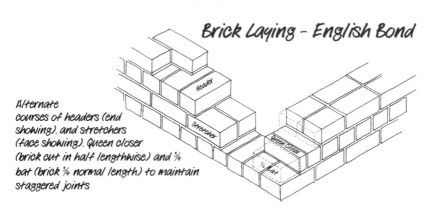

Alternate
courses of headers (end
showing), and stretchers
(face showing). Queen closer
(brick cut in half lengthwise) and ¾
bat (brick ¾ normal length) to maintain
staggered joints

Header

Stretcher

Queen Closer

¾ Bat

While the eighteenth century saw the completion of the technical development of the brick (engineering brick aside), brick had to wait until the nineteenth to move centre stage. By an unfortunate twist of fate, brick came to be virtually the standard material for the nationalised state subsidised churches that were deemed to be the means of bringing the official Christian religion to the urban masses. Had this been the only use brick found in ecclesiastic buildings, the resultant press would have been very bad indeed. As it is this genus of church has suffered under the heavy hand of time, and most of these unloved artifacts have been swept away in the white heat of postwar redevelopment. Fortunately, both the Catholics and the Dissenters had their own building programmes, and in the case of the Catholics this included a number of new religious houses, many by the leading Catholic architect of the century, Augustus Welby Northmore Pugin.

Pugin's influence on the Palace of Westminster is well known, but for the new convents and monasteries, brick came into its own, and Pugin was no less a master of this than he was of stone. Pugin's concept of the convent that he attached to the rebuilt mediaeval church of St. Anne at Bartestree, was for an essay in brick, the mellow orange-red soft-faced brick of Herefordshire, an essay that was conceptually rooted in the nineteenth century, complete with boiler house and pumped piped water, if based on the religious precepts of a millennium earlier. The convent, like its many companions from this period, thrived for a while, but this century once again finds the celibate life in recession, though brick is not.

The Dissenters built freely in brick, with the Methodists, Congregationalists and the rest often using brick to ape the

Gothic style, by no means with universal success. The twentieth century has perhaps seen more mature design, using brick as a material with its own strengths, and as a part of what increasingly has become cladding on a frame of steel or reinforced concrete. Today the brick element of a wall can be as little as half an inch thick, stuck onto a panel of insulation or cement, a far cry from the three feet of solid brickwork at St. Francis Xavier. Brick has found a future in the architectural style of the late twentieth century, where Classical and Gothic work are *verboten*, but as a facing or cladding, not as a loadbearing structural component.

Brick's twentieth century role as an attractive primary waterproofing layer is an evolutionary event. Brick is not a universal substance; some bricks are as waterproof as sponges, others are used as damp courses; most are porous. While walls remained two feet thick, bricks struggled to be competitive with stone in areas where stone was plentiful. Three things occurred in the late eighteenth and nineteenth centuries to change this. Firstly the developing coal industry reduced significantly the cost of the fuel needed to produce bricks, and that cost was further reduced by the adoption of the brick kiln, wherein the firing of the bricks could be accurately controlled and wasters reduced to a fraction of those from a clamp firing

Secondly, the canals and then the railways reduced the cost of moving coal to areas remote from navigable water, making brick production economic over much larger parts of the country (coal was in any case associated in many places with seams of clay that could be mined from the same shaft or adit as the coal to fire it). Thirdly, and crucially, application of the mathematics of structural theory to the masonry wall showed that the brick wall could be thinned dramatically, reducing the number of bricks needed, and their weight (which dictated the transport cost) to a third or a quarter of the same work done in stone.

The resulting brick wall might not be waterproof, but the nineteenth century was equal to that as well, and the heating of churches became universal, displacing the personal stoves that the rich had been bringing into their own pews (along with armchairs and footwarmers) to sustain them through the te deum of the marathon sermons then in vogue.

Heating buildings of course is a big help towards keeping them dry, but thinner walls meant greater temperature swings, and condensation channels in the inner window cills became necessary to pipe the water outside, and damp on the inside of a wall, even today, is called anything but condensation.

The thin masonry (brick) wall then, had a relatively short useful life, and by the end of the nineteenth century was being usurped by the cavity wall. Since the 1960s that usurpation has been total, and in many modern churches the brick has little or no work to do beyond keeping out the rain. Brick's continuing favour is based upon its perceived durability (well beyond our span of years if used wisely), and as yet it has no serious challengers.

Concrete; Blocks and other Curiosities

As with most things, the Romans appear to have invented concrete, part of the secret of the Pantheon, and while its production was beyond the technical repertoire of the Middle Ages, the idea of using small stones in a matrix of mortar never appears to have gone away. It is perhaps stretching credulity a bit to say that the flint walls at Clare are a form of concrete, but that is only because they are built, not poured. The development of Portland Cement in the nineteenth century made modern concrete feasible, and the idea of using the material as a substitute for stone never crossed the mind of the inventor, not even when he hit upon the name!

The idea of concrete was undoubtedly around in England before the cement that made it possible, for down many a country lane there still lives a construction form, rammed earth, that is effectively concrete sans cement. Whilst not a poured mixture, formwork is needed to build walls of mud, clay and anything else that's to hand, and straw or reed makes up the binding forces that would otherwise need cement. Finding an ecclesiastical example is a mite difficult, for, like the west nave wall built into a small church ten years ago, if you didn't know the wall was built in mass reinforced concrete, there is no way of spotting the fact today. So it is also, with rammed earth.

The very indistinguishable nature of mass concrete, unless waved like a baton by Corbusier, who has only a passing role in the history of English church architecture, consigns the material to obscurity behind render or harling. Not so concrete's first cousin, the block.

Concrete blocks are so much a part of modern construction that we need to be reminded of that era, only five decades or so ago, when stone quarried for building emerged from the quarry as neat manhandleable lumps. Low energy costs now make crushing and reconstitution so cheap that only consumer resistance prevents bricks falling victim to this lowest of low priced material. Coloured concrete blocks, and ground and polished versions are now in common, even favoured, use by architects and as such their appearance in church buildings for the foreseeable future is assured, if only as a change from brick on the outside (and the inside, often enough) and plaster.

The present regime of blocks which are manhandleable, nine by eighteen inches by two or more inches thick, is the result of a century of development; a hundred years ago experiment was made with blocks that weighed in at up to two tons. There are still a few structures extant with these megaliths, but, as with the storey height panels an inch and a half thick and four feet wide, experiments that are not successful are oft not repeated.

Chapter Eight:
Bells, Bronze, Iron and Lead

Bells have a special place in the history of church architecture, not least because 'which came first, the tower or the bells?' needs a bit of analysis. Secondly there is the question why were bells invented, and what caused the Church to appropriate their manufacture and use? Finally there is the technical matter of the bells, how they are hung and rung, what they are made of, and how did the Church, from the Middle Ages on, manage to hoist bells in most of the churches across the land? Enough questions indeed to keep the six stalwart serving men happy for a page or two.

To ask why churches sprouted towers from their earliest days, is to suggest that towers did indeed come before bells. A glance at most towers however is to cast confusion over the theory, because it is clear that towers were designed to be built in sections, as an add on that could be added on *ad infinitum*, or to a degree at least. The bell in fact predates the tower, bell casting being an art practiced since the bronze age, for bell metal, as used in this country at least, is an alloy of copper and tin, a bronze with an approximate mix of three parts copper to one of tin. The history of why people made bells and, more to the point, rang them, predates Christianity. True to form, the Christian Church knew a good thing when it saw one.

Bells quickly assumed a central place in church daily life, symbolizing the presence of God, regulating the order of the day, calling the faithful to prayer and announcing special occasions like weddings and invasions. The true bronze bell as we know it today did not exist in the ninth century, and as with so many things, the wealth of the Church was used to develop the craft, and bring it to maturity.

As a craft, the profession of bellfounding has gone through those traditional phases of technological development; foundation, growth to maturity, and old age. The craft as introduced to this country in the late ninth century was in its infancy; up to this point bells had been laboriously beaten out of iron blooms, into plates; bronze casting producing only small bells not suitable to be the voice of the Church. The problem of casting a sound, large bronze bell lay in the control of the copper/tin ratio, the stirring and venting of gases from the casting, and the control of the cooling of the finished article.

Experimentation was the key, and it was not long before the craft was sufficiently widespread to push towards its technological limits, encouraged by what was in effect unlimited demand. England is fortunate in that in terms of the historical exploitation of resources of non-ferrous metals, copper and tin are more plentiful than all the rest put together, and the mines of Cornwall that have most contributed, are also close to the sea.

From being a specialist craft, the trade of the bellfounder had become a skilled nomadic occupation by the twelfth century, with bells being cast from imported materials, or recast from old bells, on a large scale. What was now being cast was a sophisticated musical item; a single bell on its own can ring any old note, and so long as the overtones are half decent, it will sound fine. The mature English bell of the thirteenth century was the classic shape we know today, rung by the clapper striking the bow, the thickened section of the bell rim. The bow was filed or ground to an even thickness and a clear note that is assigned the term 'strike note', an octave above the persistent 'hum note'.

The art of tuning bells was one of the skills lost in the little ice age (religious and physical), to be rediscovered by Canon Arthur Simpson, the Rector of Fittleworth in deepest Sussex (eight miles north of Arundel in the Rother valley), in the nineteenth century. With a peal of bells (up to four at least), there is no need for the bells to be tuned to accurate intervals in a scale of F#minor melodic, for example (western music hadn't got that far by 1299 anyway), because ringing a peal is based on mathematical combinations, not tunes; but if the bells are of evenly distributed weights, then they will sound - well, beauty is in the ear of the beholder, after all.

When the number of bells reaches five or more, they will, in the words of the tower master 'sound awful' if they are not tuned, and this is the fate the Canon has saved us and the bellringer from, for the purpose of ringing a peal is to extract from the mathematical combinations those changes that are the most musical.

Towers then were built in anticipation of the day when the church would be able to acquire its own bell or set of bells, with the effect that from the start of the twelfth century, every church that was contemplating a rebuild or an extension, or both, that is most of the churches in England, included a tower in the plans.

To be both effective in sound broadcast, and not deafening inside, the bells need to be located out of the main body of the nave, indeed remote from any space that will be occupied while the bell or bells are being rung. The preferred design is the locating of the bellframe, a robust wood, frequently steel today, space frame in which the bells are hung, in a chamber of the tower that is some distance above the roof of the Nave, if possible. The frame holds the bells in two ways; if the bells are to be struck (chimed) only, then they are fixed to a headstock that is bolted to the frame, and a striker is positioned to hit the bow of the bell to chime it. Today, this is frequently done electrically by means of a solenoid actuator, and the bell provides shelter for the mechanism, bellchamber windows being unglazed apart from stone or slate baffles, and the more or less obligatory anti-pigeon netting.

If, on the other hand, the bells are to be *rung*, then the bellframe supports the bells on headstocks that can be rotated, and the traditional clapper is thrown against the bow by a mixture of centrifugal force and gravity. The traditional headstocks were fitted with plain bearings (of which a few remain), but have been largely superceded by roller and ball bearings that make the job of hauling on the rope a lot easier.

The rope that is not attached to the Campanologist at ground level is not attached to the bell either, but to a grooved wheel that forms part of the rotating frame that holds the bell. When at rest, the bells hang mouth downwards, and to ring changes, or occasionally a 'peal', (or, more normally, a fraction of one) the bells have to be 'put up' first, that is rotated so that the mouth points upward. At this point the clapper is leaning against the bow, and the bell is leaning against a stop a few degrees beyond top centre, so that a pull on the rope will start the bell to turn. The potential energy of the bell is released as the centre of gravity descends, and as the bell passes bottom dead centre and commences its climb back to the top of its swing, the clapper swings across as a pendulum and strikes the far side of the bow with some force.

The Campanologist, or bellringer, is thus not in absolute control of his or her bell, for, once the bell is swinging, the inertia of the bell and its rotating frame dictate that the stroke of the bell occurs at the point where the holder of the rope is not actually doing anything, it being somewhat difficult to push on a rope fifty feet long and expect to have any influence on the other end. The bellringer can in fact only pull on the rope and expect to have any effect on the harmonic motion that's going on above his head, at two points in the cycle; to slow the bell as it approaches top centre, and to pull the bell off top centre to start the next stroke. As it is impossible to see what is happening in the bellchamber, the bells are controlled entirely on the feedback received through the rope.

To ring a single bell is thus a simple matter; it can be tolled simply by putting in enough energy to swing it through a short arc, pulling on the rope as it approaches the top of its swing. To ring changes, that is to follow a numerical sequence in which the order of the rung bells changes, and hence the time between individual strokes of each bell varies, involves not simple harmonic motion, but skilled and practiced manipulation, stopping and starting the bells in such a fashion that they ring in sequence some time after they have been pulled off.

As with all technologies, the bellfounder earned his crust, not just by catering for the latent demand that existed in the Middle Ages to fill the country's towers with bells bigger and better than before, but a lucrative recasting trade as well. Recasting was, and is, required for two reasons; firstly the adding of bells to an existing ring (the 'proper' name for a covey of bells, but 'peal' is in common parlance, so long as you're not one of the fraternity), can prove difficult if the musical intervals are too close, or the tower hasn't room for one or more smaller bells that extend the tonal range towards the upper end. Secondly, bells fail due to the stresses of being rung, by being rung incorrectly, and by being rung with a worn clapper that does not strike the middle of the bow. They also fail due to poor casting.

Bells are very demanding on the frame and the tower in which they are hung, (there were no dynamic balancing machines in the fourteenth century, and the hammer blow of a swinging two ton bell, by no means the largest in common use, is of tilt hammer proportions). The cessation of church building in the mid-sixteenth century was a disaster for the peripatetic bellfounders, who found that by degrees, the lack of maintenance to the fabric of the English church caused the practice of bellringing to go into abrupt decline. There was a very real fear that vibration from the bells would be the straw that broke the bellframe, tower and all. Within a few years the itinerant bellfounder was a thing of the past (the Whitechapel Foundry was founded in 1570), and for the last four centuries casting of church bells in England has been effectively the preserve of just two firms, Mears & Stainbank at Whitechapel, and Taylors at Loughborough.

Bellringing as an occupation has fluctuated over the centuries, much as has the availability of the rings to service the art. The practice of ringing is one in which various degrees of talent are present, with the more experienced ringers touring the country to ring at churches other than their home base.

These expeditions to ring on other bells than the home ring are frequently just a visit or social outing, but may also include either a 'peal' or a 'quarter peal'. The time it takes to complete a peal depends on the number of bells in the tower and the number of 'changes' or variation of the order of ringing that are possible. Five bells generates one hundred and twenty changes, twelve bells nearly four hundred and eighty million; fortunately a full peal is only(!) a minimum of five thousand changes (5040 on six bells), for it would take several decades to perform all the possible combinations on twelve bells, rather than the usual Saturday afternoon.

Almost in defiance of the practicality of playing a tune on a ring of bells (yes, tunes can be, and are, played on tower rings at times), the Carillon was developed to allow one person to chime a tune on a set of bells from what is basically a modified organ key and pedal board. The player has to be of robust constitution, as it is fists rather than fingers for the upper registers and foot-stomping for the lower. Handbell ringing is also a tradition widely practiced, with a long association with the church and its music; the principal differences from tower ringing are the tonal scale, the ability of the ringer to manage more than one bell (up to twenty for the super energetic expert), and the volume of the end product. Up to two hundred bells can be managed by a dozen ringers, far exceeding the piano's tonal range and offering a serious threat to the organ. Muffling was mastered early on, but *piano* and all the *mezzos* and *issimos* to *forte*, are not really the medium's *forte*, though considerable control of volume is possible.

The mediaeval practice of mounting handbells on a frame and ringing them by the wielding of a pair of crude drumstick type hammers, is no longer with us, the odd orchestra percussion section apart, or perhaps it would be better to say that news of its reinvention has not yet reached the author, owing, in all probability, to his tedious habit of turning off Radio 4 at two minutes past seven every weekday evening.

Bells are the least visible but most impressive use of metal in the English church, having been the cause of construction of perhaps the most distinctive section of the church, the tower, which while not universal, is not far short of being. Only the very smallest churches do not sport a tower, and while the separate belltower, or campanile, survives in England, just, between these extremes we have a wealth of grace and beauty. The spectacular are present in Howden and Boston, while many towers support spires of unbelievable grace and weight, from the red sandstone of Ruardene, to the flying buttresses and corona of the Queen of Holderness.

Before we move on to look at the other metals that give service to the church, the last word on the subject of bells must go to Canon Simpson who, on arrival at the gates of heaven must surely have responded to the question 'and what good works have you done on earth that you should be granted entry here?' with the ultimate one-liner: 'I made all the bells of England ring in tune'.

Metals - Lead and Iron

If bronze, in the form of bell metal, is the most conspicuous use of metal in the church, in a strict architectural sense, the use of lead and iron are more important in the structure and fabric, whatever the effect of bells on the form. These two metals proved their worth as integral and almost indispensable elements of the English Church from the earliest days. Of the two, lead was by a good margin the most valuable and extensively used, the ultimate in waterproofing, and a sure sign of wealth on the part of the parish.

Second, but a good distance to the rear, came iron, not so much for the amount of iron that ultimately became part of the building fabric as door locks and hinges, or altar rails and chapel screens, but as the metal of the tools that shaped all the fabric: stone, wood, lead, glass and brick. These five materials dominated the fabric of the English church, from its inception to the middle of the last century.

True, other metals there were and are; bronze for doors, statuary, altar rails and grave markers; bell metal we have already looked at; copper for roofs and flashings; tin and zinc for roofs again; and silver and gold for the sacred vessels and symbols. With the exception of gold, there were, and are, significant resources of all these metals without having to go beyond these shores and even gold, while rare, is not absent.

Once again, the mineral resources of Britain had been scrupulously determined and exploited by the Romans, indeed it was primarily for the silver, gold, lead, tin and copper that the Romans had come to Britain in the first place. The evidence of their workings was plain to see a millennium ago, and the Romans had built roads to connect all their mining areas to the country in general and the ports in particular. To make matters even more explicit, they used the waste products of those mines as road metal, as all who know their *sumnum dorsum* from their *pavimentum* will be aware, and there was not really any great need for 'dig here' signs. In some instances

147

production of ores and refining had never actually ceased, though the methods of the Dark Ages meant that mining usually comprised digging a lot of small holes rather than one big shaft or burrow, and "continuous" was more itinerant than fixed; mines tended to wander across the landscape.

The expansion of demand that followed the launch of the Christian Church in England was not then a complete fresh start, but mineral leases, and the wealth that they generated for their owners, very quickly became an integral part of the Church's land portfolio. In time the Church, and in particular the monastic orders, played their part in the technological developments that pushed forward the exploitation of the mineral wealth of this island. The mineral wealth that was most in demand and widest distributed in the twelfth century was lead.

Lead

The ambition of every church to sport a lead roof was not just driven by fashion; there are very sound reasons why lead is an attractive roof finish. Many churches still display the scars from reroofing schemes that took advantage of lead's flexibility, and the flexibility that was in its turn lent to the designer when planning the church roof. A glance at what went before will show just how powerful a design tool lead was, and still is. In the tenth century there were basically four methods of keeping out most of the rain; thatch, turf, stone slates and shingles, and lead.

Thatch had long held sway where reed could be had; it is durable and waterproof. Straw thatch is also waterproof, but not so durable, and both had the major advantage of not requiring a lot of support; they were lightweight, and that meant that beams and rafters could span the large spaces that churches need. The downside is that to throw the water off before it comes in, thatch needs a roof pitch of fifty degrees, which results in a lot of roof for a modest span.

Turf is neither lightweight nor particularly waterproof, and has probably never endeared itself to the cleric, hermits apart. Stone slates and shingles are both double lap tiles; stone slates are heavy and need an almost Herculean roof structure; shingles are not very durable unless laid to a steep pitch.

Lead, in contrast, while heavier than thatch, and needing continuous support in the form of boarding, is happy at very low inclinations. When you have a church that, like Howden, lacked direct light into the nave, lead gives you the option to drop the pitch of the aisle roofs and generate a clerestory, without having to reduce the proportions of the internal spaces. As a design tool, lead just had to be God given, and this use on the aisle roof can be seen on hundreds, if not thousands of churches from the Saxon period to the end of the nineteenth century. Lead, unfortunately, had a down side; it was lethal to produce.

Lead as an ore is found as a compound; with sulphur it forms galena (latin for 'lead ore'), and due to its presence in hydrothermal veining in host rocks, is frequently associated with silver and zinc. Reducing lead from the ore to the metal involved two processes; separating out the other metal contaminants, and driving off the sulphur. Lead has a low melting point and boiling point, and driving off the sulphur also meant driving off the lead, at least in part, as well. The result was that mediaeval lead smelters operated in conditions where the fallout, lead and acid rain, created a killing zone down wind. The eventual solution to this was the condensation flue, where the lead was deposited on the walls of a long flue (half a mile was not exceptional), to be scraped off by unfortunate individuals whose workplace conditions were a virtual guarantee of a swift transit to the next life. The silver content was a constant source of worry, as there was a royal monopoly on mines that produced more than a small proportion of the metal as a by-product, a monopoly not removed until the end of the seventeenth century.

The end product that was so useful as a roofing material, was produced as a pig; a roughly rectangular block weighing about half a hundredweight. These pigs were transported to the point of use, where they would be remelted and cast into sheets on a prepared sand bed. If motifs or decorations were required, then these would be carved in wood and impressed into the sand prior to the casting. The size of the sheet is limited by the weight that can be manhandled into position, and by the maximum size that can be laid without its self weight causing it to creep down the roof, a few square feet being the norm.

Cast lead was somewhat overdesigned for the task, being about twice as thick as modern rolled sheet, but if properly fixed and dressed, was good for at least two hundred years, after which the remains could be remelted and recast. The lead was fixed by nailing the upper edge, or if it was the top abutment sheet, wedging into the chase in the stonework. The sides were waterproofed to the adjacent sheets by dressing over a lead roll (actually a timber section with a rounded top).

The bottom of the sheet overlapped the sheet below, which was turned up and nailed to a short vertical drip, on the shallower pitches at least. If the size of the sheet or the steepness of the roof pitch demanded extra fixings, these were formed by nailing through the sheet, and then forming a cast lead 'dot' to seal the hole.

Lead's versatility as a roofing material stems from its workability; it work hardens only slowly, and will take a certain amount of reworking and adjusting to fit a particular location, as a consequence. Secondly it oxidises at the surface slowly at normal temperatures, and forms a patina that protects the surface from further erosion, giving the all important long life. Lead also has the property of being forge weldable at room temperature, useful for making rain water pipes; and lead/tin alloys, known as solders, have low melting points that allow full metal joints to be made with both lead and other metals, permitting the easy fabrication of stained glass with jointed lead strip.

This latter use remains an important use of lead today, for there is no substitute for the lead strip that holds stained glass windows together, the combination of lead, glass, soldered copper ties and bronze saddle bars that hold the whole together, is as old as the technique itself

The use of lead enabled water from roofs to be gathered and stored for use, or directed to watercourses without the risk of washout to foundations, and fancy cast lead hoppers and rainpipes are still relatively common. Both cast and sheet lead still have a place in church architecture today.

Sheet lead is favoured for flashings and weatherings, while cast is still preferred for roofing. The techniques of working have changed little over the years, though leadburning with a gas torch is now an accepted way of forming many details, and the pencil burner is an essential tool of the stained glass artist. For working lead sheet, the wooden dolly remains essentially unchanged from its mediaeval form, and the lead roll and cast decoration likewise.

Iron

In the unique composition that is the English church, iron is the kingmaker not the king. Those churches that sport old ironwork in the shape of grilles or railings from before the middle of the eighteenth century, and particularly those items that are pre-reformation in origin, are displaying wealth in a form we cannot appreciate, because iron's usurper, steel, is now the cheapest metal on the planet.

Iron's true place, though, in the history of church architecture is in the toolbag, for it is the iron tools of feudal England that shaped the wood and stone into the glory that we can still bear witness to, and that glory would not have been achieved without the steel hardened edge tools that the mediaeval mason and carpenter, among others, put their faith in.

Iron ores are plentiful in England, just as the ore of lead, galena is widely distributed, so too are the oxides and other compounds of iron. The difference between the two metals is that while lead was lethal to work with, the ore yielded its metal at modest temperatures and metalworking from there on was more or less plain sailing. With iron the reverse is true, and for most of the mediaeval period iron is a rare metal, even semi precious. Iron ores come in several basic, or rather acidic, forms, of which the easiest to work is haematite, an uncomplicated oxide of the metal.

There are many other ores available which will yield iron if pushed, but the key to understanding iron's place in the Middle Ages, is just how hard it was for the ironworker to make the end product. Iron ore is found usually as a rock in which the iron content is usually less than half.

Typically rocks containing over 20% iron ore are workable. The first task then after the 'mine' (iron ore) is won is to remove the rock and produce a concentrated ore. This was done until the middle of the last century by hand hammers and hand picking (yes, I'm afraid this is where the females of the species come in again). Then things start to get *really* difficult. Iron will dissociate itself readily from oxygen only at high temperatures, but at those high temperatures it will readily recombine with other contaminants, such as sulphur, and the only method of reducing iron oxide to metal was to combine the oxygen with pure carbon. As the reaction is exothermic, so far so good, and the technique of charcoal burning produced excellent carbon, at a cost. Carbon however is very happy to alloy with iron, and this really was the sticking point.

Firing heaps of charcoal and iron ore produces a lump of iron and carbon mixed together, and due to the presence of the carbon, the lump, or bloom is fairly soft at about a thousand degrees centigrade. Belting it with a hammer evicts more of the carbon, and as the carbon content decreases, so the melting point of the mixture or alloy increases. The mediaeval ironworker thus reached a point where he had a bloom of fairly pure iron which was soft enough to work at high temperatures, but could only be forged, not cast, and in its raw state was too soft to take and hold any sort of an edge. At which point the intelligent observer is quite entitled to ask; why bother to go to this length for a lump of soft metal?

If weapons are an indication of the state of the art in the eleventh century, the answer to this question would be, why indeed? Tools tell us very little, primarily because they were worked with until they were worn out, and the remains recycled. Only the rich can afford to preserve things that lack immediate utility, and if we are to examine the quality of the edge tools of the period, then the only place where you will find both quantity, and a chronological succession, is in weapons, particularly swords, spears and the like.

The conclusion that you can draw from the national collections is that mediaeval ironworkers were, to our eyes at least, little better than amateurs. The reason iron tools were preferred is that there were three ways to turn soft iron into a material without equal; 'steeling', quenching, and work hardening. Steel is an iron-carbon alloy, and carbon can be absorbed into the surface of iron at high temperatures (the result is a lumpy mess known as 'blister steel', but it works).

152

Quenching is cooling from red or white heat by plunging iron in water, and work hardening is bashing the cold (ish) iron. The end result of these processes is a material that has to be ground to shape because there is nothing in the way of metal that is hard enough to work it.

Chisels, boasters, axes, adzes and saws made of tempered and hardened steel edged iron were the tools that shaped mediaeval stone and wood. Nothing else compares. Wood, soft iron, bronze, all had their place in the toolkit, but if the job, particularly the working of stone, was to be done, then the vast rigmarole that was ironmaking in the Middle Ages had to be gone through. Such was the value of iron.

With the pressure of population increasing in the latter days of feudalism, the production of iron pressed heavily on the one resource that was in short supply; wood. Charcoal retains about sixty per cent of the energy value of the original wood, but the coppice poles that make the best charcoal were also the serf's and the villein's cooking fuel. With limited supply and high prices, the pressure was always on to increase production.

When the breakthrough came, with the shaft furnace in the fifteenth century, a single furnace burnt its way through the best part of a thousand acres of coppice in a single six month 'campaign'. To a peasant feeling the chill of the Little Ice Age there was little to rejoice about in having a charcoal iron furnace for a neighbour, and surviving furnaces at Bonawe and Eglwysfach are not too close to lowland England.

The output from the shaft furnace was liquid iron, cast iron with a high carbon content that was no use for tools, but made an excellent range of natty hardware that over the next four centuries the church made a determined effort to acquire. Ornate cast iron grilles and railings, massive door bolts and handles, boot scrapers, and in the nineteenth century, grave slabs and the massive heating pipes that ousted private stoves and foot warmers, all featured on the Church's shopping lists.

From 1875 or so steel made its appearance as tie rods for roof trusses, and as the material of the trusses themselves. The bolts, straps and plates that transformed the timber roof truss into an engineering miracle were in increasing use from the middle of the seventeenth century. That ubiquitous fixing, the iron nail, laboriously cut by hand with a chisel from rolled strip, was in demand everywhere in sizes from the dainty one inch lath brad, to the hefty studs that adorned the oak doors beloved of every bishopric.

Cast iron formed the sections of the heating boilers, roaring leviathans lurking in their dungeons, fed by a new breed of church troglodyte, the boilerman. Cast iron too, formed the radiators, intricately cast as hollow sections with ornate feet and sculpted ribs, screwed together and tied to the wall lest they escape. Outside, iron found a new use; displacing the wooden gutters and lead rain water pipes with castings that came complete with added, or rather cast in, ornamentation. Revival of interest in the hypocaust led to the installation of ornate cast iron floor grilles, covering the underfloor heating pipes. Rolled iron and later, steel, rods and bars were introduced to hold the glass in the window, and opening lights in hopper or tilt mode were installed; if the location was remote enough, ingenious rope or pulley systems were added to make opening them fun.

Finally iron and steel joists and beams came to form floors, spanning the distances even the biggest timber could not hope to achieve. To these the art of the riveter added his deafening patterns, in his turn ousted by the hiss of the welding torch. Today steel is the supreme structural entity, where once it only enabled, and the chisel plays a minor part in an age where it is possible, some would say desirable, to machine everything.

Metals, however, are the bit-part players in the exploitation of the natural resources of the country to create ecclesiastical architecture, and the spotlight on the star, stone, is perhaps overdue.

Chapter Nine:
Stone - The Riches of the Earth

If an observer was to be asked to define a single element that is the quintessence of church architecture, then stone has to be the first choice. Stone is the major structural material, the prime loadbearer, the principal decorative element, and is only rarely overshadowed in any of these roles. To say that stone in an infinite variety has been the mainstay of church building for the past twelve centuries, would only stretch the word 'infinite' slightly.

Stone, as the rock beneath our feet, falls into three divisions; Igneous, Sedimentary and Metamorphic. Of these three, building stone is obtained primarily from the sedimentary rocks, those laid down, usually by rivers or seas, as layers of fine or coarse sediment and compacted into rock over millions of years. Limestones, the great carbon sink of the planet, and Sandstones, are both sedimentary in origin, and building stone classification commences by defining a stone as either one or t'other. Just occasionally of course it is neither, in which case it is one of the heat treated rocks, a metamorphic slate or marble, or an igneous granite or sill.

Before we consider the detail, a quick glance at the broad brush will help understand the distribution of building stone in England and its Celtic neighbours, for this is one area of study where rocks from throughout the British Isles feature alongside the stone of the locality. Foreign stone is comparatively rare, even though Caen was not technically 'foreign' for much of the Middle Ages.

Geologically speaking the rocks of Britain vary in age from hundreds of millions of years to a few million, from the Pre-Cambrian of the Shropshire Long Mynd, or Lewis in the Western Isles, to the Tertiary of the Isle of Wight. There are even younger rocks within these Islands, but they have no application as building stones. All of these rocks are a lot older than man's working of them.

Whilst there is not a complete stratigraphical sequence of all the rock formations ever laid down across these islands, for a relatively small land mass, the British Isles probably has a greater variety of rocks than any other similar area on the planet. That said, England has a distinct predominance of a number of rocks from specific geological eras, but complements this with certain areas that have rock found nowhere else on the Earth's surface: a finite resource indeed.

The British Isles can be likened to a tilted table, where the layer cake that is the geological strata, has been grit blasted by the hand of time to reveal the youngest rocks in the South East, and the oldest in the North and West. Erosion has left the harder rocks sticking up more than the softer, and as the oldest rocks are generally the harder ones, most of the uplands are formed in the older rocks, generally North of the Trent, or West of Offa's Dyke.

Where the rock strata of a particular formation ends we see the edge of the rocks as a scarp slope, and one scarp in particular, the Jurassic Limestone and Sandstone, cuts England diagonally in two. This feature makes the task of building stone identification a whole lot less difficult than it might otherwise be. Not easy you should note, for the task is complex almost beyond measure, but at least understandable.

To the South and East of this scarp slope we have few building stones, all from the Upper Jurassic, Cretaceous and Tertiary (the latter is very poorly represented), and these are for the most part localised both in distribution and use. The band of upland, and at times it is scarcely more than a hump in a plain, that denotes the Jurassic scarp, is not more than ten or twelve miles wide, twenty on the Yorkshire Moors, and contains an unbroken variety of the finest building stones that this island can offer.

To the West of this line, starting from the Southern end, we have granites in Cornwall, sandstones in Devon that are not Devonian in age but are part of the Permo-Triassic. The Permo-Triassic sandstones, known as the New Red Sandstone, outcrop in a great swathe across the Midlands, and onto the Cheshire and Lancashire plains. Magnesian Limestones, also Permo-Triassic in origin, are to be found in a narrow but influential band from Nottingham to Durham, and the Carboniferous Gritstones that dominate the Pennines (which are themselves predominantly Limestone) provide much of the northern uplands' dark sandstone.

The Lake District is a unique landscape famed for its slate, but equally home to a number of sandstones, limestones and granites, a reflection of its geologically turbulent past. The Vale of Eden is a further enclave of the Triassic Sandstone. Spread haphazardly across this relatively simple picture, are the intrusive rocks and inliers that produce some very special stones.

Wales and Scotland export a number of specialist stones derived mostly, but not exclusively, from the older rocks (only the intrusive rocks found as dykes and sills are younger than the Triassic). Many of these are metamorphic, igneous or intrusive.

Generally speaking, the younger a rock is, the more likely it is to be a limestone, and the softer it will be. All the best, easily worked, and most durable building stones are limestones. Most carved stone that is not red is limestone. Marbles are limestones, albeit metamorphic and totally crystalline.

So far the picture is a fairly straightforward one of a sectioned and etched geological layer cake. Here however the simple ends and the complicated begins, for within each stratigraphical horizon the local variations can be almost endless, as different sediments were laid down at the same time over quite small areas.

Taking the Jurassic scarp as an example, we can see that the whole of the exposed strata, from Hunt Cliff, near Saltburn on the North Yorkshire coast, to the Isle of Purbeck in Dorset, is comprised of rocks that differ in age by only a few million years. Starting in Yorkshire, the scarp that is sandstone trends west past Guisborough and then south to Sutton Bank, before declining into the Howardian Hills, where there are both sand and lime stones. This section is extensively used locally for building stone. The scarp is then an insignificant feature at the base of the chalk, re-emerging south of Market Weighton as a limestone, the Cave Oolite.

Crossing the Humber this becomes the Lincolnshire Limestone, thenceforth the course of the stone belt becomes a litany; Ancaster, Stamford, Clipsham, the tilestones of Colly Weston; Cheltenham, Bath, Doulting, Ham Hill, Portland and finally Purbeck, and we've missed the hundred and one variations in between. And this is just one of many horizons.

The best way to examine English stone resources is to divide the country into regions. This will give a reasonable view of what stone can be found where, because stone obeys a basic law of inertia; you don't carry a lot of the stuff very far unless someone else is carrying it for you. To religions this law has been a challenge down the ages. What better penance is to be had, than selecting a site for a new Cathedral, say York or Salisbury, at a point where you cannot actually be further from the quarry without having a navigable river to assist in the transport task?

Less self important churches make do with the supplies on their doorstep, or use water transport to make the task easier. The richer the parish, the further they were prepared to go for their stone supplies, but the regional distribution of stone, based upon the local resources, still shows strongly, right up to the end of the stone age, in the middle of the twentieth century. Let us commence a tour of the country, and the local stone, with a tour of the South East, keeping a reasonably healthy distance from London.

The Home Counties

This is a good place to start, if only because it is the poorest corner of England, and deserves to be taken first, for its stone wares are the most meagre. Stretch a point and include all the shires 'twixt Wight and Wash, and you will find only a handful of building stones of good repute. Travelling clockwise from the Thames at Greenwich we are looking first at the Cretaceous period, chalk, and in particular Kentish Ragstone.

Kent Ragstone is won from the Lower Greensand, here a mix of sandy deposits interlaced with thin bands, never more than two feet thick, of the only local building stone to be found over a wide area. Being alternately bedded with the friable greensand, the ragstone obeys the first dictum of a building stone, it is winnable at relatively modest cost of labour.

With the bed thickness modest, the stone emerges from the quarry face in thicknesses almost ideal for building work. At this point the stone's tractability effectively ceases, for the term ragstone is descriptive; a stone of hardness beyond the point where it can be worked up into smooth facing or other fine detail work. The stone has then to be used as found, unworked beyond breaking into pieces that are handlable (usually man-handlable).

With such a stone, of only limited use in plain rubble walling, it would be normal to expect only local distribution. The dearth of alternatives, the proximity of the main source quarries both to navigable water (at Maidstone, for example), and to London, a metropolis without a native stone, means that Kentish Ragstone receives a far greater geographical distribution than, say the Carboniferous Grit of the Bristol area, where a better stone is hemmed in by a plethora of superiors.

Kentish Ragstone is nonetheless a durable stone in the climate it finds itself used, and as a warm yellow rustic rubble face set among contrasting quoins and detail work, presents a handsome appearance in counties where the brick has long held sway. The stone itself is classified as a Cretaceous limestone.

While Kent Rag hails from the Greensand, and is calcareous, its immediate neighbours in Sussex and Surrey, the Ashdown and Tunbridge Sandstones, also from the Greensand horizon, are only slightly calcareous. This combination of relative youth, and lack of calcium carbonate binding, means that these two sandstones are not the most durable, suffering from weathering only too easily, in spite of the equable climate of the sub-region. Not so our fourth stone from this region, Horsham Stone.

Horsham Stone is the first of several 'Tilestones' we shall meet across England, though, like many others, it is a dying stone in that there are no active quarries, and have not been for the best part of a century. Horsham is a fissile stone, it can be split relatively easily along its bedding planes into thin slabs, which are impervious and durable enough to be used as roofing slates. Since cessation of production, a local technique has allowed the tiles in circulation to be 'stretched' to cover greater area, by means of reducing the laps normally needed to provide a waterproof roof.

Horsham stone meets the necessary criteria for roofing; weatherproof and durable. To be both, it has to be a well compacted stone, dense and not readily absorbing moisture. For the stone to be light enough to go on a roof it must be capable of being split down to under half an inch thick, and to remain waterproof it cannot attract large quantities of vegetative growth. These qualities are common to all fissile rock that see use on roofs.

Lastly, in the calcareous sandstones of the South East, we have Reigate Stone, again widely used in an area where there is nothing more durable, and poor weathering properties are no serious bar to use. This is a tractable sandstone, easily cut and carved, and sees extensive use as detail work, alongside Kentish Rag for example, supplying the quoins, lintels and arches that cannot be formed in the latter.

Chalk, the soft white limestone of the Upper Cretaceous, is generally too soft throughout its distribution across Eastern England, to supply a durable building stone. The softness of the stone has always made it an attractive possibility for building work, and much more chalk is hidden behind other stone or render than most people imagine. As a stone, chalk's crushing strength is quite acceptable for loadbearing purposes, and when protected from the weather it is durable enough, and more. In many places the chalk occurs in ideal beds a foot or so thick, and with well developed joints, often emerges from the quarry face as ready to use cubes, or can be easily split down to manageable chunks.

Perhaps the best known of the quarries for building chalk is the pit that is now a museum, Amberley, in Sussex, but small workings are widespread. Extraction of chalk is so easy, and in times past the quarry could just as easily supply chalk for limewash or whiteing, or for making up roads or liming fields, that it is now impossible to discriminate between extraction for these various uses.

Moving across the Solent to the Isle of Wight, we have a building stone from the Tertiary, Quarr Stone, part of the Bembridge series. Quarr Stone sees local use on the island, and due to its proximity to sea transport and counties lacking good stone resources, turns up on the South Coast, and as far afield as London. Quarr, and its close relation, Binstead, are creamy white limestones, and relatively soft.

Returning to the mainland and heading north through Winchester, we are surrounded by country where the hardest rock available is flint, and flint has the land to itself, with only chalk for company, and no decent beds of that either. Nonetheless chalk has been used here as a filler to wall cores, and flints 'knapped' or split in half, to form facings, but for the more expensive work imported stone has been the norm.

Further north the presence of sandstone boulders (of Eocene origin) in quantity, the 'Grey Wethers' of the Marlborough Downs and elsewhere, have supplied building stone since the raising of Stonehenge (which is constructed mainly out of Grey Wethers). These massive sandstones littered valleys (there are not a great number left these days as they are a visibly finite resource), and do not need to be quarried, merely reduced to the sizes required and carted off. To describe the resulting stonework as being of the finest kind, is perhaps stretching the truth a little too economically, but they are readily identifiable, particularly as stone steps, a duty they perform admirably, across a wide area of southern England.

At Marlborough too we must turn to the north-east to stay in the region of the little stones, and as we do so a tougher band of stone within the chalk emerges to provide a building stone, a grey limestone, Clunch. This is a true builder's stone, tractable, taking fine detail of carving and despite being a Cretaceous stone, moderately durable. Production of this stone (Totternhoe Stone) continues today to supply the repair market. Is it just possible that someone, somewhere, is using it to build new? This illustrates a quandary that many owners, repairers and planners face when stone is needed to maintain the nation's building fabric. By compromising and accepting reconstructed or reproduction (concrete) alternatives, or by robbing other structures to repair, we are rendering production of the real thing uneconomic, and ultimately condemning the buildings we are trying to preserve to oblivion.

On the outskirts of Oxford we meet a band of Corrallian Limestone, itself a feature running west across the vale to Faringdon, but here it has been worked to supply a ragstone, the Coral Rag, a coarse, hard, shelly limestone of considerable charm, to add to Oxford's more intellectual charms. East of the city, the Portland and Purbeck formations outcrop in a narrow band running towards Aylesbury, and these yield a creamy limestone that has seen extensive local use. Eastwards from the line of Ermine Street we come to a veritable stone desert, where the outcrop of clunch thins across Cambrigeshire into Suffolk and flint, present in the subsoil, or dug from the chalk, is the hardest material available.

Here, as at Clare, in the valley of the Stour in Suffolk, we find churches faced almost completely with flint, with brick and stone import details. The ruins of Clare Castle suggest that the wall core of the church may well be flint as well. Of all the counties of England, Norfolk and Suffolk, with few navigable rivers (the Wensum to Norwich allowed the use of imported stone for the Cathedral and is a major exception) and a dearth of native stone, are the counties that stand out as not having lots of stone churches, a feature rare over much of the rest of England.

Finally in the flat lands east of London, we return to the Thames at Grays, where the once extensive cement manufacturing industry was the successor to quarrying chalk for building stone. We can now move from pauper to prince.

The Stone Belt

If it were possible to estimate the importance of the Stone Belt to English church architecture, or indeed to architecture on this island, to place the Stone Belt first in terms of material supply, is merely to give the Jurasssic its due. That a narrow belt of rocks, differing in age no more than a few million years, is able to produce a series of building stones that so utterly dominated the better class of building construction from the twelfth century to the twentieth is remarkable enough.

That those building stones should posess a variety and a durability equalled by few is our exceeding good fortune. That the band of rock, a few miles wide at best (Yorkshire Moors apart), should bisect England from the South Coast to the Tees, via the Severn, is a nicety that our predecessors used to give immeasurable wealth to the land we have inherited.

The Stone Belt is for the most part a Jurassic limestone outcrop, with a scarp slope facing west or north west, a distinctive feature virtually all the way from Saltburn to Swanage. The scarp represents the end of the rocks for the most part, though there are some outliers, and the belt itself extends ten or more miles down the dip slope unless, as in Lincolnshire and the East Riding, chalk intervenes.

With the exception of the gritstones of the North Riding, all the important building stones are limestones, though some can be classified as calciferous sandstones. The nationally and internationally known stones are all in the southern half of the country, not due to any falling off in quality as we go north, but due to competition from other stones, which are increasingly common beyond the Midlands. It makes sense then to commence on the South Coast, at the Isle of Purbeck.

Purbeck

The visitor to the Isle of Purbeck today has a choice of two routes onto the peninsula; over the chain ferry from Bournemouth, a survivor from a past age of ferries, across the mouth of Poole Harbour; and the road that threads the gap dominated by Corfe Castle and the London and South Western Railway viaduct. These two structures, separated in time by eight centuries, are united in their use of the fine grey limestone that is characteristic of this area.

While this limestone is extensively used in both Corfe and Swanage, and is one of only two grey Jurassic limestones we shall meet in the next three hundred miles, it is not the stone that has made the name of Purbeck famous. The start of

163

the stone belt, like its conclusion at the Hunt Cliff, yields a famous stone that is neither oolitic nor gives a clue to the variety to come.

We do not have far to go however, no further than a moderate afternoon stroll from either Corfe or Swanage, to reach the village of Worth Matravers. This village exists primarily because of a thin band of limestone, nowhere more than a few feet thick, yielding a stone that polishes to a subtle and distinctive brown marble.

Purbeck Marble is very definitely a mediaeval church builders fashion item, the finishing contrast touch to highlight the interior. As a stone it is only seen in interior decorative work, usually as non loadbearing turned shafts. Due to the limited thickness of the beds, the marble is unique in that it is usually laid edge bedded. This prevents use outside, as it would weather badly and very quickly. Purbeck Marble is to be found in churches across the land, the quarries being close to the sea and the easy transport it offered.

On the south of the Isle are the beds that yield a creamy white oolitic limestone not unlike Portland in colour and composition, for they are an eastern extension of the Portland Beds and were marketed as 'Purbeck Portland', but we will leave the full description of this stone in the section it deserves to itself.

West of Worth Matravers the stone belt is fractured and crumpled, leading to the superb coastal scenery of Lulworth Cove and Durdle Door. The sea has devoured the scarp and the productive stone beds, which re-emerge briefly but importantly at Portland Bill.

Portland

Above all one man, Christopher Wren, has been responsible for the emergence of Portland Stone to a position of eminence that is of international status. The stone itself is part of the Portland and Purbeck formations that are limited in extent, but crop up in isolated exposures, as we have already seen, far to the east at Aylesbury, and will see again further along the Stone Belt. Portland is isolated from the Stone Belt proper, which at this point is aligned roughly with the South

Coast, the sea having breached and eroded the scarp between the Isles of Portland and Purbeck, and removed it completely between Portland and Lyme Regis.

The creamy white limestone yielded from the Portland beds comes from a sequence only some 30 metres thick, and the very particular quarrymen of ages past have chosen only the Whit Bed from near the top, and the Base Bed from the middle of this strata, to be extensively worked for building stone.

Other stone, particularly the Roach, has come to increasing prominence in recent years due to the exhaustion of the best stone. So fine is the texture of Portland Stone that its oolitic nature is not obvious to the casual observer, but it is the brilliant white colour, quite unlike any other stone when clean, and its amenable nature under the mason's chisel that sets this stone up as one of the world's finest building stones, equal to the marbles of the Mediterranean, the sandstones of India or the slates of Wales and the Lake District.

Like most of the natural resources of this island, the stone of Portland was found and worked by the Romans, but the resource seems not to have found its way into the sales catalogues of the mediaeval period, and its first major use on a church appears to have been in Inigo Jones' infamous recladding of the Gothic St. Paul's in London. The stone's suitability for classical work was evident in the general admiration received by the colonnaded portico that Jones tacked on to the front of this crumbling edifice. It was perhaps no surprise then, that when Wren tackled the new church after the great fire, Portland Stone was chosen, setting the tone for a whole series of public buildings, and leading to over four centuries of sustained quarrying on the Bill, quarrying that continues today on a significant scale.

As a resource the stone is not infinite, and if subjected to the scale of exploitation that we are seeing in the Mendips, of limestone for aggregates, for example, the Isle of Portland would rapidly become history.

The Isle of Portland would be an island but for the banking up of Chesil beach due to longshore drift, for west of the Bill, the Stone Belt is an unobtrusive shoreline dominated by the beach. At West Bay, the rocks are butted up against the greensand and chalk of East Devon and there is no discernible scarp until we have travelled several miles inland to the north, to near Ilminster.

Hamdon Hill

At Ilminster, the younger rocks to the west give way to the levels of Somerset, and the Stone Belt emerges with the scarp facing north, so we must follow it eastwards to Yeovil, and halfway twixt the two towns is Hamdon Hill. Before we look at Ham Hill stone there is a man made feature that joins the Stone Belt, here keeping a modest distance to the west, the Roman road, the Foss Way. It is quite possible to follow the Stone Belt by following the Roman road to Lincoln, and, joining Ermine Street and fording the Humber, trek all the way to the break in the Stone Belt at Market Weighton, just as the Romans did. The road may well have been built for military traffic, but there is little doubt that it follows the Stone Belt for the purpose of commercial exploitation of those stone resources.

Ham Hill Stone is justly famous for being the stone that everyone admires at Montacute House, a mile or so down the road from the quarries. In marked contrast to the Portland and Purbeck beds examined so far, Ham Hill is a stone from lower in the Jurassic Series, from the Upper Lias, and is a warm pale brown, and highly fossiliferous. A darker stone, the Grey Bed has also been worked from Hamdon Hill. Both stones are classified as limestones, though the texture is in parts sandy, and this variability is reflected in the quarries, which present as a jumble of mounds and hollows as the best stone has been followed across the hill, and the remainder left insitu.

Ham Hill is typical of the stones of the stone belt in that it is remote from navigable water (Westport is six miles away on the Levels) and the stone was restricted primarily to local use until the middle of the nineteenth century. As a top quality stone of first class appearance it occasionally is to be found further afield, but mostly in buildings built post-1850. The limited resource and the difficult quarrying conditions have made this stone special.

Chilmark

Between Oxford and Aylesbury we have met the Portland and Purbeck beds as a localised outcrop at the base of the scarp of the Chiltern Hills. At Chilmark and neighbouring Tisbury there is a further inlier among the chalk of these important rocks, and here they have yielded the slightly sandy limestone that supplied Salisbury Cathedral, some ten miles to the east, down the valley of the river Nadder. Again, this stone source supplied local needs until the nineteenth century, when, courtesy of the railways, it caught the wanderlust, and was used in London and St. Albans on the restoration of their respective abbeys. Chilmark is not the most northerly of the Portland and Purbeck beds, for there is a further inlier at Urchfont, south of Devizes in Wiltshire, where mining of the stone from a very limited outcrop enabled construction of the remarkable church there.

The quarries at Chilmark are at the practical limit of road haulage for the Cathedral at Salisbury; mass transport of constructional as opposed to detail stone, even with gravity assistance, involved the construction and maintenance of a haul road that had to be better than the dirt tracks that predominated in the Middle Ages. It is relevant therefore to cast a glance over the logistics of land transport in ages when the horse and cart were the cutting edge of technology.

To make and maintain roads in an area devoid of good metalling material meant cartage of roadstone from a distance. This is a truly monumental task, for twenty tons of roadstone will form a ten foot wide bed just twenty yards long. To build a road ten miles long, using only stone supplied from one end, means hauling a ton of stone five miles for every yard of road built. A horse, or a pair of oxen, could, in the Middle Ages, do just that, haul a ton of stone five miles in a day.

Twelve thousand loads to build the road in the first place, and about a further twelve hundred loads a year to keep it passable for the heaviest traffic. The implications of this are that transport costs are doubling for every three or four miles of haulage, and that if an article is travelling a long distance by road, then it is going to be both rare and expensive when it arrives.

To suggest, then, that the transport of heavy loads long distances was a regular occurrence seven hundred years ago is to suggest the improbable, if not the impossible. Oak principal roof beams may well have travelled far by road (popping the trunk into the nearest stream and waiting for a flood seems a lot easier), stone by the thousand ton definitely did not. When we do meet a widely distributed stone, such as the Cave Oolite, transport is invariably road—water—road, with the sea, estuary or river going the distance, and road only the short haul at either end (the road haul of the Cave Oolite at the end of its journey to Beverley Minster is about three hundred yards).

Similarly, stone supplied to London before the 1840s came by river or sea or both, from quarries that had water access within a stone's throw. Canals carried stone right from the start, but the cost still rose disproportionately with distance, goods being charged on a 'ton-mile' basis. Not until the full flow of the Industrial Revolution was society able and willing to afford to move volumes of stone around the country at will, and that expensive habit lasted less than a century.

Doulting

Of the various strata met on the Stone Belt to this point, the youngest of the Jurassic rocks, and the oldest, have supplied the building stone of the areas already passed through. At Doulting, a mile west of Shepton Mallet, Somerset, emerges the Inferior Oolite. Oolites are thus called because of the miniature spheroidal ooliths, that are the calcareous depositions, millions of which go to make a single cubic foot of stone. A cut or weathered face of an Oolitic Limestone (all oolites are limestones) does not display this subtle composition without close examination, but an old and semi-decayed piece of stone that has been frost shattered is easily identified.

The Inferior Oolite is inferior in name only, to distinguish it from the Greater Oolite, and true to form the brown, sandy limestone that is Doulting Stone is only locally oolitic, occurring in massive beds up to 12 metres thick. The masons of Wells Cathedral trekked the six miles to Doulting for their stone and received considerable assistance from gravity as the quarry at Bramble Ditch is five hundred feet above the cathedral, and only the last half mile of the road home is uphill. The restorers of the nineteenth century came as well, this time by train, and took it much further afield.

Downside

Call it a coincidence if you will, but if you have been following the Foss Way from Ilminster you may not have noticed that the course of the road has been set out, using Ditcheat Hill north west of Castle Cary as an intermediate sighting point on a traverse that starts at, surprise, surprise, Hamdon Hill, and terminates at Beacon Hill, two miles north east of Shepton Mallet. At this point it intersects the Roman road that crosses the Mendip lead mining area.

In choosing this alignment, the Romans caused the Foss Way to pass within a mile of Bramble Ditch, and a mile of Downside, before turning to the north east to head for Radstock and Coombe Down, Bath, of which more anon. At this point the Roman road is a better guide to the Stone Belt than the scarp, for here the Jurassic rocks abut the carboniferous limestones of the Mendip Hills.

There is, accordingly, no visible scarp until we have crossed the Avon at Bath and swung north, away, temporarily at least, from the Roman alignment. Some geological confusion is perhaps inevitable over the next twenty miles, for the Somerset Coalfield is a jumble of intersecting valleys and broken ground.

Downside then, like Doulting, is a stone that was known and worked by the Romans.

Downside Stone is won from the Lias, the basal strata of the Jurassic series, and is a pale, grey limestone. Liassic limestones here tend towards calcareous mudstones, and the grey, monochrome stone that is Downside gives the area an appearance that is uncharacteristic of the Stone Belt, for henceforth the Stone Belt is almost exclusively associated with the younger oolites.

Bath

Bath Stone is the genteel stone of Southern England. Probably the most widely distributed of all stone in England, and used in much greater quantity than Portland Stone, though not so distinctive. It will come as no surprise to learn that the Romans, in their systematic exploration of the natural resources of this island and consequent discovery of the warm mineral water springs of Aquae Sulis, sought out the stone supplies of the area and hit upon the Greater Oolite of Coombe Down. The Romans used this source to enclose the wellhead of the spa in the first century AD.

The Greater Oolite is distinctive from the Lesser Oolite in that it is thoroughly oolitic in structure; the shells that are a charming feature of Bath and other oolitic limestones are a firmly subsidiary element of the stone's make up. Likewise the calcite veining that characterises Bath Stone.

Bath Stone, then, is a warm, pale yellow-brown, slightly shelly oolitic limestone, made distinctive by light, almost white, narrow erratic veins of calcite that run through the stone in any direction. The stone is easily worked due to its softness when fresh, hardening on exposure to the atmosphere, and absorbing air pollution that varies the colour in different exposures to any shade between light brown and black. The stone is a favourite for cills, lintels, quoins, plain ashlar work, and decorative carving and statuary. The stone shares the honour, with only a handful of others, of being widely used prior to the Industrial Revolution, quite simply because there is no other stone that can be described as its equal in the south of England.

Working of the stone has been extensive, so extensive, in fact, that the extent of the workings from the ninth century onwards are spread over an area of many square miles to the east of Bath, in addition to the quarries and mines around and under the town itself. In an area positively stuffed with fine building stone, the use of Bath Stone prior to the nineteenth century is limited simply because the outcrop of the Greater Oolite is limited.

The area is, for the most part, overlain with Jurassic limestones that are either on, or just below, the land surface and are sufficiently jointed and weathered to supply ready for use ragstone and tilestones, without having to haul the stuff any great distance. Churches built entirely of Bath Stone, like Bath Abbey, and more than a couple of centuries old, are rare. Gothic revival ones with Bath details are almost ten a penny. Really first-rate ecclesiastical use of the stone, like the cemetery chapel at Box, demands a close inspection.

The area of exposure of the Greater Oolite is limited, and would be even more so had not the River Avon carved a gorge through the strata. Winning of the stone from the quarries at Bath has been virtually continuous for the past two millennia, with probably only a short cessation of exploitation in the early Dark Ages. By the time that the Spa was rediscovered to become the watering hole of society, the workings had moved underground, for as we have noted, the stone is overlaid by younger rocks for much of its distribution. The abandoned mines at Coombe Down now constitute a significant hazard to the residents whose homes now sit on the columns of stone, left by the miners to hold up the roof. In the nineteenth century the demand for the stone reached new heights, and a period of exploration to determine the full extent of the stone culminated with the engineer of the Great Western Railway, altering the alignment of the railway to drive it through an area that seemed likely to be a good source of the stone. The alignment of what is now known as Box Tunnel, proved the stone over a wide area, and extensive new mines were opened up between Box and Corsham, some served directly by sidings to the railway from inside the tunnel.

The excuse for moving the tunnel to prospect for stone enabled Brunel to choose an alignment that meant that the rising sun shines through the tunnel on the engineers' birthday, the 9th April. Modesty is not necessarily everyone's strong suit, and Bath Stone likewise, has little to be modest about.

Cheltenham

To leapfrog twenty miles and more over the Cotswold Hills north of Bath, is to ignore an area where the Jurassic limestones, including the Oolites, supply building stone for an area that is bounded effectively by the river Severn in the west and the headwaters of the Thames to the east. This is a region where ragstones and the thicker beds of oolite supply stone, visibly Jurassic in origin, and usually a warm yellow-brown in colour. The result is subtly proportioned churches, like that at Wotton-Under-Edge, which delight the eye, even among towns and villages patently wrought from the same material won from the same quarry.

Nowhere is far from a quarry, and while we do the delights of the Golden Valley a disservice, and many another town and village besides, to enumerate *all* the stone sources in this area, and identify the beds that supplied the tilestones, for this is an area of great stone wealth, we would be taking up a lifetime's challenge.

Cheltenham then, sits in a natural semi-amphitheatre, with enfolding hills running in a grand half circle from Leckhampton Hill in the south to Cleeve Hill in the north east. These hills harbour the Inferior Oolite, here yielding the building freestone known, for obvious reasons as Cheltenham Stone.

Flying Buttress

The pinnacle sits on the spring of the segmental arch delivering its weight exactly at the point where it will be most effective in deflecting the lateral thrust of the arch

Only the single ring of the arch is designed as an arch per se : all other masonry is dead weight and has no other purpose than to turn the lateral thrust towards the vertical plane

Source : Tewkesbury

Much of Cheltenham is graced by this material, for the scarp has been extensively quarried, and the Devil's Chimney, a man made land-stack, is a remnant of the days when much activity could be witnessed here, and the quarrymen were not above a little joke. The stone itself is a pale yellow-brown, noticeably lacking in fossils, and with navigable water not too far away (five downhill miles to the canal, probably not much further in the Middle Ages), the stone is one of the dozen or so that go to make up Tewksbury Abbey, out in the Vale of Severn.

Like all the Oolites, Cheltenham Stone is at its best when used for ashlar work, where its subtle colouring can be best appreciated, and at its worst when rockfaced, as at St. Matthew's, Cheltenham, where it has garnered enough grime to make the observer cast around for the accompanying dark satanic mills. St. Matthew's is worth a visit nonetheless, because it has some new stone, also rockfaced, and the contrast between old and new is very stark.

Tilestones

So far we have skated around the tilestones of the Stone Belt, concentrating instead on the fine building stone for which the period is famous. This is to some degree inexcusable, for if we were to count the churches built in fine dimension stone, we would find that they were outnumbered at least ten to one, by churches of humbler origin, and the Cotswolds are no exception to this rule. We have now come to the point where we must acknowledge the importance of these stones. Most village churches are built with stone supplied from a quarry only a few hundred yards distant. If the parish is a rich one then subsequent rounds of rebuilding and extensions will frequently see imported stone employed to some degree, particularly where there is no local source that can supply quoins and window tracery.

Once on the site the local stone will usually stay put, and will be recycled as necessary, but still form the bulk of the masonry. Visiting every church in England is a herculean achievement, but would pale into insignificance when compared with the task of identifying all the source quarries for those churches.

In the Cotswolds we are faced with double trouble; not only 'where did the building stone come from?', but also, 'where did the tiles on the roof come from? Well you may ask, for while the tiles on the roof are actually stone slates, or 'tilestones', and are named generically 'Stonesfield Slates', most of them have had nothing to do with the village of Stonesfield, where tilestones are mined, other than to adopt the name. In the Jurassic series the two Oolites, the Greater and the Inferior, supply what are acknowledged to be some of the finest building stones of England.

They are separated geologically by a clay band that is known as the Fuller's Earth, worked in byegone times for degreasing wool, hence the name. Immediately above this horizon is the Stonesfield Slate series, representing an era between the main strata deposits when the shallow sea covering this part of England teemed with molluscs, reptiles and mammals in a sort of muddy prehistoric paradise. This represents an interlude between periods when The Oolites were the predominant means of calcium carbonate deposition in markedly clearer waters.

A similar clay band, the Upper Lias, is in turn overlain by a further tilestone yielding strata, at the base of the Inferior Oolite. The whole sequence resembles the cyclotherms of seat earth, coal and sandstone that have given us our coalfields.

Tilestones are thus available from two distinct stratigraphical horizons, resulting in certain areas of the Cotswolds where they can be worked at the surface, and are called 'Presents', and can be mined from shallow pits as 'Pendle'. Due to faulting and erosion not all areas have a ready supply, and the surface deposits have been extensively worked to the point of exhaustion in many places, resulting in mining.

Like all ancient crafts (yes, the Romans found and worked the tilestones) waste was minimised by the use of all stone that could be obtained and split into thin enough slabs to be put on a roof, and the way to do this is to accept slates of variable size. The traditional method adopted is the diminishing course roof, where the largest slates are fixed at the bottom and the courses narrow as they approach the ridge. The different sizes gained colourful local names such as

Cussens (eaves slates) and Tants (top courses). Only a third of the actual tile is visible when fixed, and the colour and character of the roof depends to a great degree on the micro-flora and fauna that live on the tile.

Winning the tilestones involves extracting the stone in slabs up to a foot thick, and keeping it full of quarry sap (groundwater) until it can be frosted. Only after the stone has been subject to a hard frost will it become fissile. The thin slabs are then trimmed at the head and holed with a 'Pecker', a pointed pick. Trimming reduces the weight of the tile in areas where it is not needed for waterproofing, resulting in a classical 'fat cricket bat' shape. Tiles have traditionally been hung on battens using oak pegs, the shape of the pecked hole helping to grip the peg.

Most famous of the tilestones are those of Collyweston, but tilestones of essentially identical form are to be found along a great swathe of the Stone Belt, and some considerable distance either side, in an arc from Stamford in Lincolnshire to Devizes in Wiltshire, and beyond. These are probably the most durable coverings that can be seen on a roof in England, and there is little doubt that some of the tiles in use today are over five hundred years old.

Guiting and Taynton

Before leaving the Cotswolds, brief mention of these two stones is appropriate as they are typical building stones used for the better quality ashlar work, and their distribution is a contrast not between their relative worth, but between their access to suitable transport facilities. Taynton Stone, a brown streaky highly fossiliferous rock from the village of that name near Burford in Oxfordshire, sees extensive use in the county town, and is used in the interior of St. Paul's', London.

Yellow Guiting Stone is more local, the quarries tucked away in the middle of The Cotswolds south of Broadway, a pale, yellow gritty limestone much admired by visitors to the locality. Life for a limestone, it seems, very much depends on where you are.

175

The Lincolnshire Limestones

Dropping from the uplands of the Cotswolds at Stow-on-the-Wold, following the Foss Way north by north east, quickly takes us away from the Stone Belt, down onto the rolling country that will eventually deliver us into the Vale of Belvoir. This course is set too far to the west, over the sands and clays of the Lower Lias, and we needs must keep to the hills towards Stamford, there to join with Ermine Street. This is quite a long step, across north Oxfordshire and Northampton, and we are on the edge of the Fens when we arrive at our destination, Barnack, where we can take stock before turning north again. The Lincolnshire Limestones are oolitic in origin, frequently coarse and shelly, variable in colour from brown to pale yellow, and like the majority of the Jurassic stones, durable, even exceptionally durable, in the dryish climate of the east of England.

These stones have the good fortune of being in possession of a great swathe of Eastern England, whose considerable wealth in the Middle Ages was turned in no small part into ecclesiastical building, and where navigable rivers and long, gentle, downhill slopes from the quarries, eased the passage of stone to its destination. With local competition of water-borne Magnesian Limestone, and support from chalk as rubble fill, these limestones helped stimulate church building in Lincolnshire, where the competition from the twelfth century on, is from brick rather than imported stone.

Barnack and Ketton

Within shouting distance of the banks of the River Welland, a few miles from the Car Dike, Ermine Street makes a detour to visit a low hill overlooking the Fens. Inevitably the Romans found Barnack Stone, and found it very much to their liking. So too did the masons of the Middle Ages, to such an extent that all the easily accessible stone was worked out over four hundred years ago, and we can now see this coarse shelly limestone only in the buildings of that period.

A little further to the west and still within striking distance of Stamford lies the village of Ketton, where the strata hold a limestone with a pink hue as opposed to the usual cream or buff. From here the procession up the Roman road to the Humber is marked by the Oolites of the Lincolnshire Limestone; Casterton and Clipsham, then Ancaster, where, in addition to the fine-grained oolite, a coarser ragstone is also quarried.

North of the Caves

The Estuary of the Humber cuts the Stone Belt with a mile wide gash, but while the geography suggests change, the Cave Oolite is the Lincolnshire Limestone renamed, and change, although imminent, is not yet upon us. Once again the limestone outcrop is tracked by the Roman road, and once more, coincidentally or not, at the end stop of the exposed limestone belt, at Market Weighton, the Romans left the scarp and turned west for York and east for the coast. This is the last of the major Oolitic limestones, and the only major outcrop of this stone north of the Humber; a narrow belt running the six miles from South Cave to Sancton, sporting its own set of distinctive stone built villages more reminiscent of the Cotswolds than Yorkshire.

No one is left to any doubt as to the source of the stone; from the south entry to the belt off the A63 almost the first turning to the west is prominently labelled 'Stone Pit Lane'. The author, in his youthful ignorance many moons ago, was party, as junior surveyor, to converting the stone pit into a highways depot, and is duly ashamed. In times past this stone, and its polished companion the 'Cave Marble', competing only with the more distant Magnesian Limestone, and local chalk and flints, until the founding of the 'purgatory of the tile fields', found wide distribution over the County of York and the East Riding. In the rich ecclesiastical sector at least, the Cave Oolite is to be found in the fabric of South Dalton and Bainton, to name just two of the many churches that grace, even crowd, the east of Yorkshire.

While the limestone scarp burrows into the north east corner of the Humberhead levels and is temporarily lost as a feature, the topmost beds of the Jurassic provide the stone for the miniature gem that is Kirby Underdale, and more besides. Thin beds these rocks might be, but durable enough to be worth the effort, and enduring, to our continued delight, perhaps ten centuries since they first saw the light of day.

Leaving the East Riding for the North, with a graceful leap across the Derwent at Kirkham, justly famous for both the ruined abbey and the beauty of a modest defile that is christened 'gorge' in these lowlands, we arrive on the Howardian Hills. Once more the Stone Belt is beneath our feet. We can appreciate the change in the geology however; for the first time since leaving the South Coast, the trend of the rocks is to the west of north; there is no chalk scarp backing to the dip slope, only the level expanse of the Vale of Pickering. The rock too, is now increasingly, but not exclusively, sandstone. This is the precursor of the Yorkshire Moors, an extensive tract of upland underlain by a fine sandstone that is both easily won and worked.

While the Howardian Hills are famous as the site of Vanbrugh's masterpiece for the Duke, the northern edge sports the real jewels in Amotherby and Coxwold. At Slingsby, the symbiosis between quarry, village, castle and church is complete, with the quarry standing awaiting the next order of stone, over the road and just up the hill from the customers. Twentieth century transport economics has a lot to answer for.

Sutton under Whitestonecliffe to Staithes

The Howardian Hills are separated from the Yorkshire Moors proper by the Gilling Gap, and the Moors are as distinctly different from the rest of Yorkshire as they are from the rest of the Stone Belt. That difference rests on the unity of the grey brown sandstone that is the heart of virtually all the villages and most of the towns, and the glory of two of England's most famous ruined abbeys, Rievaulx and Whitby. The stone is used both as rag and as ashlar, the latter producing beautifully distinctive coursed blockwork, finely tooled and seemingly ageless. There is little doubt that the monks of Rievaulx chose that picturesque spot because the penance of winning stone for the abbey was not going to be too tough a proposition.

Although the sandstone is for the most part extremely durable, on the coast particularly, severe exposure leads to typical sandstone weathering with hollowing of the stone and loss of detail, nowhere better exemplified than on the East Cliff at Whitby. Elsewhere on the Moors, there is little to tell between the Hackness Sandstone, Aislaby Grit, Danby Stone, Rainhill Grit or any of the other hundred and one variations on the same theme. The Moors are unique in the extent of the outcrop of the Jurassic sandstones; there are beds of oolite, but their use is overshadowed by the grit.

Hiding away in its own corner of this enchanted landscape is that earliest of essays in gritstone, St. Gregory's, Kirkdale, a minster of the smallest size, albeit a mostly Victorian one.

The Lowlands of the Heart of England

Fittingly perhaps, the Stone Belt terminates in England's highest cliffs at Boulby, and we can turn away from the long neglected riches of the stone quarries, ironstone mines and mordant works that dot this northernmost outpost of the Mesozoic rocks on this island, and move west and north to the older rocks that stretch a crooked finger up from The Midlands, to push out into the German Ocean as part of County Durham. These rocks are the basal measures of the Mesozoic, the Triassic marls and sandstones of Bunter and Keuper fame, and the upper beds of the Paleozoic, the Permian sandstones and limestones. Due to the prevalence of red rocks, this series is collectively known as the New Red Sandstone. This lowland zone is readily divisible into three;

* North East England from Durham to Nottingham, in a narrow belt rarely more than ten miles in breadth.
* A triangle bounded by Stoke on Trent, Grantham and Gloucester.
* The Cheshire and Lancashire plains, and isolated areas in the Vale of Eden and around Carlisle.

These areas display distinct differences in building stones, and it is to the major exception, a limestone in the strata dominated by sandstones, that we travel as we cross the Tees at Croft Spa, of which more anon.

Magnesian Limestone

The Magnesian Limestone in many ways parallels the Stone Belt in both limited outcrop and an extensive plateau at the northern end, for this is the rock that covers almost all of the east and south of County Durham. Into this plateau, and the emergent coal measure sandstones to the west, the river Wear has etched its course to give Durham Cathedral its splendid site, but the fame of the stone is due to workings further south, where navigable rivers afford a wide hinterland. Where the Magnesian Limestone is a winner over the Stone Belt is in the fact that it is the preferred stone in circumstances where there is a good choice of stone; can compete with other water borne stone such as the Cave Oolite, and has 'come up to town', to show Londoners what real stone is.

One of the features of the British Isles is the way that rock outcrops are localised; no Oolites north of Saltburn, and no Magnesian Limestone south of Nottingham. If the stone had been used for nothing else, then the Minsters of York, Howden, and Southwell, and the Abbeys of Selby and Fountains would be testament enough to this soft yellow - brown stone that cuts and carves like butter (well, almost!) and seems likely to last till judgment day.

When Hawksmoor decided that what Westminster and its Abbey needed was a copy of the west front of Beverley Minster to smarten it up, he was wise enough to specify Magnesian Limestone. If anything the stone looks better in London than it does in Yorkshire, and while the Abbey is overshadowed on the south side by the hot air palace, there's no prize for guessing where the stone for that edifice came from either! Industry observers musing on the latest scandal of MP's mega-expensive office accommodation will not be surprised to learn that the stone for the Barry/Pugin masterpiece was not acquired without a similar shindig. Plus ça change!

The fame of Magnesian Limestone today rests on relatively few quarries; Jackdaw Crag near Tadcaster; Sherburn in Elmet and Huddleston, east of the A1 at Micklefield; Roche, near Maltby, east of Rotherham; Kiveton Park (or Anston Stone) between Sheffield and Worksop, all in Yorkshire; Bolsover Moor, near Bolsover, Derbyshire; and Mansfield Woodhouse from Nottinghamshire. These are the quarries that thrived on river transport in the Middle Ages, for the major rivers of the Humber catchment, the Ouse, Wharfe, Aire, Calder, Don, and Trent were all navigable to the Magnesian Limestone outcrop, or nearly so. Canal, and later rail transport, in the eighteenth and nineteenth centuries merely took over the river's role. These quarries are still worked, because no expense is spared to keep the buildings that are national treasures in apple pie order, and as a consequence have not been filled in, built over, had their precious resource converted to aggregate or roadstone, or been destroyed by an opencast mining smash and grab raid.

Permian and Triassic Sandstones

The sandstones that everyone recognises as such from their slightly friable surface (especially when weathered) and bright red colour, are the sandstones of the Midlands. Yet, while these red sandstones are well named, their distribution is much more widespread than might be supposed at first glance, and not all of them are red either. Sandstones are so named because their principle constituent is grains of quartz, and it is the size of these grains that give the stone both its properties, and character. Typical of the Midland sandstones is the medium to fine grained red stone from Grinshill, a hump in the Shropshire Plain overlooking the valley of the river Roden north of Shrewsbury. Easily worked up to large, even sized blocks, this is a stone worked since ancient times, with a Roman road barely two miles distant from the quarries.

Fifty miles to the north, on the southern outskirts of Stockton Heath, Warrington, there are workings in the same red sandstone, which, if a trifle darker here, is essentially the same stone, only the Roman road on the doorstep is now King Street. The pattern is repeated at Rainhill, of trials fame,

Storeton on the Wirral Peninsula, Runcorn on the Mersey, and Woolton, whence came the stone for one of Liverpool's spare cathedrals, just a short hop away over the cities' rooftops.

Further north in the Vale of Eden, we have the coarser grained but brilliantly red Penrith, Lazonby and Plumpton Sandstones, wedged in between the Northern Pennines and the Lake District. On the western side of The Lakes, the St. Bees Sandstone is from the same series, but of a browner hue. North again, over the border into Scotland to Locharbriggs, where we find the same sandstone, which has been intensively quarried and found a wide market as a detail stone over the past two centuries, the quarry near Dumfries supplying more than just a large part of Glasgow.

White sandstone

Returning to Grinshill, adjacent quarries to the Red Sandstone yield a white sandstone, and this is true of a number of locations, including Hollington near Uttoxeter. Hollington Stone is found in both the cathedrals of Coventry, but is perhaps better known after the local theme park, Alton Towers. Over to the east, and close to the Magnesian Limestone, are the red and white varieties of Mansfield, Nottinghamshire. This concludes our glimpse of the stone resources of the lowlands of England, and before we return south, there is the highland zone of northern England to examine, more renowned for its scenery than its churches, but a major source of stone nonetheless.

Highland England

Highland England divides in three; the Pennines, and the Lake District of the north, and Devon and Cornwall. Taking the northern hills first, the Dales and the Lakes meet fleetingly via Orton Scar and Shap Fell, but are otherwise separated by the Lune Gorge and the Vale of Eden. The Pennines are formed of carboniferous grit and limestone, and it is the gritstone that is the preferred building stone, even where limestone is dominant.

The reason for this is that the limestone is less tractable under the mason's chisel than the gritstone, and the extra cartage on the latter is deemed a small price to pay for improved workability. Gritstones fall into three divisions, with a fourth emerging as we travel north. Derbyshire, then, is the home of the Millstone Grit, admirably displayed at Baslow, near Chatsworth, home of the millstone that gives the stone its name.

Millstone Grit is the most widely used stone for building over a great swathe of Northern England, and in its fissile form provides massive paving slabs, and the famous diminishing course roof tilestones (now available in plastic, or rather a concrete that looks like plastic). Millstone Grit is a widely used, medium to coarse grained grey-brown sandstone; Darley Dale stone from Derbyshire, Bramley Fall, Crosland Hill and Rough Rock from Yorkshire, to name but the famous few. This stone can hold its own in an area where grit and limestones are plentiful, and where the next quality building stone, the Coal Measure Sandstone, is never far away.

The Coal Measure Sandstones of Yorkshire are everywhere beneath your feet, as the hard York pavings beloved of every town for their long life and non-slip surface. These are medium grained sandstones worked at Elland, near Halifax and elsewhere, and similar to the Upholland flags of Lancashire, and Brincliffe of Sheffield. These sandstones are not just fissile, for they supply the classic sandstones of Bolton Wood (Bradford), and Dunhouse. Durham Cathedral uses this latter stone, from Kieper quarry, which is close at hand, for once.

Thirdly, the Yoredale carboniferous series contains beds of grit that provide local stone, flag and tilestone supplies to the valleys of Yorkshire, used in preference to the limestone. As we move north, the grit beds become more important, both as landscape and building stone in Swaledale, with its procession of gritstone churches. Likewise in Durham and Northumberland, with the notable Black Pasture Stone from Chollerford, and Doddington Stone from Wooler, being more than just locally important, this last being near to the Scots border, over which we will venture in due course in search of a granite or two. Before we leave Northumberland for the Lake

District, we must note the presence of the Whin Sill, the widespread quartz dolerite intrusion, that finds extensive use as a building stone due to its unrivalled durability. Whin Sill has been regularly recycled over the past two millennia, and it is almost impossible to say when most of it was quarried, unless there is written record.

The Lake District

The Lake District is important for three unique stones, none of which is a pure 'building' stone *per se*, but two are so distinctive as to be identifiable almost anywhere, while the third is often mistaken for that which it is not.

Taking the mundane first, we have the grey-black slate of Furness, from the quarries at Kirkby in Furness, overlooking the Duddon Estuary, and currently marketed as Burlington Slate. When fixed this is difficult to tell apart from the slate of Blaenau Festiniog, but is much less common, slightly bluer, and close up has a coarser texture.

The next slate, Lakeland Green, known by its source quarries of Honister and Elterwater, is unmatched for colour except by modern substitutes. Unlike much of the stone of the rest of England, Lakeland Slate is a vivid green, not at all muted, and has been supplied both as random slates for diminishing course work, and even sizes for gauged roofs. It is in this latter form that most of the well travelled slates are to be found; the Victorian restorers found it an admirable choice. The green, slatey rocks of the Lakes find local use as random building stone, often as massive slabs of roughly split slate waste, the rock being too tough to dress or carve on any scale.

Finally we come to the bollards that stop St. Paul's Cathedral from straying; Shap Granite. As a granite it is reddish-brown rather than the silver-grey of the Cornish variety, but is distinguished, in every sense of the word, by the irregular phenocrysts or inclusions that show up so well when the stone is polished, the form most frequently used and readily identified.

As Shap was a long way from anywhere, until the railway arrived in 1846, most of the uses of this stone are modern. Occasional older pieces of Shap Granite turn up, as does the limestone also found there, currently being devoured by the million ton in the blast furnaces of Teesside, but still available for building stone from nearby Orton Scar.

The Marches of England (and Wales)

It is tempting to regard the lands immediately east of Offa's Dyke as an extension of the midland plain that has just been a bit crumpled by constant rubbing up against the mountains of Wales. Offa, however, declined to dig on the plain until he was north of Llanymynech, so south of this point our journey is across older rocks. Some of these are the oldest rocks in Britain, and nothing younger than the carboniferous coal measure sandstone of the Forest of Dean is crossed until we reach the banks of the river Severn.

Of good building stone, the borders are host to the coarse red brown sandstone, seen to dramatic effect in the Cathedral of the Forest, at Newland, and in that miniature at Kilpeck, south of Hereford. This stone, of which that from the Wilderness quarry at Mitcheldean can be regarded as typical, occurs in a wide swathe through Gloucestershire and Herefordshire.

While the name 'Hereford Stone' can be attached, this gives no more than a general name to a particularly widespread stone that in some areas is sufficiently fissile to yield tilestones. The extensive use of this tractable sandstone in an area bounded by older rocks is due not least to the absence of a readily workable limestone. As a durable sandstone it has had to cope with the competition of imported stones in an area where the rivers Severn and Wye have long offered reasonable transport arteries, arteries that have at intervals extended up the tributaries Teme and Lugg into deepest Shropshire.

Shropshire itself has limited exposures of this Devonian sandstone, though is dominated to a great degree by the newer red sandstone. The older rocks of the Long Mynd, yield the Hoar Edge Grit, still to be seen at Church Stretton. This rock yielded tilestones also, in times past, but it is time to conclude our tour of England with a visit to the West of England, where there is a modest, but unique highland zone.

185

Devon and Cornwall

That the south-west corner of England should be famous for its granites, still in widespread production when most other stone is in severe recession, is a reflection of the curious economics of the age we find ourselves living in. Granite at best is a thoroughly intractable stone, tough and difficult to split or face, and it is this durability, well beyond anything cement paste can stick together, that has enabled granite to survive as a construction stone, albeit with a limited range of uses. Let us then take the famous, or infamous, first and look at the granite that many have unwillingly hewed, for there are five principal granite masses in the south-west, and the largest by far is that of Dartmoor.

Dartmoor Granite, like most of that quarried for building stone in the region, is a silver-grey mottled colour, caused by the presence of quartz, feldspar and mica, and is dense, waterproof, very durable and takes a polish. As a stone it is to be found in local churches, as irregular blocks cleared off the fields (Moorstone), but in the nineteenth century industrialisation generated the wealth to make an intractable but extremely durable stone affordable. Hay Tor quarry started a trend that was to culminate in the ultimate refinement of piquant punishment, when the prison quarry at Princetown supplied the stone for Scotland Yard (Norman Shaw may or may not have been a prison reformer, but his knowledge of subtle torture obviously did not just extend to domestic architecture).

This use aside, granite, and there are no major differences between the quarries, is most likely to be found as polished memorial slabs (Wellington's, he of Hougoumont fame, is from Luxulyan), and kerbstones. Apart from the Land's End granite, the supplies are remote from water transport, and it's general use across England, even as rough hewn stone, pre 1800, was thus precluded.

Devon and Cornish granite, while generally supplied as silver-grey, can also be found pink and red, and varies mostly in the size of the crystals present, those with large crystals (megacrystic) being distinctive. Identification of the source quarry though, is for the expert, so we can move on to the other stones of the region without having to look closely at the other granite masses on Bodmin Moor, or those at St. Austell and Carnmenellis.

A slate is also to be found in the south-west (where there are granites, as in the Pyrenees, for example, there also will you find slate), and these Devonian slates are still worked in modest quantities from the enormous hole that is Delabole. Several centuries of production has been associated with widespread local distribution, and latterly a considerable export trade. As with all slates, the older roofs use random slate in diminishing courses, and Delabole slate is distinct in its grey-green chunky format that sets it apart from the slate of Wales. Delabole slate has similarities with tilestones, in that it contains fossils, notably the 'Delabole Butterfly'.

Just to confuse those who had imagined that the sandstone found and used extensively in Devon, was from the Devonian geological period, Devon sandstone is from the New Red Sandstone, of Permo-triassic origin, the same age as the sandstone of the midlands and north-west. This is the stone that forms the cliffs at Dawlish, and the material has been extensively quarried and used on the churches of south Devon. In appearance the stone is frequently a fairly coarse conglomerate, weathering to show the harder pebbles (including limestone and jasper) on the face, and not being particularly tractable to the carver's chisel as a result of this differential toughness within the stone.

Before we look at the special stones of England, in conclusion of a tour that has taken us through many geological ages, we return to the Cretaceous period at that delightful seaside wirescape, Beer, in east Devon. Beer Stone is a chalk that, besides giving birth to the fossil-collecting bug, also supplied vast quantities of building stone both locally, and, owing to the adjacent English Channel, to all manner of ecclesiastical projects further afield. Recent use has seen Exeter Cathedral repaired from this source, mined from nearby Branscombe.

Special Stone

Construction stone, almost by definition, is common rather than special, but as we have seen in our tour of England, there are a number of stones that have a niche in the Church, and while we are stretching a point to include monuments and statuary in architecture, the rare stones that go to form these unique works are part of our geological heritage. Many of these stones have been chosen for their decorative properties, and they are mainly, but not exclusively, limestones that take a polish and are called 'marble'. Prime among the 'marbles', as we have already discussed, is Purbeck, and we have touched on the Cave Marble of east Yorkshire. Elswhere, there is the Frosterley Marble of west Durham, Dent Marble in west Yorkshire, Wenlock Marble in Shropshire, Petworth in Sussex, and the limestone of Devon, which in its turn has been used as substitute for Purbeck.

Granites, as described above, are predominant in the exports of the south-west, and Shap has a favoured place in church architecture. Alabaster (gypsum – calcium sulphate) is a favoured material for statues and is found in the new red sandstone series, in Leicestershire and Nottinghamshire. Alabaster is only suitable for interior use, as it is chemically identical with the plaster we use on our living room walls.

Scotland and Wales

You will not find vast amounts of the stones of Scotland and Wales in English churches, not least because the English have spent at least half of the Christian era trying to batter their neighbours into submission, with varying degrees of success. The stone from Scotland is limited mainly to sandstones and granites; Peterhead and Aberdeen for granite, especially brown/red granite, Lothian and Dumfries for sandstone. Ancient use is rare, and most of the stone to be found is under three hundred years old. Also found are slates from Ballachulish, but these, like most slates, are difficult to identify from their Welsh cousins.

In Wales, apart from being the dubious source of the Prescelli Bluestones, over which battles continue to be fought by woad-encrusted warriors to this day, exporting stone has meant exporting slate. Slate is what Wales does best, and, as they have more rain than anyone else, God had to even things up by giving the Welsh something to deflect the deluge. Most of the slates from Wales come from the north, and the picture of that industry is distorted by the vast growth and spectacular decline of the last two hundred years.

None of the slate producing districts is far from the sea, and a steady export trade has been a feature of Welsh life for a thousand years. The slates you will see today are primarily from three sources; Blaenau Festiniog, Bethesda, and Dinorwic, the last having a distinctive purplish shade that sets then apart from the more usual grey/black/blue.

Other Welsh slate quarries include Nantlle, Abergynolwyn, Corris and Aberllefenni, though not all are still in production. Old roofs of diminishing course Welsh Slate are not that rare in the towns and cities of England that sea and river transport could reach. Rail transport in the nineteenth century made Welsh slate the most common roofing material in virtually every English town and city, a position of dominance only now being relinquished to the concrete tile.

Conclusion

In this gallop through the building stones of England, we have missed out a vast quantity of material just to avoid repetition and churning through stones that have no particular claim to fame. Equally, we have neglected important local stones such as the Hertfordshire Puddingstones and the Northampton Ironstones in the cause of keeping the story within bounds, even though these stones, and a hundred and one others, are part of the same rich pageant. Also left out are many one-offs, like the tale of winning the green slate of Honister Hause, where, not so long ago you could stand, as the author did, and watch fascinated as cableways and inclines brought the slate to the mill for processing.

'Yet,' you say, and with good reason, 'this is a slate that can be found throughout the country,' and indeed this is the case, and, much as it is regretted, in the need to draw a line, some stones will not get all the space they deserve, others will be mentioned by name only, and many will not even have that privilege. Perhaps it is a story for others to take up, for while stone is the grist to the mill of church architecture, it is a part of the story, not the whole. For imported stone from the rest of the world there is no place, for the import of stone has never featured large for architectural work, though marbles are widely represented in tombs and grave markers, and the building stone of Europe alone is another long, long story.

189

Perhaps, when looking at the role of stone, we are looking on from an interlude in the history of stone exploitation, and that today's techniques of smashing the stuff to pulp before even considering what to do with it next are but a short, passing phase. 'Perhaps not' is a phrase that springs to mind also. The difference between riches and wealth is after all only one of perspective and value, and in the rush to get rich quick, most of the wealth that is stone has been passed by, hopefully for others to value. The design life of most buildings today is so meagre as to debar stone; it would be a criminal waste to use it and then throw it away. Our ancestors did not, and neither should we. A rational use of resources that are by definition limited is to be encouraged.

Identifying Building and Decorative Stone

Of the more famous stones to be found, the observer will note two different types of stone from Grinshill and Mansfield, and that Shap currently shifts limestone by the million ton as well as the odd bollard of granite. The moral? It is easier to go astray than to stay on the path of righteousness! Some of the softer clunch is just as well described as chalk, and while 'cannel' is just the Scots word for 'coal', some of the harder coals find use as contrast colour in decorative work, while one is used for jewellery. How then to identify the stone on the ground?

The easiest way to identify stone is to start by deciding what it is not, rather than what it is. Stone is either local or foreign (brought from ten or more miles away). Eliminating the foreign stone is moderately difficult, but if you can identify Bath Stone (calcite veins, smooth but slightly abrasive to the touch, yellow brown, some shells) and Portland (white, feels similar to Bath Stone), then south of Birmingham you are halfway there.

Magnesian Limestone is like Bath Stone, without the oolites, only more yellow, and the calcite veining is absent. The other Jurassic limestones tend to be somewhat coarser, with more shells (some, particularly the tilestones, seem all shell), and while the colour varies to the dark brown of Banbury, their surface textures are similar. The grey limestones, those that are Liassic (muddy) or Carboniferous, have a smooth surface that is cool and soft to the touch, though the surface may be roughly dressed, and are slippery when wet. If a stone is pale grey and smooth, then it is a reasonable bet that it is a limestone.

Sandstones are more varied in hue, but feel rougher due to their quartz content, and are generally non-slip, even when wet. The New Red Sandstones (Permo-Triassic) are brighter red in hue than the Old Red or Devonian Sandstones, which tend to be more varied, with grey or green in the same wall. These sandstones weather to yield a gritty powdery surface, and often show signs of delamination (horizontal cracks in the individual stones). Millstone Grit, Coal Measure and Jurassic Sandstones are usually brown to dark grey, but otherwise are like their younger and older compatriots. Quartzites are rough like sandstones but have a crystalline surface due to being heat treated, and do not show weathering; they have a tendency to be multi coloured, from white to dark brown, and are as durable as granite. Granite in its unpolished form is usually dark grey and rough.

If what you are looking at is none of these, then it is probably the local stone, and that will usually be less rigorously dressed than stone from a commercial quarry supplying the national market. The less well finished, or the further down the pecking order (ashlar, squared, rubble, rag) the stone is, the closer it will be to the quarry. In a typical church then, you can expect to find imported stone for the window details, quoins and parapets if the local stone is represented by rubble or rag walling (if there is no local stone both will have been imported). If the stone is the same throughout then it may have travelled some distance (up to ten miles by land, a lot further if water transport is available). The richer, larger and more ornate the church, the further afield they are likely to have gone for the stone. Flint walls will be locally sourced from fields or quarries. There are no hard and fast rules on what you will find where, but this kind of back of the envelope analysis will succeed often enough with practice, and if it doesn't, it's good fun to try!

A Stone Dictionary

Stone	Where From	Type
Aislaby Grit	Whitby, Yorks	Jurassic sandstone
Alston	Alston, Cumbs	Sandstone (limestone coal series)
Ancaster	Ancaster, Lincs	Lincolnshire Limestone
Ashdown S/stone	Weald of Sussex	Calcareous sandstone
Barnack	Stamford, Cambs	Lincolnshire Limestone
Bath	Bath, Avon	Oolitic limestone
Beer	Beer, East Devon.	Cretaceous limestone (chalk)
Binstead	Isle of Wight	Tertiary limestone
Brandy Crag	Coniston, Westmorland	Borrowdale volcanics (slate)
Brathay	Ambleside, Westmorland	Borrowdale volcanics (slate)
Broughton Moor	Broughton in Furness	Borrowdale volcanics (slate)
Bolsover Moor	Bolsover, Derbys	Magnesian Limestone
Boynton	Bridlington, E. Yorks	Chalk
Birchover Grit	Matlock, Derbys	Millstone Grit
Bramley Fall	Bradford, Yorks	Millstone Grit
Bolton Wood	Bradford, Yorks	Coal Measure Sandstone
Burlington	Kirkby in Furness	Silurian metamorphic slate
Callow	Monmouth, Gwent	Hereford Sandstone
Cannel	Various	Coal Measures

Stone	Where From	Type
Carstone	Various	Iron cemented conglomerate
Casterton	Stamford, Leics	Lincolnshire Limestone
Cave Oolite	Sancton, E. Yorks	Oolitic limestone
Cheltenham	Cheltenham, Gloucs	Oolitic limestone
Chilmark	Chilmark, Salisbury	Limestone (Portland series)
Chinley Moor	Hayfield, Derbys	Millstone Grit
Clee Hill	Ludlow, Salop	Dolerite
Clipsham	Stamford, Leics	Lincolnshire Limestone
Colly Weston	Stamford, Northants	Jurassic tilestone
Coombe Down	Bath, Avon	Oolitic limestone
Coral Rag	Oxford	Jurassic limestone
Corndon	Ludlow, Salop	Dolerite tilestone
Copp Crag	Redesdale, Northumb'land	Carboniferous Limestone
Crosland Hill	Huddersfield, Yorks	Millstone Grit
Danby	North York Moors	Jurassic sandstone
Delabole Slate	Delabole, Cornwall	Devonian slate
Delph Sandstone	Wingerworth, Derbys	Coal Measure Sandstone

Stone	Where From	Type
Dent Marble	Dent, W. Yorks	Carboniferous Limestone
Doddington	Wooler, Northumberland	Carboniferous Limestone
Doulting	Shepton Mallett, Somerset	Inferior oolite
Downside	Shepton Mallett, Somerset	Liassic limestone
Dunhouse	Staindrop, Durham	Millstone grit
Elland Flags	Halifax, Yorks	Coal Measure Sandstone
Elterwater	Langdale, Westmorland	Green slate (Borrowdale Volcanics)
Frosterley Marble	Frosterley, Durham	Carboniferous Limestone
Grey Wethers	Marlborough, Wilts	Eocene Sandstone
Grinshill	Grinshill, Shrewsbury	Permo-triassic (New Red) Sandstone
Guiting	Cotswolds, Broadway	Jurassic limestone
Hackness	Scarborough, Yorks	Jurassic sandstone
Hall Dale	Darley Dale, Derbys	Millstone Grit
Ham Hill	Ilminster, Somerset	Jurassic limestone
Haslingden	Bacup, Lancs	Millstone Grit
Hereford	Gloucs & Herefordshire	Devonian sandstone
Hoar Edge Grit	Cardington, Salop	Ordovician Grit (and tilestone)

Stone	Where From	Type
Hollington	Uttoxeter, Staffs	Permo-Triassic (New Red) Sandstone
Honister	Keswick, Cumbs	Green slate (Borrowdale Volcanics)
Horsham	Horsham, Sussex	Cretaceous sandstone
Kerridge	Macclesfield, Derbys	Coal Measure Sandstone
Kentish Ragstone	Maidstone, Kent	Sandy limestone (Cretaceous)
Ketton	Stamford, Lincs.	Lincolnshire Limestone
Kirkstone	Ambleside, Westmorland	Green slate (Borrowdale Volcanics)
Ladycross	Hexam, S. Tynedale	Coal Measure Sandstone
Lazonby	Lazonby, Cumbs	Permian sandstone
Locharbriggs	Dumfries, Scotland	Permian sandstone
Mansfield	Mansfield, Notts	Permian dolomitic sandstone
Mansfield Woodhouse	Mansfield, Notts	Magnesian Limestone
Mount Sorrel	Leicester	Granite
Penrith	Penrith, Cumbria	Permian sandstone
Plumpton	Vale of Eden, Cumbria	Permian sandstone
Portland	Portland, Dorset	Oolitic limestone
Prudham	Hexam, S. Tynedale	Carboniferous Limestone
Purbeck Marble	Worth Matravers, Dorset	Jurassic limestone

Stone	Where From	Type
Purbeck Portland	Swanage, Dorset	Oolitic limestone (Portland)
Quarr	Isle of Wight	Tertiary limestone
Rainhill	North York Moors	Jurassic sandstone
Red Wilderness	Mitcheldean, Gloucs	Devonian (Hereford) sandstone
Reigate	Reigate, Surrey	Calcareous sandstone
Roche Abbey	Maltby, S. Yorks	Magnesian Limestone
Rotherham Red	Sheffield, Yorks	Coal Measure Sandstone
Shap	Shap, Cumbs	Granite
St. Bees	Whitehaven, Cumbs	Triassic sandstone
Stoke Ground	Bath, Avon	Oolitic limestone
Stonesfield Slate	Woodstock, Oxon	Jurassic tilestone
Tadcaster	Tadcaster, Yorks	Magnesian Limestone
Taynton	Burford, Oxon	Jurassic limestone
Totternhoe	Dunstable, Beds	Clunch (Cretaceous limestone)
Tunbridge	Tunbridge Wells, Kent	Calcareous sandstone
Whin Sill	Northumberland	Dolerite
York	West Yorkshire	Coal Measure sandstone

Chapter Ten:
Sketches and Timelines

As the text has demanded, we have looked at parts of individual churches to illustrate a particular point; so far we have avoided actually describing in any depth a single building, and for good reason. Without the tools to conduct an analysis, we would be reduced to the superficial of the superficial. The history of any building more than a few decades old, is an aggregation of the efforts of the generations who have cared. We can understand why they cared, now we can see how; see beyond the facts, to the philosophy, the skills and the courage of those past generations.

To start at any one church without means to deconstruct in the minds' eye the construction process, a process that by no means starts with a green field and concludes rapidly with the finished article, is to miss the very essence of an English Church. In order that we do not miss that crucial element, looking at a partial ruin, where much is laid bare that might otherwise be hid, is a good place to begin. East Yorkshire, and the Minster Church of Howden, fulfil the criteria admirably.

The Minster Church - Howden

The term 'Minster' is descriptive, not so much of a particular type of church, but of a church built by a religious order. With the resources of a wider area than the single parish available, and dating from the start of the twelfth century, to the close of the monastic period in the 1540s, Howden, like most minsters, was not a poor church. There are exceptions to this, St. Gregory's in Kirkdale, for example, is both a minster church and predates the Norman Settlement. The general rule however, is that minsters were built over a period of three and a half centuries, and most of the buildings that we see today are, like the Walrus's oysters, those of the larger size.

As a minster, Howden is a modest structure, but that is not to say that it is small. The fact that it is partially ruined is proof enough that it was once, and to a degree remains, larger than the town of Howden alone could sustain, there being no evidence that the worthy burghers of times past were any less diligent in their support of the Church than any other country town in Eastern England.

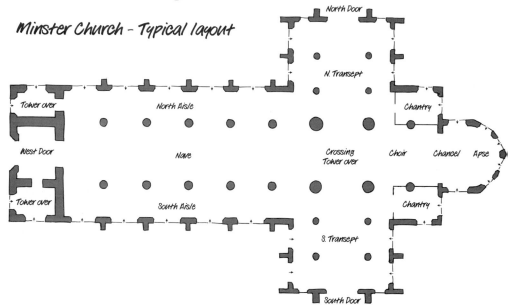

Minster Church - Typical layout

Howden lies comfortably on the rich plain that, now effectively drained, forms the Humberhead Levels. If you draw a circle twenty miles in radius from the church tower a further three abbeys and minsters are encircled. Two are undiscovered gems, the third is world famous. All four are worthy of much more than a passing glance, but Howden rarely receives its due, though scarce a mile from the East Yorkshire M62, Englands' only traffic-free motorway. The fact that the Minster is larger than the town could support, in a land both rich in agricultural and ecclesiastical terms, gives a hint that the establishment and sustenance of Minsters was carried out under a different set of economic rules from the mere parish church, and that is indeed the case.

The church that we see in part today, dates from the middle of the thirteenth century, when Howdenshire was under the authority of the Bishop of Durham. At the time the 'Shire' comprised five livings or parishes, a number later increased to six, and it was from the wealth of these lands that the resources to build a large church were garnered. Apart from an amount of river trade, the livings appear to have been entirely agricultural until the arrival of brick and tile making in the fourteenth century.

To add interest, there is no locally available stone, the nearest supplies being at South Cave, where the Cave Oolite outcrops close to the Humber bank. This source was ignored, in favour of the Magnesian Limestone of Tadcaster and Huddleston. River transport via the Wharfe and Ouse kept the cost down and allowed the use of massive stones to good effect in the south front, and elsewhere.

The church of 1250 appears to have been built to a cruciform plan with a central tower, nave and aisles, transepts and choir. Of particular note are the piers of the nave arcade, slender and delicately proportioned solid stonework of quatrefoil cross section. What is clear from the evidence on the ground is that the first church was not an overwhelming success; without any direct light into the nave, much of the church was gloomy, a gloom that the steeply pitched timber roof accentuated. Lacking a triforium, the building had a distinctly squat appearance, and would have looked and felt unfashionable within a few decades of completion.

Less than fifty years later, a second round of work commenced, almost certainly with the raising of the tower with its superbly proportioned windows in the Perpendicular style. This was almost the last straw for the tower foundations, and noticeable settlement occurred, still visible at floor level today.

The tower was followed by the raising of the nave roof to insert a triforium, and conscious of the need to keep the loads on the nave arcade within reason, the triforium was built as two hollow skins of stone, and has proved to be a complete success. As part of the same scheme, the roof of the choir was lifted to complement the nave, and the then fashionably expensive vault raised in stone to support the timber roof. A chapter house, also with a vaulted roof, completed the development, and it has been all downhill from there.

The failure of the vaulted roof to the choir stemmed primarily from neglect, but there is not really enough supporting stone in the form of buttresses to resist the lateral thrusts of the vault. After two hundred years, in 1609, the choir was abandoned, though it was a further ninety before the vault collapsed, having been 'cannibalised' of its lead roof covering some years earlier. The church thus stood in its full glory for only two of the six centuries since completion, and been partially ruined for half its life.

Howden's fall from grace has been one of slow decline, a decline we can see because the repairers and improvers of the last two centuries have not really got to grips with the scale of the work needed to put the church back into the original collegiate form. Significantly, the ruined section has not been carted away to be incorporated into the fabric of the town, though the debris has been cleared. We can only speculate as to the reason, but the most likely one is that with local brick readily available from the fourteenth century, and the high cost of stone due to the distance from the nearest quarries, by the time the choir collapsed there was no local demand for building materials that could not be met by the brickworks, at a lower cost than for recycling the stone. A tradition of brick making and brick laying, well established by the end of the seventeenth century, has thus preserved the ruins we see today, by depressing the value of the scrap stone below the worth of carting it away.

Clearly the church was a size too large for the town, and the unequal struggle to maintain the fabric is there for all to see. The spartan religious regime of the 1600s may well have been the excuse for the abandonment of the choir, but the inside stonework is almost as weather-stained as the outside in parts, telling only too well that the roof has not been in a constant state of good repair, more probably the reverse. Look too at the dates on the interments in the nave, each one, like the reusable parish coffin, representing an income when funds were at a low ebb. Today the Minster struggles to keep its head above water; the nave floor is damp, and some of the limestone to the front is crumbling. Perhaps it has always been thus.

As a church, Howden is a tribute to the Canons of the Bishopric of Durham who lavished the wealth of the six parishes on a church that has seen little, except neglect, lavished upon it since. As a work of art, it has a crowning glory, the tower, visible for twenty miles around, and quite distinctive enough to be termed unique. As an essay in design the cruciform piers in the nave arcade represent the very best of the Gothic; modest, attractive and slenderously efficient. As a three-dimensional history book its pages are more readily legible than most.

As a haven of peace and beauty in an increasingly brash and ugly world, it is in the premier league.

The Village Church - Urchfont

If Howden epitomises the sleepy country town, just far enough off the beaten track to deter all except the curious backwater explorer, it was not always so; forty years ago it boasted two railways and a brace of trunk roads, only ceasing to be a through route in the last quarter of the twentieth century, then Urchfont is the reverse, for it has never been busy. Urchfont is so rural that when the author was telephoned by the primary school, disbelief at the address, Cuckoo Corner, was total. Yet it is true, Cuckoo Corner, Urchfont, Wilts, is a valid postal address; the drive to the school is past thatched cottages. The manor park wall nudges one of the unsung marvels of post-war education, a battered third hand plywood mobile classroom (earning a crust often implies compromise with principles). What brought the author to the village, is not however, what made him stand and stare.

The village is the classic post-Roman occupation settlement of the English landscape, a unit founded to turn the wild land into till and pasture, initially subsistence, but with the passing of the decades and then centuries, accumulating wealth in the form of agricultural productivity, livestock, and buildings. There is no place for a church at the lowest subsistence level because everyone is obliged to devote all of their labour merely to survive. Religion may well be an integral part of man's survival regime, a method of focusing the activities and coordinating the efforts of a group who will always have a number of views on how a particular task should be approached.

Once that initial phase is passed, then a building to house the devotions and rites is high on the picking list. Urchfont as a village has one of those enviable spring line sites that are coveted by hundreds of similar settlements along the scarp and dip slopes of the chalk and limestone hills that run from the river Tees to Portland Bill. In this, as in the gradual accumulation of wealth over the centuries, Urchfont has no particular claim to fame. Not so the church.

Parish Church with a touch of grandeur

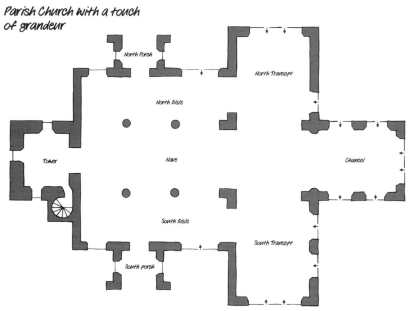

North Porch

North Transept

North Aisle

Tower

Nave

Chancel

South Aisle

South Transept

South porch

The importance of the Portland and Purbeck geological formations in providing some of the best building stones for the most prestigious buildings in England is discussed elsewhere. Here, as at Chilmark (the source of the stone for Salisbury Cathedral) there is an outcrop of these stone beds, and they have yielded stone of first quality literally on Urchfont's doorstep. The temptation to do something spectacular with such natural munificence, proved too much for parson and mason alike. The result is something unique, an ambitious experiment in stonemasonry that, whilst a partial failure (not all the original work survives), enough still stands

202

for us to picture what had to be taken down. If Urchfont had been a particularly rich parish, or an important one, it is likely that all would have long since been torn down, and the visual feast lost.

The church sits in, not on, the churchyard, which when approached from the south appears to be flat. This is an illusion created by founding the church several feet below the level of the churchyard, on a site which originally sloped away into the Vale of Pewsey. Levelling was achieved by building a wall around the north side, filling in the gap between the wall and the church, and generating an undercroft to raise the nave floor to the new ground level. A clever, but not exceptional, method of filling without cutting, to flatten the site.

The main entrance from the village leads to the porch, externally a modest lichen-encrusted stone walled and roofed structure of charm and character, but no more. Step into the porch, and for the time it takes you to adjust to the new light levels, you will wonder what is wrong with the roof. There are no posts, beams or rafters. The roof is in fact a series of interlocked stones, carved on the inner side to form a small vault, and lapped and stepped on the outer side to look, and perform, as a pitched, tiled roof. Reason tells you that the weight of the vault, unrestrained by buttresses, should long ago have forced out the walls and reduced the porch to rubble, but the structure is nearly six hundred years old, and almost as sound as the day it was built.

Long may it escape the repairers' and conservors' clutches.

Pass through the porch to the nave and two features immediately strike the eye; a chancel arch that looks as if a giant has sat on it, and an enormous transverse buttress that lumbers, rather than flies, across the north aisle to lean on the nave arcade. These two features are the lasting legacy of the solid vaulting, similar to the porch, that once spanned the nave, vaulting that squashed the chancel arch and threatened to push over the arcade that supported it. Replacing the vault, which appears to have been taken down after the transverse buttress failed to halt the inexorable effect of gravity, and before it could terminally damage the rest of the church and its parishioners, is a fine oak rafter and purlin roof, with collared queen post trusses and carved wall corbels.

If the nave has had its problems, and the original vault was almost certainly trouble from the word go, then the parish learnt its lesson when it came to the chancel, roofed with a conventional Early English style vault, suitably ribbed and bossed on the inside. Rare enough on such a modest parish church, but capped on the outside with a brilliant, if now somewhat weatherbeaten, series of carved stone ridges, complemented with a crenallated parapet pierced with quatrefoil motifs and featuring stubby but functional pinnacles to the low key external buttresses.

All this would be enough on a single church, but Urchfont goes a step further to add in a south transept, where, rather than use stone from the quarry, some bright spark has substituted flints. Perhaps they were gathered as penances?

Tended and cossetted in maturity as in its youth, this church has received the best of care from what once was a fairly prosperous parish, with a consistency down the ages that has preserved much that we now admire. True, the parish never ran to a spire to compete with the upmarketly named Bishops Canning, across on the north side of the Vale of Pewsey, even though it had the right quality stone to build one.

Urchfont's delights are made more subtle by this modesty, and it would have been spoiled if at any point in its history great wealth had been poured into its coffers. Towers and spires though, are a recurring theme in the English landscape, and why Urchfont and Bishops Canning differ in this aspect is a matter of some interest, and not a little debate.

Towers and Spires

A topic of conversation then, among the *cogniscenti*, is why do some areas have churches with just a tower, and others are flush with spires adorning almost every village? Like many solutions the key to this conundrum lies in the geology, but first we need to look at the sequence of building that most churches, abbeys and cathedrals went through. The almost continuous round of construction that was needed to make up for lack of knowledge, poor design, and poor workmanship, was a feature of the Middle Ages. Within this merry-go-round of build, extend, rebuild, extend, rebuild, demolish, build again, there were two pressures at work; the need to keep ahead of time's levelling hand, and the desire to go one step further than the village, town or city next door.

The provision of a tower as part of the basic plan of the church, was almost axiomatic, the only debate being as to its position. The inclusion therefore, of the structures that would ultimately support the tower above the roofline, in the design of the main body of the church, is essential, irrespective of what actually follows on once the roof is complete. The tower foundations and base are thus part and parcel of the nave, either at the crossing of the transepts, or at the west end, and only occasionally at the side, where it could be a notionally independent structure.

The Mature Parish Church - 10 centuries of development

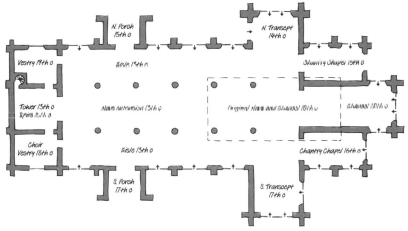

These structures also serve a second purpose; the weight of the piers or walls that would ultimately support the tower, serve as a structural arcade stop, acting as a buttress to resist the side thrust of the nave arcade. Whether this structure emerged above roof level depended upon how well the walls and columns had been built. When depended on the wealth of the parish or institution, or how high on the list of priorities going up was, compared to the other available directions.

When all these possibilities had been explored and funds allocated for a serious stab skyward, the base of the structure in the church proper had usually been in place for some time, and a new mason detailed with the task of adding the tower. This usually proved a moderately easy task, though caution dictated that most towers were built in sections, many churches having three. In most cases there was a certain amount of settlement as the masonry was added, Puxton and Howden being excellent examples.

In both these instances the settlement was enough to deter any attempt to add a spire. So far, so reasonably good; very few structures, particularly towers and spires, could be described as accurate by today's parameters. Any reasonably prosperous parish could over the centuries pull together enough resources to add a modest tower to complement their church. Adding a spire is where the geology comes in (yes, there are plenty of timber spires, but they depend to a degree on the geology, and most of them lean, too).

The evolution of skills and accumulation of experience through the Middle Ages is reflected in the increasingly complex and confident use of stone, and just about the ultimate test of man and material is the spire. While it is not impossible to build a spire in rubble masonry (Lydney has fine one), it is difficult to succeed beyond achieving much more than a squat point. To build a spire proper you need first-class ashlar work in a good stone. Spires are built hollow, usually around a timber frame, to minimise the load on the tower below. The use of mortar is minimal, because this is the weakest element, and joints are as thin as is conducive with accurate stone laying. Even when all is well, a spire exerts massive loads, usually several hundred tons, on the tower below (the largest spires weigh in excess of a thousand tons).

The effect on a tower not built to the highest specification, is to crush it, and Salisbury's spire has been doing just that to the tower piers for the past six hundred years. The spire at Salisbury is one feature of the English countryside has probably done more to deter prospective spire builders over the centuries than any other leaning edifice. The Salisbury spire is almost two and a half feet out of true, and the builders didn't have the courage to strip out the timber framing when they had finished.

Towers built in rubble masonry do not usually sport a spire, for the reason that the tower masonry is not up to the task, or doesn't look as if it is. Likewise, the quarry that supplied the stone is probably the local one, and if it was unable to produce the quality ashlar blocks to build a tower, then these articles would be wanting when needed to build a spire. Thus we have an area such as the Cotswolds, where there are many fine stone churches, but the spires are confined in the main to the areas with access to quality stone.

In complete contrast, East Yorkshire positively bristles with spires, because in the Middle Ages it was a rich land, and while there is very little local stone, even quite small villages could afford to import the best. To contrast the somewhat fantastical and just a teeny bit over the top spire sported by the Queen of Holderness, at Patrington, with the solid and statesmanlike tower at Wotton-Under-Edge, is to say it all. Wotton has its own stone supplies, half a mile up the hill on the road to Nailsworth, but they are not ideal for spire construction, and while wool and wealth have been fellow travellers in the past, hauling the best stone up the hill to Wotton has never been as attractive as hauling not quite the best stone down.

Patrington is twenty miles from a quarry that will yield anything better than a soft chalk, but is a stone's throw from a river that flows from the proverbial Eden, and the worthy burghers of Patrington had the money to pay up and take the choicest stone north of the Trent.

Stone spires then, are determined by location and geology, as well as wealth and faith. The stone spire's first cousin, the timber spire, is primarily a compromise; provided in circumstances where it was obvious that stone would be beyond the means of the parish coffers, or beyond the capacity of the existing tower. The problem with a timber spire is that it had a tendency to twist and lean as the wood seasons, and is prone to take flight in a storm, with the attendant risk of what is known in warfare as 'collateral damage'.

That said, timber needs must be clad, and the cladding can be anything from shingles through slates and tilestones, to lead, copper sheet, or 'Rosemary' tiles, to go from the bland to the brilliant, as it were. This has meant that attractive, colourful and distinctive spires have become features of modern churches, catching the eye at close range, if not dominating the immediate locality, owing to their moderate dimensions.

The temptation to add a spire during a restoration is strong, and the temptations that the restorers have succumbed to over the past centuries, is nowhere more in evidence at our next port of call, a secluded valley in the Vale of Pickering.

The Restored Church - St. Gregory's, Kirkdale

All the mediaeval churches, and many of the Georgian and Victorian churches that we see today have been subject to a degree of restoration of their fabric, and where it has been well done, few will even spot the restored sections, let alone bemoan the effect. Pity, then, poor Kirkdale. St. Gregory's Minster is one of the serious let-downs in life, for if there is anything Saxon about the structure, then it is exceedingly well hid. The setting is, without doubt, one of the best in Britain, beating nearby Rievaulx, and edging out Brinkburn. As you approach from Pickering, the river has to be forded (a real ford too, not just a bit wet in winter) and the narrow lane has neither been straightened, or widened, this century, possibly never. The turning to the church is covered by a leafy canopy, and the stroll to the churchyard gate is past meadows in a narrow, sylvan valley, where the conifers turn out not to be yews, and the church they are hiding turns out not to be Saxon.

Parish Church of the smaller size

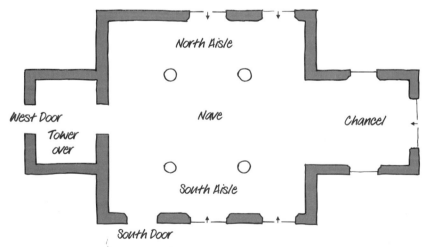

The Minster is in fact a hotch-potch of styles, but the masonry, the timberwork and the roofing is Victorian. Yes, there are mediaeval bits here and there, and the floor plan is probably more or less as it was in the middle of the sixteenth century, but the tower is a sham, and if it isn't the architects idea of how a Saxon tower should look, then it *looks* as if it is. This will not deceive many, but there are items that might, and chief among them is the tilestone roof, which looks as if it might be ancient, but on close inspection is just *too* straight and even to be older than a couple of centuries. The roof, while being a passable imitation of a Saxon beam and post, is made out of machine sawn timbers, and cannot be mistaken for anything other than repro. That level of honesty, in the roof, is about as far down the path of truth that the Victorian restorers were prepared to go, or perhaps their agenda was just different from our own.

In the churchyard the trade in burial plots is thriving; certainly you could not wish for a better place to nourish the daisies, but if you are looking for a genuine structure in Kirkdale then the only one appears to be the viaduct hiding in the trees, waiting for the restorers of the twenty-first century, perhaps.

Come and admire the scenery, the atmosphere and the Victorian church, but don't be taken in by the road signs; the Saxons fled this place two hundred years ago. We, too, can flee, as the human race has been doing for the past four centuries, to the town, and a glimpse of what resources can be devoted to the glory of God, when man crowds together. The choice of another Cotswold wool town is deliberate, because it introduces both a transitional style, and the architect, to the story of the English church.

The Town Church - Tetbury

The tally of Georgian Gothic churches in England does not run to a cricket score, and certainly nowhere near Herbert and Percy's outing at Leyton in 1932. Villages with both the resources and desire to build a new church for the Establishment in the eighteenth century were decidedly thin on the ground. While the Nonconformists, and their building programme, were picking up steam, the Catholics were, for most of the century, watching on the sidelines, debating if they dare put a toe in the water. Neither of these new entrants to the church building business was in a position to match the glory of the Established Church property portfolio, run down and semi derelict as much of it was at the time.

Prosperous towns were far more likely to invest in a suitably fashionable neo-classical building, so Tetbury's decision, eased perhaps by the desire to retain their famously visible spire, is an unusual one. Perhaps also the chosen design was a reflection of the staunch conservatism of a town far from the changing influence of the budding industrial regions, and long dependent on the staple, wool. Whatever the ultimate reason, the spire lurched on for a further century before it too was rebuilt in the original style, keeping company with a new church, a church that displays the difference between the Gothic as evolved in the Middle Ages, and the Gothic as interpreted by the architect.

By the middle of the eighteenth century it was custom and practice to appoint an architect to design whatever the Church needed, in this case a new church. Tetbury engaged Francis Hiorn, from Warwick. What Hiorn designed was a masterpiece of illusion; a church that from the outside has the appearance of a Gothic 'nave and aisle' structure, but on the inside comprises a nave and two narrow ambulatories. The chancel is effectively dispensed with. The result is a beautifully proportioned bright, light,space, with slender imitation painted wooden piers and a panelled roof. Here the gallery is an integral element of the design, and entirely fitting, being a match for the excellent box pews that, if not original equipment, look as if they are.

Francis Hiorn crafted this space to be as one with the Gothic spire, and 'crafted' is the correct word, because while what you see in a mediaeval church is what holds the building up, here the piers are hollow timber casings, the 'vault' painted plaster; illusion from the pen. Tetbury then, epitomises the emergent architectural profession, a commission executed by a man from sixty miles up the Foss Way (a day's journey by post, each way, just to visit site), using the materials and techniques of his time to recreate the appearance of the English Gothic Church. Hiorn successfully dispensed with the heavy arcade and triforium, and succeeded in making the glazing in the clerestory fill the nave with light.

210

In this task he was aided by the use of plain, as opposed to coloured or stained, glass, both being unfashionable at the time. With only a light timber roof to support, and the mass of the ambulatories to buttress the walls, there is no real need for a lot of stone between the windows, which are as wide as the roof purlins, and the overall proportions of the church, can sustain.

The space that was created in the eighteenth century, is surprisingly economical in its ability to admit as many people to the service (as opposed to the church), yet retain the trappings of the Gothic. There is no room for the exotic tombs, no nooks or corners where exotic carving of wood or stone can find a breathing space; this is a functional space, solely dedicated to worship. All who wish to listen and participate may do so. The clergy have no lengthy chancel to retreat into, no screens or arches to hide behind. Whatever Hiorn's brief, his solution has stood the test of time in a manner that all designers can, with delight, envy to the ninth degree.

A masterpiece his Victorian successors would have done well just to copy.

While we may still deprecate the restoration work of the Victorians, and bemoan the fact that from the records of those restorations we know just what has been lost, the technology of building conservation is very definitely a debatable approach to building repair. What you cannot fault our nineteenth century surveyors of the fabric for is their *enthusiasm*. Like most of the human race, they were never happier than when they had something to complain about, and with neo-classical alterations and repairs to Gothic fabric, they were on very solid ground when grousing.

New materials, particularly wrought iron, and later steel, were seen as the wonders of the age that could remedy the ailments of the elderly, just like plastics, epoxy resins and stainless steel today. Who are we to say that what we now count as good practice, will not receive a bad press a century hence? The whole concept of conservation, rather than restoration, it can be argued, substitutes specialists in materials science for masons and carpenters. Is this effective management of old buildings or a method of extinguishing the skills that created them? The debate, it seems, has yet to begin.

Action to suit their words was more the restorers' line a hundred and fifty years ago, and much as a beam that has provided lunch for twenty generations of death watch beetle crumbles at the touch, so too did many churches in the nineteenth century. The reasons are not difficult to deduce; a modest drip of water from a leaking roof will not cause many people to do other than find another pew, and it only happens when the wind blows from a particular direction anyway, so there's no need to worry. Unfortunately that drip will feed wet or dry rot fungus, which in their turn will encourage the wood boring beetle and before the century is out, there is a nasty sag in the roof. As it happens there is a similar drip into the top of the wall, and that one is leaching out the lime from the mortar, and as the roof starts to sag, so the wall starts to bulge. In no time at all, the parish has an emergency on its paws.

When the builders move in to make safe and open up to see what's wrong, all the other one hundred and one little faults pop up too, and the project starts a merry and expensive dance known as 'hunt the sound work'. And if you are tempted to think this is a rare event, rest assured this is the norm, not the exception. The only known antidote to this malaise is to do *your* bit and pretend that the rest is OK. That is very normal too.

When the restorers came to our next church, Crawley, what they found was quite probably a bit like Winnie the Pooh's house for Eeyore; visibly a church but sagging in all directions. The steps taken to bring order to the chaos were, as we shall see, solid, sound and unpretentious; the result highly satisfactory.

The Village Church Restored - Crawley

Crawley is a small village, not far removed from the ecclesiastical majesty of Winchester, but on a different planet in the real world. The parish church of St. Mary's, will tell you a lot about the village and its past that you will not learn from the present well-to-do duckpond and half-timbered pub. There is a veneer of prosperity that gilds Crawley today, and if you are deceived into thinking that it has always been thus, then you will be fortunate to discover the church and the clear tale it has to tell.

As a village, Crawley had reached a low ebb at the end of the nineteenth century, when a 'retired' cotton magnate, Ernest Philippi, arrived from Scotland and proceeded to buy up the village lock and stock, and turn it into the twee little retreat we see today. Photographic records show that prior to this transformation the village was far from the rural idyll, more a series of hovels that the poor would have been pleased to desert for the city life. Centuries of unremitting toil against poverty can have been the only lot of the villagers, and this is the tale that the church tells.

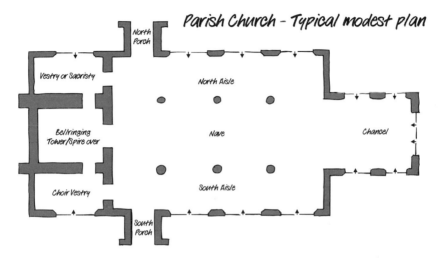

Parish Church - Typical modest plan

The present church is in essence fourteenth century in plan and structure, sporting an unashamedly Victorian roof, covered with the bright orange-red delightfully-named 'Rosemary' tiles, from the maker's impressed mark, giving a cheerful splash of colour to the outside.

In plan, the three compartments of tower, nave and chancel are typical of a modest village church, with an extension to the rear housing the organ. Of the church's predecessors only a fragment of Norman arch moulding remains, built into the rear face of the chancel arch. The walls are faced with flints, either gathered from the fields or laboriously won from the beds of the upper chalk. The walls may be all flint, or facings concealing chalk blocks, as do the bricks of Beverley's Friary. In either case the durability of flint ensures that what we see today was almost certainly first worked before the Norman conquest, and reused over again until it found its present resting place.

Ashlar and carved stonework are used sparingly, for the quoins, windows, sanctuary arch, and the tower drip mouldings and crenallation. It is this sparseness of good stone, only five miles from navigable water, that emphasizes the historical poverty of the parish, and provides the church with its most endearing feature.

Without the resources to purchase good building stone in the fourteenth century, the parish were unable to widen the church by the traditional means of arcades and aisles. The adopted solution was to use octagonal oak posts to support the beam and post roof trusses, and their purlins. These posts, together with their curved purlin braces, survive to support the Baltic Fir of the Victorian roof. The main roof posts have disappeared, and we can only speculate as to whether the chancel roof is a copy of the original, or the result of what the Victorians thought ought to have been.

The nineteenth century roof is interesting in that the simplicity of the roof structure, with the rafters, purlins and close boarding, and the plain collars at high level, give the nave an uncluttered appearance with excellent proportions. Whereas the same design would have sufficed for the chancel, the use of struts and ties almost imitates a barrel roof in appearance.

The tower is in two sections, with the top a later addition, housing a ring of six bells; it has a competitor, for it is mirrored by a tower at the dower house across the road, formerly the rectory. The timber open south porch has similarities to, and may be contemporary with the timber framing of the village pub. Of the interior fittings, there is nothing of substance from times long past; most of the timber work is Victorian, with modest semi-box pews with raised timber floors, and an organ that squeezes into its loft, somewhat out of scale with its surrounds.

St. Mary's is not a rich church, and has never been; it is modest both in its original concept and Victorian restoration, a restoration that has preserved both the feel and the substance of a poor parish of the Middle Ages. There is little that can be said to be great work, either in material or in execution, yet the whole is far greater than the sum of the parts, and the modesty of the building is a great part of the attractiveness. Relative wealth in this century has not spoilt this salt of the countryside.

On the wider canvas, wealth ultimately sorts out the sheep and the goats; poor parishes a long way from the stone and timber wealth of the countryside, no matter how devout, are unable to do anything other than reflect the paucity of their surrounds. Crawley is after all, only five miles from a navigable river that gives access to the stone resources of the south coast, including Purbeck, Portland and the Isle of Wight. Yet those imports amount to only enough to deal with the minimum external and internal quoins and tracery. Kirby Underdale, perhaps a mite smaller than Crawley, hasn't had to scrabble in the fields for flint, has been able to order enough of the best to both build and rebuild to its modest plans, and is palpably richer, in material wealth at least.

When we come to the larger village and town churches, this disparity in wealth, not just for a day, as with Pope Pius II's Pienza, or for a mere hundred years, but on a timescale spanning millennia, produces contrasts that are literally eye opening. One intriguing way of analyzing this past is to set the timelines of contrasting churches alongside, and while the smaller churches of Crawley and Kirkdale are not really important enough to throw up much in the way of insight, Howden and Urchfont are a much better prospect.

Timelines: Howden Minster and Urchfont

Date	Howden	Urchfont
c700	?First church	?First church
c900	—	?Second church
c1100	Second (Norman) church	—
c1230	Third (Early English)	Third church
c1250	Transepts added	—
1270	New choir, roof raised South porch added	—
c1300	—	Enlargement, ?Nave vault
1320	—	Transepts added
1330	—	Chancel vault
1340	Choir completed	South aisle added
c1350	—	Nave rebuilt, first bells installed
c1400	Chapter House. Tower commenced	North aisle added
1430	—	South porch added
c1470	—	Tower section added
c1500	Tower completed Grammar school added	—

Date	Howden	Urchfont
1609	Choir abandoned	—
1630	—	North aisle reroofed
1696	Choir collapses	—
1750	Chapter house roof collapse.	?Gallery installed
1787	—	South transept reroofed
1791	—	South aisle reroofed
1843	South porch becomes vestry	—
1864	—	Gallery removed
1900	—	General restoration
1984	Chapter house reroofed	—

The comparison between the fortunes of two churches down the centuries is one that makes for considerable insight into the way the Church operated, and to a degree, continues to operate today. Howden Minster was built at the whim of the chapter of the Minster. That building programme, and the magnificent edifice thereby generated, reflects both the ability of a six-parish living to throw large volumes of cash at a project, and the way in which that whim was discharged at irregular intervals to add this section or that to the church. The tower alone seems to have occupied them for any great length, probably because they were playing with fire, or, rather, suspect foundations, and knew it.

With the end of the collegiate church, the town quite simply had neither the resources to maintain a building well beyond their needs, nor any sort of tradition of stumping up the cash when something needed doing. Those parts of the Minster that we see today survive because they are well built, much better built than Urchfont, which is what it is for very different reasons.

Urchfont is not a small church. As village churches go it is one of the middle rank and has a worth beyond its measure because of an accident of geology. As a church, the parish must have put almost all its surplus over subsistence into not just the church we now see, but the ones that preceded it. This church has never been left long without work of maintenance or improvement of some sort. Howden effectively went for three hundred years without anything beyond the most basic of maintenance, and not even a great deal of that.

Urchfont has been tended regularly over the whole of its eight hundred year life. It is this long term care, with regular tending of the fabric, that ensures Urchfont's survival, and explains why other similar churches were beyond recall when the restorers of the nineteenth century arrived with the funds, and found that a new building was needed.

The parishioners at Urchfont may never have had the resources to build as they might have liked, and what was achieved, while unique in concept and execution, in strict structural terms teeters the fine line between success and failure. In this latter respect it is not particularly different from a host of others. These two churches are the product of a period of political and religious stability that has been rare in the Christian sphere of influence. The contrast between the times when the people of Urchfont were vaulting the nave or the priests of Howden planning their tower, and events in that broader sphere, is an illustration of the principle that stability is a prerequisite of building in honour of God.

These local timelines compare dramatically with those of the wider Roman Church, where the benefits of a stable and lucrative relationship between church and state, and a country (relatively at least) at peace with itself and neighbours, were not so easily obtained.

Timelines 2: The Church in England, the Church Politico-religious

Date	England	Politico-religious
c300	—	Spread of Christianity in Roman Empire
312	—	Conversion of Emperor Constantine
410	Roman withdrawal, Church withdraws too.	—
450	First major migrations Anglo-Saxons move in.	—
529	—	Benedictines founded at Monte Cassino, Italy.
563	Columba founds the Iona community.	—
597	Pope Gregory I sends St.Augustine to be first Archbishop of Canterbury	—
664	Synod of Whitby ties Church to Rome.	—
790	First Viking raids from Norway	—
900	Edward the Elder unites England	—
c1000	Commutation of Plough Alms, Soul Scot and Church Scot into Tithes.	—
1042	Edward the Confessor confirms Church's pivotal role in state affairs	—

Date	England	Politico-religious
1054	40 Benedictine monasteries now established	Eastern Church leaves Rome.
1066	Last Viking invasion, from France.	—
1070	William I appoints Lafranc as Archbishop of Canterbury, to 'reorganise' the church.	—
c1080	Rise of Patronage (effective ownership of church and Parson by Lord of Manor)	—
1098	Romanesque churches	Cistercians founded to restore 'austerity' to Benedictines. First crusade.
1100	Archbishop Anselm upholds Papal supremacy against English kings.	—
1115	—	Foundation of monastery at Clairvaux starts expansion of Cistercians
1147	—	Second crusade.
c1160	40 monasteries on Durham Cathedral rolls alone.	—
1189	—	Third crusade.
1202	—	Fourth crusade.
1209	Church building programme in full forward gear. First Gothic style (Early English).	Albigensian crusade in SouthernFrance, heralds Papal intolerance of dissent.
1218	—	Fifth crusade
1221	Dominican Friars arrive	—
1224	Franciscan Friars arrive	—

Date	England	Politico-religious
1228	—	Sixth crusade
1233	—	Inquisition founded.
c1240	Carmelites and Augustinian Friars arrive.	—
1248	—	Seventh crusade.
1270	—	Eighth crusade.
1309	Decorated Gothic supercedes Early English style.	Papacy relocates to Avignon.
1320	—	Catharism wiped out by Inquisition (S. France)
1380	Perpendicular Gothic.	—
1517	—	Martin Luther's Theses
1519	—	First reformed church.
1529	—	Diet of Speyer fails to suppress Protestantism.
1534	Henry VIII parts with Rome.	—
1545	End of Gothic church building programme	Council of Trent launches counter reformation.
1549	Act of Uniformity. Book of Common Prayer.	—
1550	—	Counter Reformation under Popes Paul III and IV
1552	Mk II prayer book	—
1559	Mk III prayer book	—
c1560	—	Religious wars on the continent.
1598	—	Edict of Nantes gives Protestants in France religious freedom.

Date	England	Politico-religious
1662	Mk IV prayer book (current version)	—
c1670	Wren's half century of London Churches commences.	—
1685	—	Edict of Nantes revoked Mass migrations due to religious persecution.

The conclusion to be inferred is that until the Conquest, England was in effect no better off than its continental neighbours. Wars, and the migrations that resulted, disrupted trade and agriculture to the extent that long term planning and building were pointless, if not impossible. The Conquest changed all that; Lanfranc's reforms put the Church in the driving seat at a time when feudalism was laying golden eggs. Even better was the ability of the English Crown to externalise its disputes until 1485, fighting virtually all its petty wars on someone else's hallowed turf (mostly French).

Not picking an argument with the Papacy was also a good move, especially after 1200, and the net result of this was a period of five centuries where war or religious conflict (the latter usually being the more bloody of the two), were more or less absent from these shores. The church builders were virtually unimpeded in their task, either by lack of resources, or by violent diversions. The rest of the domain of the Church of Rome had no such good fortune; regular skirmishes between monarchs and the occasional full blown war laying waste to swathes of Europe; over a century to put down a slight schism in southern France; divisions within the Church that led to the excursion to Avignon, and enough crusades to keep the most bloodthirsty Templar happy. Philip the Fair put the Templars out of business in 1312 for being just too aggressive, and for being beyond papal control, but warfare on the Continent seems to have been the rule rather than the exception in the Middle Ages.

The Papacy, however, throve on the back of the Crusades, which caused migrations and a lot of deaths in Europe, more than in the Holy Land. When the eastern sacred places were finally lost to the Saracens, the Vatican could be seen to be holding a fistful of military aces, including a track record of violence that would have drawn admiration from Attilla himself. What it did not do, though, was create a peaceful devout European union of Catholic states, and as a result England is uniquely embellished with churches, because it had the sense to keep the mire of European politics at arm's length. That arm, just as long as the strip of sea that separates this isle from the Continent is wide, has been regarded as being of crucial military importance right up to the present day.

Without that sleeve, English church architecture would certainly be missing much of its heritage, even when we allow for much of the heritage that went missing after the events of the first half of the sixteenth century. Why that heritage went missing is worth a glance or two, for it illustrates the ease with which people can put nil value on the works of their ancestors, especially when wealth can be turned into ready cash.

Consider then the position of Henry VIII in the decade following Martin Luther's defiance, and crucially, the protection Luther's monarch offered to keep Martin out of the hands of the Inquisition. That is exactly what Henry did; consider his position, and he took his time over it because he was only too well aware of the resources the Church could devote to fighting a Holy War (the English Crown had actually contracted a bishop to fight a war on its behalf). The divisions that such a war would generate within the country had the potential, at the least to bring about the fall of the monarchy, and to generate bloodshed on a disastrous scale.

The ability of the Church to continue the building programme, in spite of the decline of the religious houses, was a factor that augured massive wealth, but it was the lack of religious force within both the Church and the country at large, that eventually decided Henry that the risk of incurring, and being removed by, the Pope's wrath, was worth the reward. That reward comprised the lands and wealth of the church, the two being almost synonymous in the mid sixteenth century.

To say that this grab by the state put an end to the Gothic age is superficially true, but if you look at what was happening elsewhere, where the Church's ship of state was being tossed on seas made mountainous, not by the greed of monarchs, but by the wish of ordinary people to be free to worship God as they deemed appropriate. Few people understood the scientific corner the Church painted itself into by asserting Ptolemy over Copernicus, but the refusal to change, even when shown to be wrong and ridiculous, alienated a lot of people. Once such divisions are visible, the drive that is needed to push forward a building programme is the first casualty; if you cannot agree on how to honour your God, the last thing you are going to do is start laying out on bricks and mortar.

Luther's theses, were not just the wedge that split the union of the Church of Rome, but as far as England was concerned, proved to be the casting of the first stone, bringing to an end an era of unprecedented building activity. That this was accelerated and assisted by the state making off with both the goose and most of the saleable golden eggs, is true, though the event smacks a little of opportunism after the die was cast. The root cause of the end of substantive church building activity was not an attack by a greedy monarch on a defenceless church, but Luther's rocking to their foundations the core beliefs thrown up by theologians down the ages, to buttress the founding tenet of 'I believe in God'.

One coincidence, if you can call it that, of the suppression of dissent after 1200 in Europe, and the wars that resulted, is the arrival in England of a veritable procession of religious orders. It may be both callous and unfair to assert that these orders were arriving in England because it seemed to be the only part of the Church's domain where war was not likely to break out. Given the strength of the Church in England at the time, and the sheer numbers and wealth of the monastic houses, the need for a further series of monks and nuns to further the religious fervour of the country, seems dubious. The suspicion is that the soft option of a life in a devout, rich and peaceful land proved an attractive temptation to many in the Middle Ages, who made England their destination as a consequence.

The foundation of monastic life has been redefined many times down the ages, but usually involves some sort of a vow of poverty, and virtually always one of chastity. The difficulty with such a vow is that an individual without a family to support does not have to work very hard to keep body and soul together. Any vows combining poverty and hard work, without the regular giving away of the surplus, would appear difficult, if not impossible to keep. When you look at the great ruined monastic houses of Fountains or Tintern, for example, the buildings represent just a part of the surplus over subsistence generated by the monks. Even by the relaxed work ethics of the thirteenth century, only moderate efforts would need to be made to raise a large building within the monastic system. Modern monastic buildings include significant structures raised practically single handed; wealth generation on a large scale. The parish church however is visibly more demanding of its builders, who had families to raise, the lord of the manor and his retainers to support, and various other demands placed upon them by the feudal system.

We cannot see the goods and chattels that the followers of the monastic life used to fill their buildings, but over the centuries, the parish church, minster and cathedral alike, were given, acquired, or had specially made, a vast range of decorative items, that at times threatened to overwhelm the receiver. While not strictly architectural, these items of furniture and religious bric-a-brac, are often of a unity with their abode, and we can assert their valuable contribution to the Church down the ages, even if the welcome they received has not always been wholehearted.

Chapter Eleven:
Furniture, Fittings and
Decoration

This title succumbed to the temptation to add the words 'and decoration' to furniture and fittings, because so much of church furniture is decorated, and some of the items appear to have little function other than to carry decoration. True decoration demands a section of it's own, and what we are looking at here is the accumulated items that, while not necessarily being in the church are obviously part of it. If that sounds a strange notion, then think about how incomplete a church would be without the gravestones in the churchyard. The first thing to realise about church furnishings is their vulnerability to change and decay; while the fabric of the building comes in for alteration, demolition and rebuilding often enough over the centuries, furniture can literally come and go on a whim overnight.

Craftsmen working on a particular item, be it a stone tomb or a choir stall, will always prefer to work in their own workshop, bringing the finished article to the church for final assembly and finishing off. Removers come in either stealth or violent mode, both sorts have a preference for the hours of darkness, or at least times when they think no one will be around to notice. What we now see in English churches, is what previous generations have decided we should see. This by no means represents either what was there when the church was first complete, or what the church has accumulated by

227

degrees down the ages; clear outs have been regular, either as a result of a philosophical change of opinion, or as an attempt to restore what went before.

The first item to grace any church is always the altar, unless it is Nonconformist and then we can dispense with it instead. Where fixed, the altar has suffered no less from the whims of fashion than has any other item. The original concept of a plain table covered in a white cloth has seen many variations down the ages; pre-reformation altars had to be simple to survive in the age of the Puritan, most appear not to have survived. The 'simple table' beloved of the Puritan is a difficult concept to adhere to, and a slab of 'simple' marble obviously needs a pair of 'simple but elegant' carved and polished blocks to stand on, and the only quarry producing marble at the time when this is needed is of course at Carrarra, and while it will look alright on the floor of the chancel or sanctuary, it would be more appropriate if it were set off by a matching polished marble floor as well.

You can see how people get carried away to excess, and how as little as a generation later along comes a purist who starts off by saying that the altar is not in keeping with the original fabric of the church, it should in fact be a 'simple table', only this time in unpolished granite, and of course it is imperative that the original floor be exposed, only when that happens everyone can see why it was covered in the first place, and half a mountainside of Cornish granite now has to be shipped to replace the marble. And so on.

Altars then have a tough time, and if altars are constantly on the move, especially in the larger churches where there are several possible positions, then the chancel or sanctuary is equally a piece of furniture, leading a slow but merry dance of fashion down the ages. The sanctuary, to give it its original name and to admit of its more desperate function, seems always to have been built with a level difference between it and the nave. That at least is one constant to hold on to.

Equally the only furniture to start with was the altar. Then came the candlesticks, the wall hangings, scenes painted on the walls and ceilings, flags from victorious armies, banners from knights, coats of arms, minor and major statuary; in the smaller churches room had to be found for the choir stalls;

chairs for the clergy, reliquaries and eventually, tombs. A brave archbishop suggested altar rails to keep animals at least out of the sanctuary.

The crowd that dwelt in this space prior to the clearouts of the restorers, particularly of the nineteenth century, were certainly jostling for elbow room.

Likewise, no one has ever been able to agree on is just how high above the nave floor the floor level should be. One step, two, three even? Should we have altar rails? The traditional rail of wrought iron and mahogany is traditional this century past perhaps, but in times long ago the rood screen has had its part to play, and that has frequently been a religious sticking point.

Rood or Chancel Screens

It will come as no surprise to reveal that the reason the same object is in possession of two names is because of its fall from grace and resurrection under an assumed name. The word 'Rood' is a trifle obscure, an old English word for a crucifix and the crucifix in question was hung (and still is in certain churches) from a beam that crossed the axis of the church at or underneath the chancel arch. In the relentless search for something new to lavish resources upon, in the late thirteenth century the idea was hit upon that the area between the floor and the rood beam could be filled in with a screen that would separate the nave and its congregation, from the chancel and the clergy. This screen became a physical representation of the religious apartheid that the Dominicans and the Franciscans were sent out into the world to bridge.

Nonetheless the rood screen became popular, and if those few that remain are anything to go by, lavish is not an improper word to describe them. In its simplest form the screen was not so much a screen as an openwork carving, impairing but not eliminating the view from the nave. In York Minster we see the ultimate in carving; physical representations of all the monarchs of England from the Conquest to Henry VI, amid a veritable riot of embellishment. Not surprisingly, there is no view of the choir beyond, and the screen is deep enough to support the organ pipes and windchest, or part of it. This is quite an appropriate use as the rood gallery, on top of the rood screen where it was large enough to support one, was the venue for choirs, accessed via a small, usually spiral, stair.

Come the Reformation, rood screens had an understandably bad press, and the new Established Church of England, even if it could agree on little else, agreed that rood screens were a bad thing, and would have to go, but, if you were very fond of the one in your church, it was permissible to call it a choir or chancel screen and retain it. A few churches duly acquired choir screens to replace their old rood screens, but the general consensus was that the clergy were adept at hiding from the congregation, and didn't need a screen to help them do it.

Choir Stalls

Choir stalls are one of the glories of the wood carver, and are discussed in the music section, along with their misericords. No one seems to have taken particular exception to their presence in either the choir or the sanctuary/chancel, and as a result we have examples that cover the mediaeval period as well as the seventeenth, eighteenth and nineteenth centuries, with the older ones likely to incorporate work from later periods. The Thorntons' eighteenth century contribution to the sixty eight seater at Beverley Minster, for example, is the norm, not the exception. Even oak suffers wear and tear and accidental damage, and not all damage is accidental. The Victorian restorers had a penchant for pine alongside oak, and while there is good work in pine, it is still not to be compared to the real thing. As with all things where there was only a limited requirement for structural competence, choir stalls became an art work, with their original functional purpose disguised, if not lost, in the detail.

Pulpits

The pulpit is an attempt to resolve a conundrum that plagued the Church throughout history, a conundrum only solved by twentieth century technology; how, in a space as complex as the larger parish church, minster or cathedral, can speakers make themselves heard by all who wish to hear. Hogarth's famous painting of a congregation asleep during the sermon is not just a reflection of excessive length or lack of interest or poor delivery, but a very real illustration of the fact that, what with echoes and unplanned reverberations, the last place you would expect to get up on your hind legs and spout, and expect to be heard, is the inside of a large, crowded church. The lengths that the Church went to, just to make its clergy heard by the captive audience, is a reflection of the poor acoustic properties of the internal space of the Gothic Church.

The Classical and Nonconformist churches in comparison appear to have had a little insight into the problem, and the simpler spaces with the audience stacked in galleries to be as close to the speaker as possible, made for much better listening.

The pulpit started life as the lectern, a simple, later much more ornate, bookstand on which the bible can rest (most of the older bibles had much larger print than normal to enable the speaker to read from the text without burying their nose in the book, and as a consequence were far too heavy to hold for an extended period). Delivery of the sermon was carried out standing up because it was necessary for the lungs to deliver full voice all of the time, and that cannot be achieved while sitting down (Opera is just the same, for exactly this reason).

The lectern was not entirely satisfactory in use, because the step or steps up into the chancel meant that the sermon was either delivered from behind the arch, which impeded the sound broadcast to the nave and aisles, or from the floor of the nave, where the speaker was much less visible. Re-jigging the step to provide an area in front of the chancel arch for the lectern was the first small step to providing a pulpit, for a fixed, raised area gave demonstrably better sound broadcast, especially as there was either a wall or a pier behind the speaker to bounce the voice into the nave.

Thus fixed, the parson's sermon delivery was ready for a little more elevation, a modest and well proportioned enclosure, with a small spiral stair, carved balustrading, bookstand, nothing too elaborate. Oh, and a sounding board, and a seat for the clerk, a little lighting perhaps, and some simple carved stonework for the base. We have been down this road before, and will again, without shadow of doubt.

Pews

In the phrase 'the weak to the wall', we have the measure of the pew in mediaeval times; there were none, only a stone ledge around the perimeter of the nave where those who were too weak to stand through the service could take their ease. As the village or town church was the only large covered space, in which were performed all manner of, for want of a better word, 'plays', the fact that there was no great amount of furniture, either fixed or loose, was a great advantage. Furniture was not in over supply in the Middle Ages generally, and while we are not content until our houses are stuffed to the point where navigation is difficult, the average hovel in the thirteenth century had little to be upset by the comings and goings of the menagerie that regarded it as home. So too the church, downwind of the chancel step at least.

By the start of the seventeenth century changes were in the air; well-to-do townsfolk could, and did, afford to furnish their homes in some style, and were accustomed to sit down for a significant part of the day. Standing through a church service became a chore. With increasing divisions in the distribution of wealth came also personal hygiene; the rich started to wash regularly, if not their clothes then their bodies at least.

Fraternising with one's less well-off neighbours at too close a range became undesirable. The advent of the pew came just at the right time to save the rich from the poor, the rich's knees from the floor, and their noses from the odour. To the church it meant pew rents in a time when church lands were being disposed of and livings were shrinking. The effect of the pew, which to start with was anything but the ordered rows of identical seats we see today, was to cut the capacity of the church at a time when it was being cut in other ways as well. As pew rents covered not so much the pew itself but the space it occupied, the design and installation of the pews themselves was left, it would seem, very much to the owner.

The results were generally reasonable, but as with all things human, there just had to be a lunatic fringe, those with more money and power than sense or faith, and these few have left a small but wonderful legacy of how not to do things.

Sadly the restorers of the nineteenth century had a field day on giving short shrift to the wilder excesses of the pew builders, and we are left to picture only with the mind's eye the wealthy churchgoer of the early eighteenth century, sitting in his family pew complete with easy chairs, warming their hands and feet at a cast iron stove, tended and fuelled by a family servant, with the flue pipe discharging its wood smoke (they might just have had the decency to burn charcoal) into the nave for the benefit of the rest of the congregation. We do not have to picture the scene at Croft, near Darlington, where there still stands the pew that needs a staircase to access it, for all the world like a competing pulpit, only larger and more elevated.

By the middle of the eighteenth century the box pew had found favour; it was, and still is (at Tetbury for example) a restrained and effective way of fitting a large number of people into a church while not permitting too much in the way of undesirable social interaction, keeping the parishioners well divided. Seated in such a box pew, the average person of two hundred and fifty years ago would have seen little of the people in front; many women would have been invisible except to those in the same pew. The parson would have been invisible except when in the pulpit, and the whole congregation disappears when kneeling to pray.

The box pew was in fact the precursor of the modern pew, with the seat back raised to eye level, or further, and incorporating a hinged kneeler and a prayer book shelf, set at a constant seat pitch so that the pew can be closed by means of doors at the ends. All the Victorians had to do was lower the seat back, remove the doors, and add the heating pipes to produce the arrangement we see today.

Galleries

Galleries emerged, took their short flight of fancy, and in the Church of England at least, departed to a well deserved oblivion in the space of a couple of hundred years. One that is left is worth a visit just to remind us how crowded churches became when a serious effort was made to cram in as much furniture as possible. When objects, 'd'art' and otherwise, brought in rents to a church that was not as rich as it would like to be, the naturally avaricious do not generally worry overmuch as to the aesthetics. So an excursion to St. Mary's, on the East Cliff at Whitby, is essential to appreciate what the restorers were bent on removing, and the fact that this one survived is a reasonable indication that it was by no means the most excessive, probably the opposite.

The emergence of the gallery, so easily fitted into a new neo-classical style church, and offering a new dimension to the auditorium that is the nave, is not to be wondered at; the transfer from the theatre, where this stacking of the punters round the stage was essential to enable the dialogue to be heard, is merely a little lateral thinking, exactly what you would expect from the emergent breed of the architect.

Where things began to go astray was in the Gothic church, where the whole space is generated from the proportion and line of the structure. To carve up the view, the generation of which had occupied thirty generations of clerics and master masons, was to invite an aesthetic disaster, which was duly delivered. The gallery was hung, drawn and quartered before it had a chance to appear in the dock. That it managed to survive for a couple of centuries is surprising, until you take a look at what was happening at ground level, and below.

Tombs

The further in, the more you pay, runs one churchyard ditty, and down the centuries those few whose last resting place was inside the church door, were on the whole not entitled to relief under the Elizabethan Poor Law. The practice of burial inside the church is an ancient one, a privilege to be bought by great deeds or misdeeds, or great wealth. A tradition, from the twelfth century onwards was that the living of the parish was in the gift of the lord of the manor, and many of these minor gentry, and some not so minor, saw it as their right to be interred in the church, often in a family tomb built for that purpose. The tombs that were fashionable in the Middle Ages are familiar to all; graven effigies on raised tombs (the soft stone, alabaster, along with the local 'marbles', were favoured materials), there being many survivors that the restorers could not tear away.

Also from the Middle Ages, and quite unlike anything else, is the Percy Tomb in Beverley Minster; it no longer has a tomb, but the carved canopy that is its great glory has no equal in England. These survivors are the residue of what was swept away during the Reformation and the century of neglect after, before the fabric of the Church began to attract Mr. Wyatt and his contemporaries' attention. Wren famously stood on an old grave slab when surveying St. Paul's (the 'Resurgam' incident); this ditching of the memorials of past generations is a regular event, always attracting publicity, usually adverse.

The Church in the seventeenth century saw the sale of burial spaces inside churches as a great money-spinner. Those churches with crypts could sell burial space and a memorial in the church above. As a result the favoured plots in the nave were soon taken, and the flat slabs that bear witness to this are still with us today. The eighteenth century saw a craving for tombs of the larger size, and a preference for marble monuments that were anything but modest. Aisles, side chapels and even the main operational and circulation spaces of churches began to fill with these carved lumps of Carrarra Marble, Cornish, Aberdonian and Shap Granite, and other exotic stones from all over the world. Hence the need for galleries.

Decoration

If this topic is not where everyone expects to find it, in the section on the development of church architecture, this is because, in spite of the tendency to consider decoration as architecture, decoration is just that, decoration, and architecture is architecture, whether it is decorated or not. To put it at its simplest, a pier is part of the architecture because it has function (it helps hold up the building), and form (its proportions are, or should be, worked out to be pleasing to the eye). The lintel that rests on top of the piers is also architecture, because it too has function and form. Both may be decorated with fluting or friezes, which may add to their beauty, but the whole would still qualify as architecture without the decoration.

Let us therefore consider decoration on its own merits, as detail to the greater canvas of architecture.

Decoration falls into three categories; as an integral part of the manipulation of the proportions, or as a solution to a particular problem, e.g. window tracery; as an applied decoration to the fabric of the building, giving grace and beauty without any greater architectural context; and as freestanding items such as memorials, choir stalls or crucifixes, which are part of the fixtures and fittings.

As with all things, the sum of the whole is greater than that of the individual parts, which is why mature buildings feel more complete than their younger counterparts, and buildings without their fittings are bleak places indeed. To a degree, decoration and fittings are a reflection of the care and attention lavished upon a building, especially where there is a long and continuous chronological sequence.

Taking decoration as an integral part of the building as our first stop, remembering that until the Romanesque gained sway over the Celtic, decoration is minimal, and as a way of altering the proportions, mostly absent. With the Romanesque came the thick walls and the massive nave piers that look out of proportion, and with this massivity came the need to do something to scale it down. As far as the nave piers went, the attempt still with us today is the zig-zag patterns that are a feature of Waltham Abbey, for example; as a slimming aid it has little to recommend it. The thick walls were a different matter, and the method of working doorways with decorated conical arches was a complete success, many surviving to this day as unequalled examples of decoration not determining form, but disguising the construction method that generated it.

The classic conical door arch of the Romanesque (Kilpeck is a particularly fine and famous example), when built with a tympanum, needs no centering. The first ring of masonry can be placed on top of the curved head of the tympanum, and successive rings cantilevered or corbelled over until the full wall thickness was achieved. The decoration serves to unify each ring into a single carved whole.

With Romanesque work these examples of decoration are evidence of considerable ability, but while the decorated conical arch was useful and of great beauty, it was marginal to the building as a whole. This is unsurprising, when it is realised that what we are looking at is the first serious attempt to weave complex decorated stonework into the fabric of a church. With the first of the gothic styles, Early English, decoration is well to the fore and increasingly mature, but as yet not completely dominant. Clearly, from the middle of the twelfth century on, the clerk and mason were sufficiently confident of their abilities to address the questions of proportion in the Gothic church by integrating the decoration into the structural fabric, or where the decoration could not be so integrated, making it look as if it was.

The need to glaze the new style of window with many square feet of glass that could only be made in panes a few inches wide, meant that stone tracery, particularly mullions, were needed. As supports for the lead framed glass, these could have been simple vertical dividers, a form eventually reached, but not at all simple. A much better effect is obtained by giving the mullions curved heads to replicate the curves of the window head proper, and allowing room for a trefoil or quatrefoil motif in stone as well. By adding decoration, the length and thus the slenderness ratio of the mullion is reduced, resulting in a more robust design than if the window were plain. Decoration of this kind helped solve some of the issues of scale that began to arise as the Gothic system began to explore the limits of the materials, particularly the limits of stone used in small sections.

If the challenge posed by the scale of the larger windows needed in the Gothic was addressed in part by the subtle use of applied decoration, then decoration came into its own to slim down the massive piers necessary to carry roofs, particularly vaulted ones. The first piers that supported the arcades of the Romanesque naves were disproportionate to the spaces they helped enclose. Massive piers, up to ten times the diameter of their classical counterparts were deemed to be needed where a vault was intended.

This was in essence caution, for there was no comprehension of the loads these piers had to support, and the mason reacted accordingly by putting into the piers almost as much masonry as in the wall that would have replaced them. Some brave soul decided that where a vault was not to be supported, this amount of masonry was not necessary, and the Early English pier was slimmed down to a single drum of stone. By judicious use of a base to spread the load of these slim piers, and foundations beneath the base, loads could be supported with confidence. With the vault though it was a different matter, the mason was experimenting in the unknown, and quite simply dare not reduce the pier to a modest dimension. Here decoration came to the mason's aid in the quest for true proportion and line.

While a circular drum of stone as thick as the wall it supported, could perform the task of holding up the roof quite adequately, by the time space had been allocated to a base the columns slenderness is more properly termed stoutness. Worse was to follow when it was realised that more light, from a clerestory, was needed, and that the nave proportions need must include three horizontal divisions in the shape of arcade, triforium and clerestory. The slenderness of a huge drum could not be trimmed up by making the pier the full height of the nave; such an arrangement would have destroyed the springing of the nave arcade, and made the building far too top heavy for its own good.

The solution was as sophisticated and delicate as it was massive; disguise the true proportions of the piers by adding shafts to the exterior, whose slim lines could carry just as far as was required; to the arch spring; to the spring of the triforium arcade, or right through to the clerestory. So while the piers were slimmed down to the point where they were adequate but no more, their perceived proportions became positively sylph-like.

On its own, the use of shafts achieving this would have been justification enough, but having a group of shafts on each pier meant that each shaft could be terminated at the point that gave the most desirable effect, and as shafts and arch ribbing intersected, great skill, in the interplay of line through the arch haunch and pier top, could be displayed by the mason. This effective manipulation of the proportions of internal space is all down to the use of decoration; the Gothic has it, and uses decoration in a way not constrained by the order of the past, but to refine the proportions of arch, vault and wall as never before.

As with the pier, so with the roof, the vaulted roof at least. The Romanesque had failed to provide a solution to the covering of the nave with a stone vault; the barrel or quadripartite form was just too heavy, and the pointed arch as first developed addressed this structural problem with complete success. The reaction to this mastery of the vault led quickly to the application of decoration in the shape of delicate ribbing and intricately worked keystone bosses. The end result however was something completely different; the fan vault.

At Urchfont we can still see the remains of an attempt, sufficiently long lived to be credited a partial success, to apply solid stone, as distinct from rib and infill, to a church roof. The conclusion is that Urchfont's clerks and masons were not alone, and that there were many attempts to work up a roof in solid stone, and it was a long time before the fan vault provided the solution. The reason why all this effort was made is a little less obvious, but it is fairly clear that the motivation was to create a fully decorated roof of solid stone that outshone all predecessors, including that pestilential pagan edifice, the Pantheon.

The fan vault realises the ambition to integrate structure and decoration, because someone realised you can achieve the same effect as a rib, merely by obeying the rule of thrust at the joints in the stone. If the plane of the joints between adjacent stones is perpendicular to the line of thrust along the lines of the notional ribs, then no matter what the shape of the rest of the stone, or how it interlocks with its other neighbours, the 'ribs' in the solid vault will transfer the thrust of the vault to the piers. The result is a soffit of a vault that is curved in such way as to reflect the structural nature of the work, but will take the imagination into another dimension when carved to reflect the stresses in the stone as if it were some sort of petrified tree. Heaven only knows how many failures came before success.

This persistence to produce a canvas for the carver, a canvas whose decoration reflects the deeds of the stone, is one of the great wonders of the Gothic; the deliberate, and ultimately successful attempt to outdo all previous vaults in terms of skill and imagination. Without the decoration the work is apparently mundane, hiding its structural brilliance from

239

the viewer. With the decoration, the work is masterful, a total symbiosis of decoration with structure.

Decoration Appliqué

With the development of the fan vault, the line between decoration to manipulate the proportions of the building, and surface decoration is blurring, but at the dawn of the Romanesque surface decoration is found on piers to nave arcades and window mullions; and doorways aside, on not a great deal else. Romanesque is still recognizably classical in it's use of cushion capitals and circular section piers. The step from modesty to just a teeny bit over the top, is one of confidence and wealth, and it commences in earnest with the first of the true Gothic styles.

Early English in essence is a cautious style, for the mason had much more on his mind than mere flights of fancy, needing all his skill to pull the fabric into shape. That hurdle overcome, there were seemingly endless surfaces and designs just waiting to be carved; dog tooth, billet mould, label stop, intrados, ballflower, blind arcade, finial, hood mould, beakhead, cable mould, annulet, extrados, diaper, poppy head, tympanum, organ case, and coffering, are just some of the places and motifs that bedeck the church fabric. Eventually we arrive at that excuse for exuberance, the misericord, which is functional in that it achieves a purpose (saving the legs of the choir) but would it have existed if the excuse of decoration had not been readily available?

The reason for this outpouring of skill in surface decoration, and we must bear in mind that what we can see is only what subsequent generations have deemed fit, and that the hand of time has failed to erase, is not too hard to find. In spite of all the politicking that went on in the upper echelons of the church, and all the wealth that was squandered on high living; the parish church in particular, whatever the realities of power, belonged to the people of the parish, no less to the serf than to the lord of the manor. The church was their meeting place, their place of worship, the location for all their rites of passage, their final resting place.

This commonality of purpose in all the parishioners, bridging the inequalities of the feudal system, and the sheer permanence of the building, that led all to look on the church as theirs, and to lavish care and attention upon the fabric generation after generation. Without this, the fate of the parish church would have been the same as that of the monasteries; erasure from the face of the earth. Decoration suffered badly at the hands of the reformers, with much destruction of the 'false images' so reviled by Thomas Cromwell, but it was the third decoration medium, decoration in the shape of paintings and statuary, and painted statuary, that came in for iconoclasm in a big way.

Art For Art's Sake

The ability to build a new church or extend an existing one is not in the hands of your average mortal; that power rests with but a few. The desire to give something in honour of your God, or in remembrance of times and people past, is however universal, and for those who, for reasons of wealth, could not run to a building, or part of one, then the commissioning of some work of art, or the execution of such a work, was the next best thing. That we can still elbow our way into the churchyard after over a thousand years of giving, without having to climb over praying knights stacked ten deep in the twenty-fifth lych gate from the fourth west door, is not a reflection of the parsimony of the parishioner, but down to the fact that clearouts have been regular, if painful, events, and that time wears heavy, even on the inside of a church.

The list of 'decorative' items that seek a home inside or outside a church is a long one; tombs, gravestones, memorial slabs and brasses; statues of angels, saints, knights and kings; banners and trophies of war; reliquaries, crucifixes, religious tableaux, altars and side chapels devoted to everything from God, through Our Lady and a multitude of saints, to war. For the most gruesome use for a chapel you needs must visit the Tower of London, where there is a chapel devoted to the disposal of the remains of all those people with whom the kings and queens of England violently disagreed. There are iron, wood and stone screens; silverware, vestments, curtains and wall hangings, hassocks and cassocks, chandeliers and candlesticks, chairs, benches and pews. Time and a little careful manipulation could transform this to rhyme, but the reader can appreciate that without the occasional good clear out, churches would be warehouses, stuffed full of much treasure of dubious value.

To those who have gazed at the west front of Wells Cathedral, the rood screen at York, or their favourite reredos, inside or out, carved wood and stone statues will perhaps seem a favoured form of decoration. Overall this is less axiomatic; statues are expensive, can only be carved from certain stones for the larger pieces (wood statues are small because wood tends to split as it seasons, and large wood sections take up to a decade to season and are then hard to carve), and the difficulties in transporting large stones around is something only the ancient Egyptians solved, prior to the Industrial Revolution. Many churches do not have a single stone statue, unless it is an angel on a nineteenth century plinth in the churchyard. Others will have one, the richer churches a handful, with only the privileged few a plethora. It is not that unusual to find statues made of plaster of Paris, and no matter how devoted the commissioner, or dedicated the carver, as works of art most statues fall short of brilliance. It is in the representation of the everyday aspects of country life, frequently as bas relief, and often as sub-plots or bordering or infill to a larger work with a religious theme, that the church carver has set his stall for the generations to admire.

If the average stone or wood carver was no Michealangelo or Grinling Gibbons, the level of skill displayed is still high, high enough to give power to their imagery, particularly in the representation of life around them. In everyday images life is caught; the cupids with faces of endless perfection and innocence (child-like because the chance of reaching adulthood unscarred by life was slim); images of local people, worthy or otherwise; stylised plants like convolvulous, vine or poppy; foxes, rabbits, geese and mice. With these are older churches crowded, and they are well done because people put their lives into them, literally and metaphorically.

What we can no longer see are the paintings on the walls; not only did they go out of fashion, but in a climate of neglect, the first thing to degenerate is the paint on the wall, and we can only speculate that what was there was not that far removed from what can be seen today in other parts of Europe. Today's artwork is more often seen in textiles; tapestry, embroidery and similar needlecraft, handmade by parishioners, replacing worn work or adding to the church's store. This is why the church survives; people *care*.

Segmental pointed arch - Endless variety

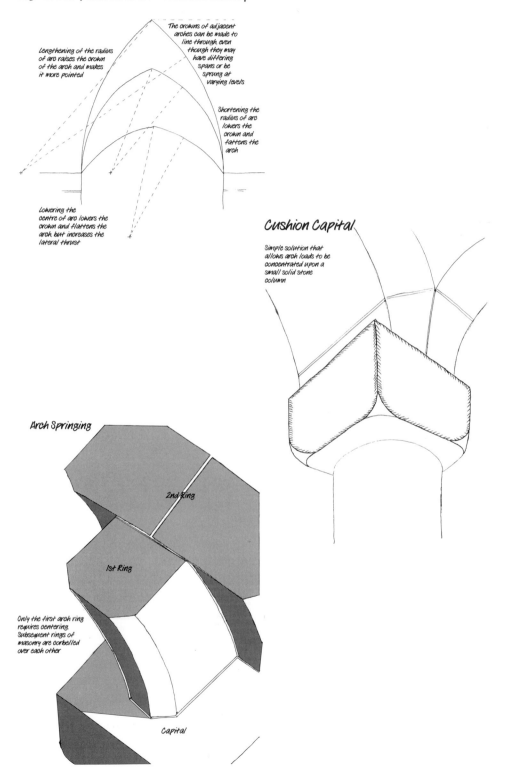

Lengthening of the radius of arc raises the crown of the arch and makes it more pointed

The crowns of adjacent arches can be made to line through, even though they may have differing spans or be sprung at varying levels

Shortening the radius of arc lowers the crown and flattens the arch

Lowering the centre of arc lowers the crown and flattens the arch, but increases the lateral thrust

Cushion Capital

Simple solution that allows arch loads to be concentrated upon a small solid stone column

Arch Springing

2nd Ring

1st Ring

Only the first arch ring requires centering. Subsequent rings of masonry are corbelled over each other

Capital

244

Chapter Twelve:
Explaining the Obscure

In any tale there are threads that escape the weave, words and phrases that do not slip off the tongue without the brain waving a flag and saying 'now, what *is* that?' Rounding up these escapees and stitching them into the fabric is the job that makes the tapestry complete, and assists a greater understanding. This chapter is devoted to those evaders of the text, and to the words and phrases that have been used a little freely without an explanation.

Aisle

Side section of a Gothic church, parallel to the nave and generally narrower and with a lower ceiling. Separated from the nave by the nave arcades. Aisles were the gothic solution to the problem of not being able to span spaces much wider than about forty feet (the size of the largest timber commonly available), allowing churches to be double or more this width. Aisled churches were first built without a nave clerestory, but the spaces were dark due to the limited light that could enter through the windows in the aisle walls.

Ambulatory

Narrow passage or corridor running parallel to the nave of a church. Frequently of no practical use other than to create the appearance, from the outside, of a traditional aisled church, though used in certain circumstances to allow the clergy to process down the nave from a sacristy adjacent to the chancel.

Ancaster Stone

Oolitic limestone from the Lincolnshire Limestone series, fine grained, cream in colour, and having extensive local usage. Quarried at Ancaster, South Lincolnshire, six miles north east of Grantham, close to the Roman Road, Ermine Street, and the site of the Roman town Cavsennae. A coarser stone from the same beds is known as Ancaster Rag.

Apse

End of the nave or chancel where the arcade, instead of being terminated, is turned through a half circle and buttressed. This avoids having a large amount of masonry at the end of the arcade to resist the thrust of the end arch. Instead the lateral thrust is taken by buttresses, occasionally flying ones, and the arcade is continuous from one side of the church to the other.

Arcade

Series of arches supported by piers, each pier supporting the springing of two adjacent arches. The lateral thrust of the arches balance each other except for the two outer arches, where there is always massive masonry to accept the lateral loads, unless the arches are tied. An arcade built semi-engaged to a wall is known as a blind arcade.

Architecture

The art of building design, or the result of that art. The word is a lot older than the people who take their professional name from the root word, having its origins in the classical world of the ancient Greeks and Romans.

Arch

The arch is the foundation of the Gothic style, just as the trilithon is the Classical. The arch was developed in the semi-circular style during the Roman period when it was extensively used in building and civil engineering, and also in the rotated form as the dome. The Gothic represents a phase of rapid development of the arch into a number of styles, including segmental, pointed, semi-elliptical, flat.

The arch comprises a series of shaped stones - voussoirs - that lock together by virtue of their shape, when supporting their own weight and imposed loads. Arches rely on friction between the adjacent voussoirs, and the plane of thrust of the load passing perpendicular to the plane of the voussoir's face, or nearly so. Increasing the imposed loads improves the stability of the arch so long as the line of thrust remains near to the ideal relationship. Unequal loads, particularly upon the haunches, leads to failure by the centre of the arch being forced upwards.

Arches are constructed on centering, a shaped wooden or metal frame that forms the arch profile and incorporates wedges to allow for removal once the arch is completed. The wedges are essential as they allow the arch to be struck without having to destroy the centering, which is loadbearing while in position, and can be reused several times.

Most arches in architecture, with the exception of those in flying buttresses, support only modest loads due to the phenomenon of interdependency, which enables masonry to cantilever over quite large openings, leaving the arch to support its self weight and a small amount of masonry close to the voussoirs. Loads from roots, vaults and towers/spires are usually taken directly onto piers, avoiding the large lateral thrusts that locating loads onto arches generates.

Semi-circular arches are used in Romanesque work, and have a constant span/rise relationship of 2:1. This inflexibility led directly to the development of the Gothic style.

Segmental arches form an arch with a segment of a circle, always less than 180 degrees (OK, somewhere there is a segmental arch of more than half a circle, but not in general use). Segmental arches are typically found in flying buttresses and may be as little as thirty or forty degrees of arc. The large lateral thrusts generated by the large span/rise relationship, often 3:1 or more, makes this arch form unsuitable for architectural work.

Pointed arches are the Gothic form, and started out as two segments of arc leaning against each other. This is the most common form. The purpose of the Gothic arch is not to bear large loads, a purpose for which it is quite unsuited, but to provide continuity between the piers that take the structural loads, or in the vault to transmit the roof loads, which are comparatively modest, to the wall piers.

The strength of the arch in this form is the variability of the span/rise relationship, allowing arches to cross a space at various angles from the same springing and rise at different rates to the same ridge line. This flexibility allows the construction of quadripartite and sexpartite vaults. The span/rise can be as little as 1:3 or less, a factor that gives the 'architect' control over the proportions of the spaces generated by the use of piers and arches.

Later pointed arches are to be found with a flattened form, almost semi-elliptical, to span wider openings in accordance with later styling. This form is no more efficient at carrying loads than the narrow pointed variety, and tends to be restricted to window and door openings, where the lateral thrust generated by the masonry above can be absorbed by the adjacent stonework.

Flat arches are not a contradiction in terms, but a skillful manipulation of the relationship between the load, always modest like the opening span, and the angle of thrust through the inclined faces of the voussoirs. The effect is more a visual feature than a true arch, and is to be found in neo classical work, where like as not the 'arch' will be backed by a timber lintel.

Ashlar

Smooth-faced stonework of the very best kind, where the stone is squared and given a smooth face by sawing, splitting and tooling, with the final finish being rubbed smooth after the stone is laid. Only relatively soft stone is amenable to this intense working, the most common being the Bath and Portland Oolitic Limestones, the Magnesian Limestone of north-east England, the Permian and Triassic Sandstones of the midlands, and the exported Sandstones from Scotland.

Back Gutter, Box gutter

The back gutter is a universal necessity to a parapet wall, sitting in the gap between the end of the roof and the back of the parapet, and originally discharging through carved stone spouts better known as gargoyles. Most gutters now discharge into cast iron pipes of nineteenth century origin, with ornate castings. Some early lead arrangements survive also, the back gutters being in lead on timber boards.

Ballflower

Decorated stone carving, often a dripstop, label stop or keystone to a rib, where the leaf or flower motif is stylised and the surrounding stone is undercut to the extent that the work appears to be hollow, with the foliage enclosing a space within the carving.

Balustrade

Stone, metal or timber railing defining the edge of a stair, balcony or pavement, comprising vertical plain or carved balusters, joined at the top to a handrail or coping.

Barley Twist

Wood decoration where the circular shaft of a chair leg or similar object is carved to present as a tight spiral or helix. The work is executed on a lathe, but only as a working frame, until the nineteenth century, when carving was mechanised by use of a clamped tool and leadscrew.

Batten

Thin wood strip used for hanging tiles or slates, or for lining a wall or ceiling to take a lath and plaster or plasterboard finish.

Batter

The inclination or rake of a wall or buttress that is not vertical, but leans towards the load, usually described as 'batter 1 in 15', meaning that the wall slopes inward one unit for every fifteen vertically.

Beam

Loadbearing, usually horizontal, member in which the top face is in compression, and the bottom in tension. The first beams were timber logs or poles used in the round, then squared, a form that persisted until the end of the sixteenth century, when rectangular sections came into use, driven by material scarcity. Cast and wrought iron beams were developed in the eighteenth and nineteenth centuries, along with iron reinforced 'flitched' timber beams (there is one of these behind the classical facade at St. Francis Xavier, Hereford). Iron and steel I or T sections, reinforced concrete, plywood, and a host of other modern beams are to be found today. Stone beams or lintels' capacity to bear tensile loads on the bottom face is very low, and will crack under self weight, even when used in only short spans.

Beams fail in three ways: tension, compression, and shear, their load capacity being a function of the strength of the material to resist these forces, the span of the beam, its depth, width, and the load being borne. Span/depth ratios determine a beam's proportions, and empirical formulae based upon these ratios are still enshrined in English building law.

Bearing

That portion of a lintel that is supported by the quoin, pier or column. Bearings tend to be equal in length to the depth of the lintel, a proportion that is both aesthetically pleasing and allows for movement in the wall, without risk that the opening will ultimately prove to be wider than the lintel that bridges it is long, resulting in a partial or total collapse.

Bed, Bedding Plane

Sloping or horizontal junction between layers of sedimentary rock, originally laid down in chronological order (lowest first), typified by a crack a few millimetres wide along which the rock will cleave. The vertical distance between the bedding planes defines the use to which the stone can be put. Thin bedded rocks, say up to three inches (75mm) thick are used as walling where there is nothing better available, but their prime use is as flags or tilestones. Stone up to about a foot (300mm) thick, especially if it has well defined joints that make winning easy, are known as building freestones.

Thicker bedded stone, such as Bath or Portland, has to be sawn or split into handleable dimension stone, stone produced in a set number of standard sizes, nine or twelve inches thick being common. Stone is used with the bed perpendicular to the load, so most stone is laid 'on bed', that is with the bed horizontal. With some homogenous stones the bed is not obvious, and must be marked in the quarry. Nonetheless wrongly bedded stone is not uncommon, and stone thus laid has a short life. Purbeck Marble is almost always laid 'edge bedded', due to the thin strata that yield this stone. As a result this marble is only used for interior work, usually decorative shafts that could not be produced as a single piece otherwise.

Beer Stone

Cream-grey stone taken from the Chalk at Beer on the East Devon Coast, seen to best effect at Axminster and Exeter Cathedral.

Belly

The tendency of a badly built or overloaded wall to push outward under load, or as a result of water penetration. Usually due to the failure of the wall core.

Benedictines

The original Christian religious order, founded in 529 at Monte Christo, spreading with Christianity to the whole of England by the time of the Conquest, and thus one of the chief beneficiaries of the Norman Settlement. Subsequent reform (Cistercians, etc.) did little in the long term to reform the orders considerable wealth (wealth in the Middle Ages was defined by land, and the monasteries had plenty); monks found it quite difficult to be poor. The order is still one of the largest in England, having returned with Catholic emancipation.

Bishopric

The basic unit of administration within the Church of England, the bishop's diocese being the group of parishes over which the bishop has authority. Each bishop has as his home a palace (some are literally that) and a cathedral as his spiritual home. The bishop is assisted in his work by the chapter, the priests responsible for the day to day running of the diocese, and bishops have had a seat in the House of Lords (the lords spiritual) since the Middle Ages. Appointment of bishops is still a political event, owing to the monarch being head of the Church, and the monarch in turn being advised by the government of the day.

Blind Arcade

Wall where the stonework is carved proud in the form of an arcade, and the wall face recessed, The arcade columns and arches are effectively semi-engaged with the wall, but the wall is the structural element, the arcade the decoration.

Bracket

Projecting stone, wood or metal support to a corbel or balcony.

Brunelleschi

Italian goldsmith-turned-architect who is generally credited with cracking the conundrum of the large dome built without centering. The dome of Florence Cathedral, completed between 1420 and 1436, is in fact not hemispherical, but at 140 feet in diameter is larger than any centering could then support. Rumour suggests that he worked it out in Rome by studying the remains of the buildings of the Roman Empire.

No dome survives on English Gothic, but Wren used a very similar construction form at St. Paul's, London, two hundred and fifty years later, adding a third shell to make the outer and inner forms look proportionally correct. Brunelleschi's dome, which still stands, has only the two shells, the outer curving upward from an octagon base.

Bullnose

Half round moulding applied to the edge of a cill or step to protect building users from injury, and the stone or timber from rapid erosion or impact damage. Can also be used to describe a rounded arrise to a quoin.

Buttresses

Body of stonework built at right angles to a wall, or continuing in the same plane beyond a quoin, and normally not as high as the wall it abuts, but stepping inwards with massive capstones to the plane of the wall. Buttresses can be ornamental, or can be for the purpose of resisting thrusts at right angles to the wall. Most buttresses are integral with the wall, but where movement has occurred a buttress can be built leaning on the wall, with the masonry courses sloping towards the building.

Campanile

Freestanding bell tower now very rare in England. A sensible compromise to avoid overloading existing towers with a bell frame and a ring of bells, or where the tower had been built without the necessary access. Essential accessory for the church that already has everything.

Canon

Senior priest responsible for an important parish, or a number of parishes; frequently the prime mover in new building work.

Canopy

Stone or timber cover to an altar, tomb, statue or other piece of decorative work; usually nonstructural and frequently highly decorated in itself. The canopy may present as a cantilever, be supported on columns, or suspended on a chain or chains.

Cantilever

Projecting beam, or series of beams, e.g. a corbel, having one fixed end and one free end. The compression and tension faces of a conventional beam are inverted, with the lower face being in compression and the upper, tension. Cantilevers are extensively used in string courses and classical pediments, where the tensile element is often iron or brass bars bedded in the upper face and secured to the main body of the wall.

Capstone

Top stone on a pier or buttress, usually large, often worked up to form a finial. The stone performs the same duty as a coping.

Carstone

Ironstone cemented sandstone, found as 'nails' in mortar beds, and as a stone in its own right in North Norfolk, and used in areas where other, more durable or tractable stone is absent.

Casting

Production of objects by pouring moulds with metal or concrete. Sheet lead was originally cast on a sand bed, into which decorations could be pressed, to be reproduced on the lead face. More recent castings are reproduction stonework, balusters and copings, distinguished from their natural stone counterparts by a softness of line to arrises, etc, and often a break line along the two halves of the mould. Other cast items include bronzes, especially statuary (there are bronze doors in existence) and from about 1550, iron, especially door scrapers, railing finials, and floor grilles.

Cat Slide

Roof form generated by the use of two different roof pitch angles on the same roof, the steeper pitch above the shallower. Common on aisled churches where the nave and aisle roofs are run together without a clerestory between.

Cement

Mixture of crushed chalk and clay, fired in a kiln to a hard clinker and ground to a powder. Mixed with sand, or sand and lime, to make mortar, and with aggregate to form concrete. Reacts with water (reaction is exothermic) to form a hard grey stone like substance similar to a marlstone. Cement is hydraulic, i.e. the reaction continues in the presence of water, as distinct from lime putty mortars and concretes, which are only lightly burnt and which require air to harden.

Strength of cement develops slowly over many months, but initial set can be modified by accelerators and retarders to give an initial set in a few seconds, or as long as several days. Dangerous material in the hands of inexperienced users as it has entirely different characteristics from lime mortar, used exclusively post Roman times to the mid 19th century, and extensively until the mid 1950s since when cement has been dominant.

Cementstone

Coarse stone formed of fragments of stone set in a limestone matrix.

Centering

Temporary timber or steel bowstring truss, in which the shape of the top beam is the same as the arch, which is to be built upon it. Centering takes the dead weight of the voussoirs that form the arch, until they are a complete ring, or rings, and able to support themselves. As the term bowstring implies, the bottom beam of the truss is in tension, and until the development of modern trusses, the longest length of timber available dictated the longest span of an arch, in practice about forty feet. Domes are also built on centering, though this is not essential, as each completed ring can be interlocked with the course below, and is self supporting when complete.

As centering is heavily loaded when the arch is complete, there has to be a method of transferring the load from the centering to the haunches of the masonry that is the permanent work. This is done by installing wedges between the centering support (often a permanent corbel which will serve as a scaffolding point in future maintenance work) and the centering. These wedges can then be driven out, gradually transferring the loads as they are removed.

Chamfer

45 degree cut to the edge of a stone or timber section, or to a quoin to remove the sharp corner. Often used as a method of softening a corner or opening.

Chancel

Section of the church, also known as the sanctuary, reserved for the clergy who perform the services. usually raised above the nave by one, two or three steps, an altar rail, chancel arch, rood screen, or a combination of all these. In many churches the chancel is smaller than the nave, and the chancel arch is then a structural necessity.

Chapter House

Gothic 'add on', typically detached, or nearly so, polygonal building located adjacent to the chancel or choir. Churches rich enough to afford a chapter house were usually rich enough to lavish decoration upon it, and most surviving examples are adorned with fine stonework, and frequently have a vaulted roof. Takes its name from the Chapter of priests who gathered to oversee the administration of the church.

Charnel House

Repository for bones from the churchyard graves. It was frequently normal practice for graves to be reused (still the done thing in Austria today) and in many soils the larger bones do not decay very quickly.

Chase

Groove cut in stonework to act as a channel for condensate from a window, for example, or to carry modern appurtenances such as electrical cables or window operating rods.

Choir

Section of the church between the nave crossing and the altar (not always present) housing the choir stalls.

Cill

Base stone of window or bottom section of window frame. Receives water run off from glazing, and frequently condensate via weepholes from inside the church. Cills are either flush with the wall, or project to form a drip, both details being common, and both leaving a section of masonry that is either too often wet, or not wet at all, both leaving a shadow on the wall.

Cistercians

Religious order founded in 1098 in Cistercium (Citeaux) in Burgundy, France. Order based upon the labour of the monks providing all physical needs. Under the direction of Bernard of Clairvaux, and others, the order grew rapidly, initially at least eschewing the riches that had been garnered by the Benedictines, but ultimately producing the largest and probably the richest abbey in England, Fountains, near Ripon in Yorkshire. The order declined rapidly in the fourteenth century due to monastic life going out of fashion. The order retains a presence in England today, together with an order of nuns (Bernardines).

Cleave

Splitting of stone is the preferred method of reducing large lumps to both manageable sizes and usable blocks. For blocks of stone to be split and cleave into even pieces with the line of the split running as intended, the stone's centre of gravity should lie in the plane of the split. Stone cleaves easily if split in half, and progressively less well as the proportions diverge. Soft stone will cleave better than hard, and some hard stones will not cleave other than in half.

Thus to form a quoin in a hard stone (a stone with two faces at right angles to each other and perpendicular to the two bedding planes) a stone four times the desired size will be needed, split in two to give a flat(ish) face, and then in two again to give a second face at right angles to the first. Uneven cleaving results in an odd piece of stone and a lot of chips.

Clerestory

Third and topmost element of the gothic nave, resting on the triforium and usually formed as a series of arches and windows designed to throw light into the nave (early aisled churches built without a clerestory tended to be dark). Term has subsequently been adopted to describe any high level windows. Pronounce it how you will, but 'clear-story' sounds good.

Clock

Church clocks, also known as tower clocks, are the oldest clock form known in England. Typical clocks utilise the dial face, originally with only a single hour hand, weight drive and pendulum escapement, and determined local time until the adoption of GMT in the 1840s. The traditional church clock was, and frequently still is, a large piece of machinery weighing several hundredweight, comprising two sets of gear trains, one for the hands, the other for the chime, set in an iron or brass frame.

The oldest gears are of the peg and lantern form, later ones are brass, cut using special indexing lathes. The drive to the hands is via extension rods, and where four faces are driven, bevel gearing. Hooke type joints are set in the drive rods to account for minor inaccuracies in the alignment of the machinery and the faces. The weight drive is usually applied from cables wound onto the drive drums, the cables crossing the floor of the clock chamber on pulleys to the weight shaft, usually located in a corner of the tower. Weights can be many tens of pounds and hand winding is vigorous exercise.

Some form of dust-proof enclosure is now the norm, and electric winding is common.

Coffering

Indentation in flat soffit of a ceiling to break up the ceiling into a series of squares or rectangles separated by beams or ribs that intersect to form a grid pattern, usually with decorated borders. Can also be used in curved work as on a barrel vault or dome. A good example is the ceilings at St. Paul's Cathedral, London. Coffering was developed, no perfected, by the Greeks, who worked the coffering out of solid marble. Most historic coffering in Britain is in timber framing and lath and plaster. There is a modern form, usually in reinforced concrete and undecorated.

Coloured Glass

Plain glass to which a single tint or colour has been added, as a pigment at the molten production stage.

Colonnade

Series of linked trilithons (posts and lintels) usually in a straight line though curves do occur, in which each lintel shares its post with its neighbour. Stonehenge represents the earliest form extant in England. System perfected by the Greeks who established the rules of proportion, and introduced the base, capitol and frieze. Copies made by the Romans, themselves copied in the Renaissance, and copied yet again in the eighteenth and nineteenth, and to a lesser extent, twentieth century. Not to be confused with the Arcade, which has arches. Used primarily to front a building, forming a porch, for example.

Column

Vertical support, usually structural though occasionally decorative. Derives from the timber post, hence the common circular cross-section. Variations in the cross-section appeared with the advent of the Gothic style, first with simple quatrefoil and then with successively more intricate attachments of shafts to form what is better described as a pier. Columns originated with a base, a copy of the stone block used to keep a timber post off the ground and prevent rotting, again increasingly decorated; and a capitol, perfected by the Greeks as part of the various orders of architecture. The capitol again underwent transformation from the Norman cushion to the ornate Gothic. Solid stone columns are worked into drums of stone whose height equals the thickness of the bedding plane from which the stone was won, and are then dowelled together with iron or bronze cramps bedded in molten lead. Larger columns are assembled by cutting stone to templates and bedding in mortar, in the same manner as a conventional wall.

Convection Currents

Churches were originally built without glazing, simply because glass was too expensive. Later all windows had glass fitted and then the Victorians added some form of heating, since extended and updated. Owing to the height of most churches, heating systems set up air movement in the form of convection currents, with the most important air movement being a cold current descending from the nave and passing at foot level through the pews to the aisles. The siting of heating pipes under pews is designed to destroy this circulation, and mitigate the penance of prayer in a chill wind.

Coping

The top course of stone, usually incorporating an overhang to form a drip, on an exposed wall, i.e. a wall not covered by a roof. The top surface usually slopes to drain water off the stone's surface, known as weathering. Coping stones are usually large in order to stabilise the wall top, and to provide a primary waterproof layer to protect the wall below.

Corbel

Projecting, frequently loadbearing, stone or course of masonry supporting the foot of a truss, or masonry work above, which is then said to oversail. Corbelling out is one method used to support the base ring of a stone hemispherical vault where it sits on a square, hexagonal or octagonal masonry base, bridging the corners.

Cornice

Projecting carving in stone, or moulding in plaster or cement, usually at ceiling, inter floor or roof eaves level, typically present in classical work as a moderating detail giving emphasis to the horizontal lines of a facade or interior.

Coursing

Formation of horizontal bands of brick or stone in random walling, either as a feature, or as a reinforcement. Also used in ashlar work, where it is termed a string course.

Cramp

Bronze or iron, now stainless steel, flat or circular section bars used to secure important sections of stonework together, e.g. columns and cornices. Usually set in molten lead, occasionally mortar, now epoxy resins. Ruined work often displays the holes for cramps, which have been recovered for the value of the metal they contain.

Creasing Tile

Small flat section of clay tile used to form an undercloak at a roof edge, or to infill under ridge or hip tiles.

Creep

Slow movement of materials out of their original fixed position due primarily to thermal cycling. Lead on pitched roofs is particularly prone to this, and masonry will creep along a suitable slip plane, such as a damp course.

Crenellation

Common decorative articulation of parapets to mimic the defensive wall and loophole arrangements on mediaeval defensive works to castles and town walls.

Crossing

Intersection of nave and transepts, frequently surmounted by a tower, sometimes a spire in addition. The four piers at the corners of the crossing are usually the largest in the church, intended to support the loads of further phases overhead, whether or not those phases eventually materialised.

Cruck

Building form generated by splitting a suitably shaped tree in half and leaning the two halves together. In use since at least 900AD, possibly earlier, with many survivors, including some churches. Size of the building is limited to the domestic scale due to the size of timber available.

Crypt

Undercroft of church, frequently the result of having to excavate for good foundation strata in poor ground, used for burials and exploited to provide an income.

Curing

Lime and cement mortars harden over time, their working strength improving as they age. This process is known as curing. A lime mortar will set in a few hours, be hard in a few days, and still be gaining strength twelve months later. This is due to the fact that lime mortars only set in the presence of air, and are thus said to be non hydraulic. Lime mortars in very thick masonry can take many years to cure. Cement mortars cure more readily, and can be accelerated or retarded as needs be. Owing to their requirement for water for setting, they are known as hydraulic mortars.

Cusp

Literally a 'point', usually referring to the pointed sections of glazing left in Gothic tracery by the curve of the window head and the division of the window by circles or quatrefoils.

Dado

Panelling, usually wood but occasionally stone, forming a horizontal band three or four feet high on a wall immediately above floor level. Topped by a carved or moulded Dado Rail.

Dais

Raised area of a floor, usually one or two steps above its surroundings to allow for an audience or congregation to better view the ceremonial or proceedings.

Damp Course

Many stones and bricks are porous and soak up groundwater. Slate, and later bitumen dampcourses, or courses of impervious brick or stone are used to prevent rising damp staining walls by depositing nitrate and sulphate salts on the wall surface.

Deal

Term for joinery quality softwood, timber that will take planing and polishing. The most common material for the Victorian pew.

Death watch beetle

Small, wood-boring beetle characterised by large flight holes, and a preference for slightly rotted oak as a diet. Attracts mate by barely audible rapid drumming of its head (legend says that this is only audible in the quiet of a room where someone is dying, hence the name). Not a serious pest unless accompanied by wood rotting fungi.

Decorated

Middle period of Gothic architecture, descriptive of the decoration that followed on from the adoption of the Early English style and characterised by the extensive use of carved work such as dog tooth moulds, ball flower drip stops, finely worked tracery to windows and grouped shafts to piers.

Demi Columns

Columns inset into walls as to leave only half of the column visible. Also known as semi-engaged columns.

Diaper

Decorative carving, usually Gothic, representing a stylised flower set in a square, frequently repeated to form a border or a string moulding to an arch.

Dog tooth

Decorative moulding to arches, etc, formed as a stylised dogs canine tooth, repeated as a string.

Dominican Friars

Order founded in 1212 (but, sadly, not in Whitehall) to bring the teaching of the Church to the people by preaching. Still in existence today with nuns and lay departments. Surviving buildings from before the Reformation are very rare.

Doric

Greek order of architecture identified chiefly by the design of the capitol that connects the column to the lintel.

Dormer

Roof window set in its own small gabled roof, not flush with the main roof pitch, intended to admit light to an aisle or nave. Function taken over largely by the clerestory.

Downdraught

Chill air movement in a high enclosed space, caused by thermo-syphonic action, very common in the nave of a church.

Drill marks

Many stones are won by stitch drilling the rock beds and driving in wedges and feathers to split off the blocks. Where not all the faces are to be worked, the drill holes survive as semi-circular chases in the back of the stone.

Drip Moulding

Functional and decorative moulding over the head of windows and doors to throw water off the wall, or divert it to the side of the opening.

Dry rot

Every building owner's worst nightmare, a fungus that just loves to devour wood, only needing a modest amount of drink to thrive, prepared to fetch and carry its own water, and prefers neglect to an excess of attention.

Early English

The first of the Gothic styles to use the pointed arch. Characterised by the wide traceried window, divided into two by a central mullion with the decoration above the spring of the arch.

Entasis

Slight swelling to classical columns designed to emphasize the effect of perspective from the viewers position at ground level.

Epistyle

The surround or architrave to a door.

Entablature

The section of classical construction that sits upon the top of the column and capital.

Falsework

Stone, timber or plasterwork put in to hide the structure of a building, or to alter the space or proportions of an element.

Fan vault

Solid stone vaulting where fan like tracery is worked on the face of the stone to produce the effect of a stylised tree canopy. Perhaps the most elaborate integration of fine building and decoration.

Fibrous plaster

Lime plasters were usually reinforced in the base coat with hair, often horsehair, but other animal hairs are common, providing a' shrink free base for the finishing plaster. Non animal reinforcement is used when fibrous plaster is needed today.

Fillers

Materials designed to add bulk to composites such as mortar or plaster, usually comprising anything suitable that was waste and to hand. Furnace wastes and coal dust are common, crushed brick and stone equally so.

Firring

Tapered timber to give a slope to a flat roof, placed under the roof boarding.

Flashing

Leadwork let into a wall or tucked under a string course to waterproof the joint between the wall and an adjoining roof.

Flint

Hard calcareous nodule, white on the outside, grey or black inside, found as surface deposits with clay, and as thin beds in chalk deposits. Extensively used as stone walling, either neat or split, in eastern England east of the stone belt. The chequerboard work common in Kings Lynn is in flint, as is similar work elsewhere.

Flitched beam

Timber beam reinforced with iron or steel plates, a popular solution to long span beams from the nineteenth century on. There is a particularly impressive one behind the facade of St. Francis Xavier, Hereford, though not on public view.

Flying buttress

Arched support in gothic architecture taking the lateral thrust of the roof vault above the line of the aisle roof and directing it into the ground via a buttress that forms part of the aisle wall.

Footing

Thickening of a wall at or below ground level to form a foundation on the soil that is wider than the wall itself. Footings predate the use of mass concrete for foundations.

Franciscan

Religious order of monks (the Friars Minor), and nuns (Poor Clares), founded 1209 and 1212 respectively by St. Francis of Assisi, to live in poverty and preach repentance, under the approval of Pope Innocent III. The Franciscans arrived in England in 1224 and set up house in the towns and cities, rather than the countryside. Survival of their buildings, such as the Friary at Beverley, are rare, but the indications are that the vow of poverty did not last long. The order survives today, having being reintroduced upon emancipation of the Catholics, and the Poor Clares at least have built a new convent within the past decade.

Freestone

Wildly inaccurate term used to identify any stone that is relatively easily won and worked, typically those rocks that yield well jointed and bedded stones that will cut, dress and cleave easily.

Frieze

Decorated strip above the entablature in classical architecture, later referrals can be to decorated strips internally also.

Frog

Pressed indent in a brick to reduce weight.

Frontius, Sextus Julius

Roman engineer and writer whose works on water supplies in the late first century AD survived to be the basis of mediaeval water engineering, being used as a model for the supply of water to the Cathedral at Canterbury from the start of the twelfth century.

Gargoyle

Carved waterspout, used to throw water off roofs in place of the more frequently used rainwater pipes. The gargoyle has come to be synonymous with the uglier things in life, as the topics all had to have a big mouth.

Going

The tread of a stair, or more precisely, the distance between two successive tread nosings on a stair. The vertical distance is the rise.

Gothic

Term describing the ecclesiastical architecture of the period 1100 to 1550 and coined during the seventeenth century as a term of abuse. Derived from the Visigoths, who were responsible for the sack of Rome in 410 AD, and in original intent was intended to mean primitive and barbaric (when compared with classical architecture).

Gutter

Channel to take rainwater off roofs, or at ground level away from buildings. gutters can be in stone, lead, cast iron, wood, or these days in aluminium or plastic.

Gypsum

Naturally occurring mineral, calcium sulphate, now extensively used as a plaster, but chemically the same as alabaster, a soft stone used in statuary.

Haunch

Lower part of an arch, that section above the springing.

Header

Brick laid so that the end is visible, as opposed to the face.

Herringbone

Brick work or stone work laid so that the beds incline at 45 degrees to the horizontal, and the individual units interleave so no plane of bedding appears.

Hip

Roof where the eaves runs all round building, the small end pitch is known as the hip, with corresponding hip rafters and hip tiles. Plain tiled roofs can have the attractive bonnet hip tiles.

Hog's back

Roof where the pitch is steeper at the eaves than at the ridge, due to a change of pitch at some point, or points. The reverse is a cat slide.

Hopper

Lead or cast iron box taking water from a gutter and discharging it to a rainwater pipe. Both cast lead and cast iron versions can be very ornate.

Hopton Wood

Cream limestone from quarries near Wirksworth, Derbyshire. Beloved of masons and sculptors alike, extensively exported from the nineteenth century onwards and can turn up almost anywhere. Distinctive for its fossil crinoids.

Hypocaust

Originally a Roman idea where fires warmed floors from underneath, the idea was revived in a modified form in the nineteenth century where heating pipes were laid in ducts in the floor and the warm air circulated up through decorative cast iron grilles.

Inclusion

Lump of 'foreign' matter in stone, of which perhaps the best known are those in the Shap granite bollards outside St. Paul's, London. Particularly noticeable when stones are polished, inclusions are quite common in both sedimentary and metamorphic rocks. Inclusions can render stone less durable, and iron inclusions in sandstone can lead to streaking as the iron oxidises and leaches out.

Jack rafter

Sawn softwood roof timber laid to the pitch of the roof and taking the load of the slates or tiles. The classic sawn size was three inches by two.

Joints

Timber is jointed to provide a method of load or force transfer from one member to another, from a hip rafter to a tie beam, for example. Up to the time of Palladio (the sixteenth century) all timber joints were compression joints, limiting clear spans to the size of the largest beams, as no tensile timber joint had been developed. Wrought iron straps and pins, with wedges to tighten them, changed this, allowing long trusses to be made. Bolts and flitch plates followed on in close order.

The old timber joints had all the familiar names; mortice and tenon, dovetail, cross halving, tusk tenon, still in common parlance. Modern joints are made with 'connectors'. Hmm.

Joist

Floor structural timber of rectangular section; early beams tend towards the square of a squared trunk, and floors for the early galleries were constructed in a series of bays, with small beams spanning to larger beams. The use of softwood and the rack saw led to the modern joist, up to five times deeper than wide.

Journeyman

Trained craftsman who had completed an apprenticeship, and was judged 'competent' but not yet a master craftsman. The term comes from the fact that this class of workman was often obliged to travel to obtain employment and experience. In practice most of the routine skilled work fell to this level of craftsman, with the fancy work being performed by the 'master'.

Keystone

The centre stone (or brick) of an arch, completing the ring of masonry, and frequently decorated or set proud to emphasize its importance. As the final stone, allowing the centering to be struck, it was the key to the arch, hence the term.

Lime mortar

Limestone or chalk, fired at modest temperatures to calcine, that is reduce the limestone to a powdery consistency that can be then mixed with water (slaked) to form a lime putty. This putty will cure to a hard mortar if exposed to the air, so traditional practice allowed for keeping it in pits and covered in water. Plastic bags are used to facilitate its transport today. Prior to this lime was dispatched in barrels and had to be kept dry owing to the reaction between the quicklime and water being exothermic.

Lime putty can be used neat, on ashlar work with thin beds, for example, but is normally mixed with fillers; sand, gravel, crushed shells, small coal, stone dust. In areas where sandy limestones led to indifferent mortars, the technique of 'nailing' with slivers of flint or other durable stone pressed into the mortar bed, was used to protect the mortar from erosion or the attention of insects, particularly bees.

Limestone

Stone composed entirely or principally of lime, calcium carbonate, of which the major rock formations, youngest first, are: Tertiary Limestone (Bembridge Limestone) Chalk, Corallian, Portland and Purbeck stone and marble, Jurassic limestones of Ham Hill to Bath and all the way to the Lincolnshire limestone and the Cave Oolite (the Oolitic limestones and others) Magnesian, and Carboniferous. Rocks older than the carboniferous are not lime rich enough to qualify as limestones, except in limited exposures.

Limestones are subdivided into the Oolites, easily worked fine grained stones such as Bath or Portland stone; Ragstone, tough often sandy limestone that is difficult to work, though the term is a general one, not exclusive to limestone; Fissile stones, often highly fossiliferous and used as tilestones (limestone makes poor paving because it gathers a film of slippery algae) 'marbles', either true (heat treated) or limestones that will take a polish, and specials, found in a single location, as at Barnack, with unique qualities of colour, texture or composition.

Living

Part of the structure of the Church in feudal England was that the parish gave the church, rather than the priest, an income. That income was known as the 'living', and was traditionally the gift of the lord of the manor, who had a powerful say in the choice of the priest, and could increase or reduce the income the priest received out of the total that the parish gave to support the church.

Thus a church could be rich in terms of income, yet the priest receive little if out of the lord's favour. The priest had the means of raising direct income, such as the sale of indulgences, but at the parish level actual power was limited.

Luther, Martin

German cleric of the early sixteenth century, famous for nailing his ninety five theses to the door of Wittenberg Cathedral in 1517 (Wittenberg lies on the Elbe, south west of Berlin), thereby provoking the schism that concluded the Gothic Age, and gave birth to the Protestant churches, which in turn produced the Counter Reformation. Luther objected to the doctrine of infallibility, and urged reform of the Church to rid it of its less desirable traits. He was eventually excommunicated for his pains, and would probably have fallen into the hands of the Inquisition but for the protection of the state.

Magnesian limestone

Band of tractable limestone running from Durham through Yorkshire to Nottingham, renowned for its fine building stone. The largest monastery, Fountains, was built of it, as are both the Palace and (parts of) the Abbey of Westminster; York and Beverley Minsters, Lincoln Cathedral, and hundreds of lesser churches in the east of Yorkshire and Lincolnshire.

Marble

Metamorphic (heat treated) limestone that can be polished to a high gloss surface finish. True marbles are not found in England, but several limestones take a polish, of which the most famous and widely distributed is Purbeck Marble, from a single bed in the Purbeck limestones of Dorset. Others include Dent (a Carboniferous limestone) Ashover (Derbyshire) Draycott (Wells, Somerset) Frosterley (Weardale, Durham). True marbles are dominated by the marbles of Italy (Carrara is the one everyone has heard of) and Greece, where slabbing marble is still an extensive industry.

Mason's Marks

Marks made on facing stonework identifying the mason who carried out the work. Very common but need to be looked for. Signatures are usually in a semi - runic form, each mason having his own.

Millstone Grit

Tough sandstone from the Carboniferous period, extensively used for millstone production (Baslow Edge near Chatsworth in Derbyshire is littered with escaped stones that evaded their owners on the journey down from the quarries, or were perhaps part of an extreme form of egg-rolling contest) hence the name. The Pennines are formed of this stone (the other is the carboniferous limestone) and it is extensively used for building, and in its fissile form, flag and tile stones.

Minster

Church established under the authority of an order of the Church rather than the efforts of the parishioners. Minsters were usually granted the 'living', or income, from one or more parishes (Howden had six) and were not controlled by the Lord of the Manor, but by the abbot of the order or his bishop, depending on individual personalities, there being a considerable latitude in the wielding of power within the church hierarchy.

Models

Before the invention of scale drawing in the eighteenth century (the French made it a state secret after they invented it) models were the most effective means of conveying three dimensional ideas from the builders to the clergy, and were in common use, probably from the twelfth century on. Models were standard form by the sixteenth century, and Wren had at least two made of his proposals for St. Paul's (one survives at St. Paul's, the 'Great Model', though this was not what was built).

Monasticism

The practice of setting up religious communities dates from the earliest days of the Church, with the laying down of the first rules for the governance of these communities by St. Benedict. The Benedictines remain a major element in the monastic movement after fifteen centuries. Until the welding of the Celtic Church to Rome communities were often mixed, with men and women in the same establishment. The monastic movement received a double boost to its fortunes with the Norman Settlement providing land and resources, and the burgeoning population of the Middle Ages the recruits. Orders and establishments grew very rich, even the 'reformed' Cistercians, and the later orders, the Franciscans (Friars Minor) after whom so many town and city streets are named, with various coloured habits.

The Black Death of 1348-50 changed all this, leaving monasteries seriously undermanned, and a wealth of opportunity elsewhere, and by the start of the sixteenth century most religious establishments were struggling to push their numbers into double figures, where a hundred and fifty years earlier hundreds were 'in orders'.

The Dissolution of the monasteries, and the subsequent religious recession put an end to the monastic life until the middle of the nineteenth century, when both the Established Church and the newly-freed Catholics re-established orders which flourished for a few decades. These establishments have withered to a toehold at the end of the twentieth century.

Mullion

Originally used to describe a vertical stone divider in a window (the horizontal one is the transom), now generally applied to timber, steel, etc.

Narthex

Covered entry within the body of the church, usually but not exclusively, at the rear of the nave, underneath the west window. The Narthex acts as a draught lobby, allowing the doors of the church to be left open in welcome if needed.

Nonconformist

Strictly speaking, those who did not wish to conform to the Established Church with the sovereign as the head of the Church of England, of which the Methodists are perhaps the best known, and who proceeded to set up their own churches and chapels in the eighteenth century. Not to be confused with Protestants in general, of whom the Nonconformists were but a part.

Nogging

Timber in short sections between vertical members (studs), to hold the studs in position and control twist and bowing as the wood seasons.

Nuisance pipe

Overflow pipe from a hidden gutter or hopper to warn of a blockage, gaining its name from the most effective ones, which make a nuisance when working properly. The author installed one at a convent, arranged to discharge over visitors who rang the front door bell.

Orders, Architectural

Greek classical architecture was divided into three orders; Doric, Ionic and Corinthian, distinguished primarily by the decoration of the capitals to columns.

Oversailing masonry

Masonry that is corbelled out over the line of the wall below it to form a cornice or a feature band.

Palladio, Andrea

Italian architect of the renaissance, 1508-80, multi-skilled and credited with the design of long span lattice trusses, and the neo-classical architectural style that bears his name.

Perpendicular

Style of Gothic architecture, representing the final phase of development, with windows the full width of structural bays and decoration that threatens to go over the top.

Pointing

Fine gauge cement or lime mortar used to provide the finished line of the mortar bedding between stones and bricks. Can be coloured to match/contrast with the rest of the wall, and flush, weather struck or recessed to provide a shadow line.

Pollution

Atmospheric fallout causing colour change, damage or erosion of masonry, glass, timber. Effects have been most noticed on masonry, due to acid rain and soot deposits eroding limestone, especially statuary. Most noticeable are loss of detail and the spalling of surfaces due to salt accumulation. Surfaces that are not washed by the rain can turn black (especially Portland Stone) and the accumulated deposits can reduce the stone to powder.

Puritanism

The extreme reaction to Catholicism, involving the removing of all images, large numbers of which had been gathered by the Church in the five centuries prior to the Reformation, including stained glass, statuary, wall paintings, saints' relics, etc. Puritanism's first disciple in England was Thomas Cromwell, who led the 'rooting out of images'. Puritanism was generally a little too pure for most people, and the established Church of England eventually plumped for a more catholic compromise.

Quatrefoil

Decorative motif in the form of a stylised four petal flower or leaf, used as tracery in windows along with trefoil (three leaves/petals), or for motifs in stonework.

Quartzite

Tough sandstone formed of quartz crystals, displaying considerable colour variety, difficult to work but waterproof and unaffected by pollution. Probably the most durable building stone.

Queen and King closers

Cut bricks in a solid brick wall, to maintain break joints.

Reveal

The return of a wall that forms the opening for a door or window.

Riven

Natural surface of stone that has been split, usually referring to slabs that have noticeable current bedding on the face (bed) and are used as pavings.

Sarum Use

Latin book of prayer in general use during the Middle Ages ('general' is perhaps a misnomer, as few could read; perhaps there was a literate handful in each parish). Replaced by the Book of Common Prayer (English). The relative scarcity of literate Latin scholars in the general population led to the extensive use of stained glass and wall paintings to illustrate the services held in the mediaeval church. Painting helped bridge the gulf between the clergy and the Latin of the Mass, and the general population. Regional variations included York Use and Hereford Use.

Shadow mould

Stone or timber string course, architrave, etc, where the moulding is designed to cast a shadow on an otherwise flat surface, to break up or emphasise a particular feature or junction between two surfaces or materials.

Slenderness ratio

Ratio between the length and the breadth of a structural component, beam, column, etc., which has a major bearing on the component's load carrying capacity.

Soapstone

A stone similar to Alabaster, a gypsum, Calcium Sulphate.

Soundboard

Angled board over the pulpit to reflect the voice of the reader towards the congregation, rather than allow it to disappear into the roof.

Spall

The most common cause of brick and stone failure, where the accumulation of salts in the outer face of a wall causes the face to part company with the wall. A sliver of stone or brick, perhaps only a couple of millimetres thick detaches and takes the original detail with it. The other principal failure is delamination, where the stone splits on its plane of bedding.

Spandrel

Curved section of a window formed by the curve of the window head and the window tracery.

Springer

The first stone at the base of the arch, having a horizontal bottom bed and a sloping top face.

Stick and stack

Traditional method of seasoning (drying) wood before use, involving the use of thin sticks to separate sawn planks in a stack to allow air to circulate.

Stile

Vertical timber forming the edge of a door (swinging and hanging stile) or its frame.

Stretcher, Stretcher Bond

A brick laid with its long face showing (the end is the 'header'). Can also refer to ashlar stonework or any stone where the blocks are of even size. Brick or stone laid to break joint with the stretcher face showing, is laid 'stretcher bond', with the vertical joints (perpends) staggered on consecutive courses. Cavity walls are usually in stretcher bond, solid walls can be laid stretcher bond but are more usually laid with headers and stretchers forming patterns (Flemish bond, Garden Wall bond, etc.) and staggered bonding is maintained by king and queen closers.

String course

Horizontal projecting course designed to alter the proportions of a wall.

Stucco

Decorative wall or ceiling plaster, applied as moulding and other relief decoration.

Sulphates

White powdery salting to walls at low level is usually caused by the deposition of sulphates due to water, often ground water, evaporating off and leaving behind small crystals. Frequently associated with rising damp (most churches do not have a damp course), the salting can lead to the decay of the surrounding stone.

Transom

Horizontal divider in a window or door, sometimes called the 'mid rail'. Larger windows may have more than one transom.

Trifoliate

'Having three leaves'; decoration where three lobes are grouped in a circle similar to a clover leaf.

Triglyph

Classical decoration to a frieze comprising three vertical parallel sided indents set close together.

Trilithon

The classical assembly of two posts and a lintol that is the foundation of Greek Architecture; in its crudest form, the stones at Stonehenge are assembled into Trilithons.

Tympanum

The infill panel between the arch of a doorway and the top of the door, where the door head is horizontal rather than curved.

Undercloak

Tile or slates at the verge, used to form a durable base to 'kick' or lift the edge slate on the roof and prevent water from running off rather than down the slope of the roof.

Undercut

Working of stone or timber so that the carving is three dimensional rather than bas relief, yet still retaining the background base. Used for rib bosses, label stops, etc, where the base stone is structural.

Vitruvius, Marcus Pollo

First century B.C. engineer and author of the work, De Architectura, whose republication (it was never 'lost' but was not widely known or used in the Middle Ages) in 1485 cast the stone that put the Gothic to flight. Perhaps the books' most lucid contribution to architecture is the section on arches, recognising the lateral thrust generated, *viz*; 'In all buildings where piers and arches are used, the outer piers are to be made wider than the others, that they may resist the thrust of the arches'.

Voussoir

Component of the arch, a stone cut with two faces that are radial to the arch and thus perpendicular to the line of thrust that passes through them.

Winder

Tread of a stair where the inner width is less than the outer, and the stair curves as a consequence. In a spiral stair the tread diminishes to nothing at the inner end, which in a stone stair forms a drum that is the central support. In most church towers there is a stair with winders, usually spiral, and not infrequently this is set in the outer wall which has a characteristic bulge on the outside as a result. The spiral stair appears traditional, though vertical and near vertical wooden ladders are also to be found.

Xenolith

Irregular shaped lump of different coloured stone in granite, producing distinctive identification marks (see Shap Granite). Xenoliths are not weaknesses, and cut and carve in the same way as the rest of the stone.

York Stone

Yellow brown sandstone, famed for its non slip properties, and extensively used as top quality paving. Part of the Coal Measure carboniferous gritstones, and originating in West Yorkshire.

Ziggurat

Babylonian pyramid and nothing to do with church architecture, but all the other letters find a place, and Z should not suffer needless discrimination.

Select Bibliography

Many sources of information were gleaned in search of information for the preparation of this work. While most of these texts are of limited interest to the reader, in researching the various shades of architectural and religious opinion of the last three hundred years, and the history of the Christian world over the preceeding fifteen centuries, a number of books were read as much for their general interest as for the information they contained. These works are listed below, are not exclusively, or even primarily eccliesiastical in their content, and are not to be described as primary information sources.

The author also had access some years ago, to a number of relugous texts, dating from the middle of the seventeenth century on, that passed through his hands while in the process of restoration. These texts, like the well known and widely available work of Edward Gibbon, give an indirect window into thinking in the ages of relugous and political turmoil; because they do not address directly the issues as political treatise, the axes they grind presume a particular stance on the philosophical questions of the day, a stance that frequently gives greater insight into the times than the text itself. Needless to say, there are many shades of opinion, and many conflicting views, and while from today's viewpoint the words 'extreme', and in some instances, 'bigoted' slip easily onto the tongue, these works are, like Rupert Brooke's poetry of the Edwardian high summer, reflections of widely-held opinions of the time, rather than evidence of the racist or jingoistic extremism of their authors.

Briggs, M. S.	*Goths and Vandals*
Bird, V.	*Portrait of Birmingham*
Gibbon, E.	*The Decline and Fall of the Roman Empire*
Hall, I. & E.	*Historic Beverley*
Hatje, J. E. (ed)	*Encyclopaedia of Modern Architecture.*
Mee, A.	*The King's England; York, East Riding; Nottinghamshire.*
Murray, P.	*The Architecture of the Italian Rennaisance.*
Pevsner, N.	*The Buildings of England; Middlesex.*
Singer, C.	*From Magic to Science*
Statham, H. H.	*A History of Architecture*
Summerson, J.	*Sir Christopher Wren*

Acknowledgements

The author wishes to thank all those individuals and organisations whose contributions, intended or accidental, have made this book possible. As individuals I would thank Rob Thewlis, for his valued contributions in keeping the author on the geological straight and narrow, and Rob Jordan, who is the tower master of All Saints, Hessle, and of the text (see page 143). Of individuals who have unwittingly contributed by being drawn into conversation as part or their, and my, work, there are many; the generation of organ builders, masons, carpenters, architects, surveyors and sales representatives, currently charged with the task of keeping today's heritage for tomorrow. They must remain anonymous, for anonymity is part of the part they play.

Contributions from organisations have come in the most unlikely forms; an alliance between a water company (who supplied the water) and a Diocesan archive (whose books were flooded) gave the author access to books that would otherwise have failed to cross his path. One of the major banks, and the author's habit of navigating England without a map, resulted in the discovery of the church at Crawley, while returning from installing ATMs in Hedge End, or was it Bournemouth? After a 1am start and a 2pm finish, it's hard to be categorical, though that day included passing Hougoumont, which gave the association with Wellington, St Paul's and Luxulyan. A similar combination, involving a leading high street retailer and a manufacturer of cementitious floor screeds, contrived to take the author to Clare. Not all who wander are lost, but it is often difficult to tell betwixt the twain.

The people who have most contributed to this work are of course those who, through the course of history, have given a labour of love (including a due measure of blood, sweat and tears) that has made the English church what it is today. As with all building projects it is the prime mover who is remembered, not the doers, and where we find craftsmen remembered, it is the master, if at all. Women, who today are the staff of the church, taking on the roles of parson and warden to add to those of organist, seamstress, cleaner and flower arranger, are even less well represented in history's roll of honour. To all these folk who have cared and continue to care, the parish church is a monument in memory of their lifelong devotion. When, after all, did you last see a roll of honour in a church recording the flower arrangers from 1550 to the present day alongside the roll of the parish priests, let alone the roll of cleaners? In the porch of many a church you will find a flower rota (names of peeresses have featured) but flowers are the ultimate ephemera, the handwritten paper rota following the blooms into the dustbin of history almost at the drop of a petal.

Without all these individuals from a land not now well filled, but crowded with folk, there would be no tale to tell. Behind me, as I write, a young organist, one of the next generation to care, perhaps, is rehearsing the left half of a duet by Gabriel Fauré. The rain pattering on the roof reminds me that I promised to sort out that damp patch on the western gable of the village chapel, of which my wife has just been elected deacon.

To all these people this work is dedicated, and to all of them I give my thanks.